Ed Sacks

The Renters' Survival Kit

**Real Estate
Education Company**
a division of Dearborn Financial Publishing, Inc.

Publisher: Kathleen A. Welton
Acquisitions Editor: Patrick J. Hogan
Associate Editor: Karen A. Christensen
Senior Project Editor: Jack L. Kiburz
Interior Design: Lucy Jenkins
Cover Design: Jones House

Published by Dearborn Financial Publishing, Inc.

Printed in the United States of America.

94 95 10 9 8 7 6 5 4 3 2

Library of Congress Cataloging-in-Publication Data

Sacks, Ed
    The renters' survival kit / by Ed Sacks.
        p.   cm.
    Includes index.
    ISBN 0-79310-588-9
    1. Rental housing—United States.   2. Landlord and tenant—United States.   I. Title.
    HD7288.85 U623 1993
    333.5′4′0973—dc20   93-10463
                                                                          CIP

Ed Sacks's Tenants' Bill of Rights

A Tenant Should Have the Right To:

A clean, safe place to live;

Heat in the wintertime;

Hot and cold running water, drains that work;

Windows that work, screens and storm windows;

A working toilet;

A front and back door that lock;

Roofs, ceilings and walls that don't leak;

Privacy and protection from intrusion and harassment from the landlord;

Repairs made quickly and properly;

Roach-free, rat-free and mouse-free living;

A structurally sound building;

A building with smoke detectors, fire extinguishers and fire escapes;

Make complaints about violations of rights without retaliation;

Remain in the apartment until choosing to move out;

Move out when necessity arises, for any number of legitimate reasons;

A lease that guarantees these rights in writing;

Enforce these rights by repairing and deducting, rent reduction or withholding, tenant actions and in a court of law;

Prompt return of all deposits and interest due;

Protection against property seizures, lock-outs, evictions or denial of lease renewals without probable cause and due process of law; and

Recover damages from violations of rights.

Contents

Index   237

Acknowledgments

I wish to thank the following persons and concerns for information and assistance in the research of this book:

Judith Donner, Orkin Pest Control; Frank Headler, EcoWater Store; Cheryl Graves and Sheila Thomas, Access Living; Donna Griner, U-Haul International; The Altom Oil Company; Jim Winkler and Jack Wallin, Dole Vale Division, Eaton Controls; Harry Plawlowski, U.S. Environmental Protection Agency; Elizabeth Knospe, 7th District Federal Reserve Bank; Tony Abruscato and Keith Klein, Mid Town Bank and Trust Company; Dan May, U.S. Department of Justice; Jaci Feldman, National Training and Information Center; Bob Fleckal, Commonwealth Edison Company; John McCabe, National Conference of Commissioners on Uniform State Laws; John Mueller, Peoples Gas Company; Maribeth Robb, Water Quality Association; Larry Festenstein, McClier Engineering; James Grow, National Housing Law Project; Bill Wilen, Legal Assistance Foundation; Kathy Stevenson, National Clearinghouse for Legal Services; John Hamil, American Civil Liberties Union.

Introduction

When my first landlord took three weeks to remove a glob of plaster from my bathtub drain, I thought it was exciting to live in a big city so I could tell my friends about my experiences of sponge bathing in the sink during a heat spell. When my second landlord explained that the kitchen cabinets were "extra," urban roughing-it was no longer exciting. When my third landlady withheld my security deposit after *her* dog piddled on my kitchen floor while she was making one of her frequent unauthorized inspections, I was not amused. When my fourth landlord broke a series of promises about renovations, making me wait a month (between apartments) only to arrive (with a 40-foot moving van full of furniture) to floors wet with varnish and doors that were kept closed with nails, I decided first to get mad (easy) and then get even (much harder). Thus, this is the genesis of my involvement with tenant rights and relations.

Landlord number four fought and lost a lawsuit filed by the apartment building's quickly formed tenants' union. He paid us money every month for three years as part of the judgment. He also left town. Since, at that time, every tidbit about tenants' rights was cleverly hidden from most renters, I had to do extensive research. I put what I learned into my first book so my experiences could be shared. I continue to be involved in tenants' rights and dispute resolution issues, and this is my third book about renting.

Ed Sacks's *The Renters' Survival Kit* is not about getting mad or getting even; it is about making wise choices. The book begins with selecting a unit and moves on to dealing with rental problems, including repairs and rent withholding, and then to lease breaking and security deposit refunds. There is no need to go through all the agony and research as I have, especially if you can benefit from my experiences.

More and more people are renting their living spaces these days, primarily because they can't afford to buy. Other folks are forced back into the rental market because of financial setback, divorce, job changes, retirement or other life-style adjustments. Thus, demand for rental units will stay steady or rise. As a general rule, the purchase costs of commercial (rental) housing, land, construction and financing are more pricey than they were ten years ago. Property taxes also take more absolute cash than they have previously. The point for tenants is that demand will continue to force rents to be a higher and higher percentage of their income, while the cash squeeze on owners and managers will make them try to skimp on services as they keep rents as high as the market will bear.

Consider this book to be a friend who has been through it before and has developed many tips and tricks. Even better, you don't have to be embarrassed to ask a question. The checklists, worksheets and sample letters and forms are as helpful as my advice. They help you evaluate your situation, guide you toward decisions that you will feel comfortable about and sometimes just keep track of what needs to be done. They also let you assert your rights.

It makes a lot of sense to be cautious when renting. Even though tenants' rights laws exist all across the country in various forms, a lease is a contract. Breaking leases isn't easy. The lawyer you hire or the judge who hears your lawsuit *might* also be a landlord, so staying out of court is preferable to fighting within a legal system based primarily on the rights of property.

How To Use This Book

Keep this book handy. It is a reference book—your guide to survival in the rental jungle of apartments, condos, co-ops, lofts and houses. Browse through the entire book once just to get the feel of it. Then dive right into the parts of the book that specifically concern you. Skip chapters that contain information you do not need just then. Read only what you have to read when you need to read it. For example, first-time renters will need to look at chapters 1 and 2. People who are moving need the refresher course contained in chapters 3, 4 and 6. When the troubles start, chapters 7 and 8 will fill the bill. And when all hell breaks loose, read chapters 9, 10, and 11.

The appendixes are always useful for general information. There are sections about tenants' rights laws, sample letters, an inspection checklist, lease riders, tenants' association sample bylaws and a collective bargaining agreement. If you are afraid to take a legal action but need relief, please talk to a lawyer.

This book is a continuing project. Readers are encouraged, even requested, to send me copies of their local laws, court experiences, and the whys and ways of the local housing system. Send them to Ed Sacks, P.O. Box 578803, Chicago, IL 60657. For those of you with modems, you can reach me on CompuServe at account number 70531,3533, and on ConflictNet via Internet at *edsacks@igc.org*.

Renting—The Whys and Wherefores

> ### *The Ideal Rental Unit*
> - Attractive
> - Comfortable
> - Affordable
> - Right Size
> - Located Conveniently

The goal of renting is simple: Find an attractive, comfortable and affordable place that is the right size for your needs and is located conveniently. Finding such a place is seldom easy. I put apartment hunting right up there with wallpaper removal, tax audits and root canal work. Not only do you have to traipse all over hell-and-gone, there are also a hundred questions about the units you're looking at that you can't get readily answered. It is a trip into *terra incognita*, that fuzzy place on the map of life with the inscription "unknown beyond this point."

The goal of this renters' kit is to make that fuzzy land as clear and known as possible. To do that, the kit has worksheets and checklists that are helpful in sorting through the myriad decisions you make, consciously or not, when you rent. I'd like to ease you into the process by starting with the basics.

According to a May 1992 National Association of Home Builders survey, 70 percent of tenants consider the cost of rent the first consideration when taking a unit. Location is chosen second. Security, neighborhood and community assets follow. So, if you have the luxury of choice, this seems to be the hierarchy. Sadly, many renters do not have such luxury. A study released by the Center on Budget and Policy Priorities, in cooperation with the Low Income Housing Information Service, reports that more than 66 percent of renters in the nation's 44 largest cities pay more than 50 percent of their income on housing! Nationwide, approximately 50 percent of tenants pay more than 50 percent of their income on housing! In this regard, 84 percent of renters are paying more than the government-recommended limit of 30 percent of income on rent! When you are paying so much, you must be an informed buyer to ensure value.

Tenant-Landlord Relations—Duties, Obligations, Common Sense and Decency

Adversaries or a Business/Client Relationship?

Once upon a time, not so long ago, landlords had no duties! They rented out a piece of land, with or without buildings and/or improvements, and that was that. The tenant had the obligation of paying the rent no matter what, maintaining the property and leaving when the lease ended (or when the tenant couldn't or wouldn't pay the rent anymore).

A landlord in New York City at the turn of the nineteenth century sued his tenant for nonpayment of rent after a fire destroyed the house the tenant had rented. The landlord argued the common law: that the landlord's only duty was to offer the tenant the *opportunity* to use the rental property, not the guarantee of any particular use, in exchange for the rent money. Furthermore, he argued that he and the tenant had a contract wherein the tenant agreed to pay rent regularly for the duration of the lease. It was the tenant's job to determine the suitability of the property and the lease terms. Once signed, the landlord had no obligation except to allow the tenant possession of the premises until the lease expired. It had always been that way.

Imagine the landlord's surprise when a court ruled that this tenant had no obligation to pay rent on a burned-out hulk! This example, highly abbreviated, is the basis of the modern relationship of landlords and their customers.

Residential rental real estate is a huge business, with more than 50 percent of some large-city populations renting apartments. Rental expenses for many tenants are the largest recurring outlay they have. Landlords tend to be very mistrustful of their clients, stacking local and state laws with all sorts of special interest rights of property and quick, harsh remedies. Until quite recently, tenants were forced to completely accept one-sided arrangements and found themselves without defenses before the landlords' courts. Is it any wonder that unlike other mutually useful and interdependent relations, parties to renting tend to be adversarial?

For a lot of good reasons, it is important to arrive at and remain in a business/client relationship with your landlord. For one thing, it is easier to conduct your daily life if you are not fighting with somebody. For another, if you are on pleasant terms with a person, that person is more likely to help you when you need it. You want to feel and act as if you have equality and power in your relationship with the landlord because you do! You pay for something, and you expect to get what you pay for. In areas where tenants' rights laws exist, this is relatively easy to do; in other areas, you'll have to be more creative and persistent. Adversarial encounters announce the failure of a relationship, usually confirming its imminent ending.

What Is a Good Landlord?

A landlord has statutory, case law and contractual obligations to a tenant. At the very least, the landlord is expected to hold to what is required. Most fundamentally, the landlord must make sure the rental unit is safe to live in, properly heated (and cooled) and physically repaired when needed. This is called maintaining habitability. The landlord is expected to deliver all the services that are promised, especially those things made part of the lease. The landlord is expected to obey the laws and not violate the civil rights of the tenant. The landlord has a responsibility to ensure to the tenant the peaceful use and enjoyment of the apartment by not harassing the tenant, by promptly responding to tenant needs and requests with courtesy and by making sure all tenants respect other tenants' needs for quiet and access. A landlord has a continuing obligation to be honest, which includes proper handling and return of a tenant's security deposit.

What Is a Good Tenant?

A tenant has legal as well as commonsense duties. The most common duty is to pay the rent when due. The tenant should also respect the landlord's physical property by not damaging it and by conducting himself or herself in a respectful and nondisturbing way toward the rest of the building occupants. If the tenant has lease obligations, these need to be honored. Not very complicated, is it?

Making the Rental Relationship Work

Difficulties with the landlord can arise for many reasons: mistrust, fear, personality conflict, stubbornness, power plays or conflicting goals. These emotions and attitudes come from both sides. Some can be overcome easily through open communications, while others require explanations, negotiations and compromise. It is your choice as a tenant to analyze your needs regarding the degree to which you want or need to get along with the landlord.

Why do you want to get along? There are several good reasons: to get the apartment you want, when you want it and at the price you need; to obtain the cooperation of the landlord in completing promised work and responding quickly and adequately to your requests, from maintaining to rule waiving; to have your lease renewed without mishap.

Communications means talking to the landlord in a friendly, businesslike way when you need something. It means telling the landlord promptly about a problem, being reasonable about what you expect and being practical about the time schedule. Talking is most important. If you wait for a little problem to grow in magnitude or irritation, your encounter with the landlord may become unnecessarily confrontational.

This is not to encourage you to be passive or bend over backwards to be nice; I am simply suggesting that you give courtesy a chance. As you engage the landlord, figure out what problems or attitudes the landlord carries and position your requests accordingly. At the same time, don't make broad assumptions, that is, don't let your own fears, stubbornness or power conflicts cloud the issues or expand the problem. Don't assume, for instance, that because you request a lease change that you will be given grief. At the same time, don't go ballistic the first time you make a complaint. Be as cooperative as possible. As an example, after you move in, if you want something repaired, you'll need to give the landlord access to your unit, and you might have to be flexible as to when the workers can enter and how much warning you'll be given. Appreciate that the landlord has other problems to handle and other priorities.

If civil communications break down, you can expect sparks. You may have to assert your tenants' rights (see chapters 7, 8 and 9), take administrative or legal action, fight an eviction (see chapter 10) or face an attempt not to renew your lease.

Understanding the Rental Process

Basic Definitions

Let's define residential renting: *Paying somebody a fee in return for the opportunity to occupy a space suitable to live in. The fee covers specific uses and a fixed period of time.* This definition could get very fancy, and in fact, as you read this book, it will. But why muddy the waters right now? When I talk about renters, tenants and lessees, I am speaking about and to you, the folks forking over the rent money. When I talk about apartments, I am also talking about studios and efficiencies, condo and co-op units, coach houses, town houses, lofts and freestanding units including single-family dwellings. When I talk about landlords and lessors, I mean the person or company that signed the lease and/or to whom you directly pay your rent. Landlords broadly include supers, concierges, managers, agents, housing agencies and owners. When I speak of leases, I mean the arrangement between the tenant and landlord relating to, but not limited to, rents and other terms and conditions that let you stay in your apartment. Leases can be written or verbal, cover a week or a year and contain special rules or incorporate conditions imposed by law but not actually written into the lease or spoken about.

Basic Decisions

Let's assume you've decided that you want to or have to rent. You've evaluated the alternatives of staying where you are now: living in your own home, living at home with family, living with others, living in a dorm or institutional setting or living in a hotel situation. You've also decided that it is economically advisable, feasible or necessary that you rent. Now you need to start your strategic evaluation plan.

Finding the right apartment has several components beyond the questions of location and monthly rent. As a matter of fact, the other considerations can be more important. I'll talk about cost and location later.

Living Arrangements

Begin by asking yourself questions about space and living arrangements. Are you going to live with other people now or in the near future? If you are married or in a companion relationship, you'll need to find a unit with enough space and breathing room for the two of you. If you have children, you need extra bedrooms or sleeping spaces plus play spaces. Are roommates part of the plan? You'll need separate bedrooms, adequate bathroom facilities and perhaps an entertainment area that can be separated from the sleeping area. Are you going to care for a relative? Will you need two bathrooms or two bedrooms interconnected? Do you entertain out-of-town visitors frequently? What type of space do you need to accommodate your guests?

As you think about living arrangements, you know that you don't need a three-bedroom house if you live alone and never have guests. You also know that five roommates and one postage-stamp bathroom may create disharmony. If you are seriously dating and may want to live together soon, take that into consideration when sizing up your potential digs.

Size and Space Requirements

Space is the next consideration. Make sure you have space for an audio system, extra beds, plants, baby crib, books, space heater, large-screen video, a desk or home office, a piano, stuffed furniture, toys, closets for clothes, china cabinet, living-room altar, portable darkroom, electric pasta maker, microwave, Puss or Boots, life-size statue of Elvis and grandfather's urn. How many rooms do you really need? In which rooms are size, ceiling height, angles or window exposure important? Use the "Requirements Checklist" at the back of this chapter to get a grasp on what space you require.

Underlying Requirements

Now that you've got the hang of this, we'll try something a little more detailed. What are your needs and expectations? Try this as a metaphor: Now that you've decided on ice cream, will it be chocolate or vanilla, low-fat or pure cream, single or double, cup or cone, sugar or plain? When you taste the ice cream, do you want it to crack your teeth with coldness or coolly slither down your throat?

Needs

Applying this process to the decidedly nonsensual activity of apartment hunting, what kinds of questions need to be answered? Foremost in many persons' minds is the question of safety: "I need a secure place—one with a fence, intercom, double locks and a well-lit entrance." Others will want a building with a swimming pool or enclosed porches because of small children. I know I always want parking as part of my package, as well as a doorman who can receive my messenger and UPS deliveries. I've lived in several places that didn't have closets. Do you need them? What about storage?

Amenities can be considered needs. When the rental sales agent pitches the apartment to you, the amenities will certainly be touted. These include an appliance-stuffed kitchen with oversized freezer compartment and ice maker, extra burners or double ovens with the stove (by the way, it may be customary for *you* to provide these appliances), a microwave oven, kitchen range hood and ventilator, double sink, a dishwasher and garbage compactor. Would you like a bathroom with separate shower and tub, bidet or heater lamps? Are electric drapery closers something you can't live without? Maybe you need a grocery store, cleaners, a pharmacy or an auto mechanic on the premises?

There may be special items you don't need—for example, kids in the hallways, senior citizens cracking peanuts in the lobby or party timers. There may be items you don't want to pay for that come packaged with the rent—for example, unlimited access to the weight room, golf course privileges, boat docking rights, etc. Maybe you *don't want* 24-hour, front-desk security!

Some needs are easily identified, while others are not. But the subtle requirements can be just as important. We've mentioned safety, noise versus quiet and a generally compatible building or neighborhood environment as common needs. What about door ramps, elevators or bathroom facilities with bars and grips? Would you feel safer with a video monitor as part of the intercom system? Who takes out the garbage and to where? Not every building or complex will fulfill your special needs. The nice-looking Mediterranean complex up the hill might not look so nice as you trudge up that hill with three bags of groceries during an ice storm or on the hottest day of the year. Think subtle.

Expectations

You expect to be happy about your rental choice because it meets your needs *and* you can live there comfortably without other complications. Thus, you create a picture of what it will be like to live in your new place. In your mind, you see how the furniture fits and the sun filters through the windows. You also have an idealization as to what life will generally be like if you rent this place or that. Think about your life-style issues, your prejudices and your way of doing things. Just what do you expect?

You might expect a doorman to come flying with an umbrella when you go out to find a cab, or you might expect the janitor to keep the laundry room clean. You might expect the hallways to be vacuumed every day or that the building be as silent as a church in August. You might expect the office in the building to accept your deliveries or the landlord to stay out of your place unless invited. You might expect repairs to be made rapidly or to meet people in the lobby, laundry or game room with similar interests. You might expect the heating and cooling to work or a Christmas tree with lights in December.

If you have certain dietary, political, religious, ethnic or ethical needs or beliefs, you uncritically expect not to be upset or offended by activities or actions pertaining to your living situation. A vegan vegetarian, an Adventist or a Hindu might have problems with barbecue grills under his or her window. An observing Jew might be uncomfortable about a Christmas tree or creche in the lobby or front of the complex. A recovering alcoholic might not want to be around beer drinking at the pool. It might be a bad idea as a Bosnian Moslem tenant to rent from a Serbian Orthodox landlady with the expectation of peace and quiet or lease renewal.

Subtle yet very powerful expectations relate to your *address* or the special distinction a building or complex might hold. There might be a class or prestige aspect that could make you feel very uncomfortable later. For instance, you might be an outspoken Democrat who moves into a Republican building. Your political friends won't step foot inside, and the condo committee or management orders you to remove your political bumper stickers and campaign posters.

Expect heat from neighbors or management if you are going to throw a lot of parties in a building where other tenants work very early or late shift jobs and are trying to sleep as you fire up the compact disc player. So mention your expectations to the agent and size up the building's capacity to meet those expectations *before* you sign an application. I discuss expectations from a different perspective in the section on strategies that follows.

Realities

Your home is your castle, but castles for rent? Many people as they shop for their rental unit have a certain attitude or expectation not yet discussed. It relates to finding the "perfect" place. This attitude mixes a desire to find the best there is with a reassuring/self-congratulatory conclusion that indeed the best was obtained. This sets the tenant up for a big letdown that in turn may engage the slow-grinding grist wheel of dispute later on during the lease. You know how you feel when you buy a new jacket and then spill something on it? Little death! Have you ever seen that look of horror on a new car owner's face after the first scratch is discovered? How about the irate restaurant customer who demands a free meal or money back because of some minor flaw?

There is nothing perfect, rental units included. If you think you have found your castle, look again, because it won't stay that way for long. There's no problem with this. You don't own the place. It wasn't built for you. You probably didn't choose the paint or wallpaper. You didn't buy the appliances. Essentially, all you can or should expect is that you get the good use of the premises without problems or hassles. Nit-picking and unrealistic expectations can be the cause of a lot of useless grief. The issues are realism and reasonableness.

Anticipate and prepare! There will be noise when you least want it. Some neighbor is going to complain about your TV set. The heating system will go kerflewey on the coldest day of the season. The manager will have bad breath. The hot water will invariably run out during your shower every morning at 7:45.

The realities here include not getting what you thought you were paying for, not having any control and experiencing results or effects that are disagreeable or even harmful. One reason for taking care in selecting your rental unit is to avoid some of these types of problems, but no one can always confidently predict when a situation will arise. The longer and more permanent your connection to your apartment, the more you'll need to check it out before you move in, the more you'll demand services and the more it will be necessary to compromise and work out problems. Reasonable expectations lead to reasonable solutions.

Short- and Long-Term Renting Strategies

Why talk about this subject now, before you actually start looking, or why talk about it at all? The reason is that you must have another area of thinking before you start the hunt. How long do you plan to stay in the apartment you are now seeking? Will you move in a year or less because of schooling or graduation? Are there marriage or job transfer plans coming up? Is this a short stay because you are buying a house? Is this a long-term venture because you are tired of moving or can't afford to change every year? Are you ready to settle down and buy furniture and custom drapes? Are you saving for a mortgage down payment?

If you are only staying in town for a short time, your best strategy might be to rent a furnished apartment or live in a residential hotel with an oral or short-term weekly or monthly written lease. The cost will be reasonable even if the early-attic or recent-thrift-store period of decor leaves you lacking. You don't have to buy furnishings, move them in and out or worry about a long lease. You expect to stay for a short time and can tolerate the circumstance because it is predictably short.

You may opt for other short-term strategies to rent below your needs as you save money, learn about an area before buying, start a new relationship, transition out of an old relationship (divorce anybody?) or prepare to transfer jobs or schools.

Example: I have a friend who decided nine months in advance to leave town. As her old lease came up for renewal, she condensed her belongings into two rooms, sold the rest at an apartment sale, negotiated a month-to-month lease and moved into a tiny apartment. She paid for her out-of-town move with the apartment sale money and saved enough more with her reduced rents that she could afford to start her new life with some cash. She also didn't need to worry about breaking a lease. In return for all this, she put up with noise and low water pressure. In the short run, it was worth it. She adjusted her expectations, sacrificed what was needed and was reasonable about the raft of tenant issues we are discussing. Under other circumstances, such as a full year's lease and higher rents, she would have taken her landlord to the mat and bit his ear off.

A long-term renting strategy might be to live frugally and save money until you can buy a place of your own. Again, you can tolerate some circumstances better if there is a good reason or the end is in sight.

A totally different long-term strategy must be employed when you want to remain in the prospective apartment (perhaps house?) for several or many years. First, you must be more thorough in your prelease inspections. Second, you might try negotiating a multiyear lease that will ensure that any carpeting and custom decorating you pay for will have a useful life. Third, by offering to sign a multi-year lease, you may be able to get concessions from your landlord for decorating, appliances and lower, predictable rents.

There is another and important aspect to long-term strategies. It relies on all that has been discussed in this chapter. Choose your unit well. Make sure your space requirements are met. Temper your expectations to reality. Be reasonable. Since you have long-term goals in mind, during the course of the lease you'll have to be prepared to compromise in order to sustain a satisfactory relationship with the landlord. In addition to doing your homework on your apartment, evaluate the "personality" of the management company, landlord, manager or whoever. You will have to deal with the "other side" from time to time concerning consternating issues. If you can keep your cool with them, and they you, your long-term strategy will be successful. If you get into a fight, you'll be unhappy and may even lose.

Rents

I've saved discussing rents until last because it is the driving force in rental agreements. How much you pay determines what you'll get. The concern is how much can you afford? As a tenant, that question means how much money can you pay to the landlord. To the landlord, it means whether or not your salary, present circumstance and credit record allow you to qualify for the unit you are seeking. What you think you can afford, what you can actually afford and what the landlord thinks you can afford can easily be three separate numbers.

Net Rent

The monthly payment specified on the lease is called *net rent.* As a general rule, this number includes the basics of your lease, usually just the apartment and cold water. Sometimes hot water and heat are part of the package. Less often is air conditioning included. Rarely does your basic lease include electricity. The net rent is just the starting point in figuring what it will really cost to take a particular unit.

Gross Rent

What it costs you each month *in toto* is called the *gross rent.* Great name, isn't it? Start with the net rent and add in all the extras: gas; hot water; electricity; air conditioning; parking; surcharges for using the deck, playroom, pool, game room or laundry room; storage; security services; telephone; television cable; elevator fees; furniture rental; and what else? Whatever you have to pay on a monthly basis for shelter goes into the gross rent.

Example: You and your companion want to rent a two-bedroom town house. The net rent is $885 a month. Your proposed lease requires that you maintain the small front yard. One parking space is provided, but you have two cars. Sitting down with the

"Net Rent/Gross Rent Worksheet" found at the back of this chapter, you add up what this lease will really cost.

You call the local utility companies and ask what the budget amounts for their services will be. The *budget amount* is a prorated monthly payment based on the past 12 months' usage in that unit. If the unit was empty for part of that time, an adjustment may need to be made. This lets you estimate how much it costs to heat, cool, provide hot water and cook when broken down to a set of monthly bills. The same is true for the water bill. If the building or complex resells these utilities to the tenants, you would get a set of monthly estimates from the management. In this hypothetical case, there is no gas bill. The electric budget bill amount is $195 per month. Water and sewer charges are $45 per month. You will have to pay the management company another $12.50 a month for automatic lawn sprinkling and $40 for a second parking space.

If you want use of the pool, you will be charged $20 a month for one pass or $50 a month for unlimited usage for you, your companion and your guests. You already know your monthly phone bill, $65. You can't get a good TV signal without cable, which costs $34 for basic service plus $3 for each additional hookup—for you, this is a total of $40.

Your unit is wired for a security system installed and maintained by the management. If you wish to subscribe, there is a basic charge of $20 per month for calls to the police and fire department if the alarm goes off. For an additional charge of $75, a security officer will investigate any alarm, drive by four times a day to inspect the exterior and check all the doors while you are out of town. You would like full protection. A check with your insurance agent reveals that a tenants' policy (contents; theft, fire, vandalism; and general/medical liability) will cost $25 a month. When you finish the addition, your gross rent potential with this unit is a whopping $1,452.50! Can you afford the gross rent?

This example clearly contains add-ons that you might not have access to or need. But even the basic utilities pump up the rent. Are you going to rent furniture or appliances? Add these into your gross rent figuring. Then there are always the "sleepers." For example, the apartment you're looking at includes electricity as part of the basic rent. In the summertime, you are surcharged $50 per month for each window air-conditioning unit, whether it is used or not. There are three units in the proposed apartment. The cooling season is arbitrarily determined by the landlord to start "when it gets hot" and end "when no longer necessary." The cooling season is always at least four months long, which adds $600 to your rent. In this case, you have a $50 a month sleeper in your lease.

I know of sleeper fees for elevator use in high rises—pay and ride or walk! Some leases, especially those for freestanding units, some condos and some apartments rented by ma-and-pop types tack on property tax increases (or the whole tax), condo assessments, municipal street and sewer and water special assessments, and scavenger and/or recycling fees (the garbage man). A sleeper clause that requires you to have the carpets professionally cleaned can also add the equivalent of $25 to $50 to the monthly gross. Ah, the schemes to pick a tenant's pocket are many.

In chapter 4 I'll discuss how you can qualify on your credit report for the privilege of signing the lease and paying the rent. Here it is important for you to qualify yourself in terms of what you can afford to pay. As a rule of thumb, don't commit yourself to pay more than 30 percent of your take-home pay as gross rent.

At the beginning of this section, I mentioned that what you *think* you can pay for rent and what you can *actually* afford may be different amounts. One reason for this is that net rents and gross rents are different, and most renters think net when they need to think gross. Another reason is that a renter, particularly a new renter, may not have developed an overall monthly budget strategy that covers the rest of life's normal expenses, such as food, clothing, medical needs, credit cards, car and student loans and an occasional movie or concert. The "Credit Qualifier Worksheet" at the back of this chapter has a section on budget estimating to help you put rent into perspective.

It is important that you are able to *afford* the rent because it is very important that you be able to *pay* the rent. If you get caught up in debt, there are serious ramifications beyond irate phone calls from creditors and lawyers. You could be evicted, and in some communities this means being blacklisted as a tenant. Your credit rating could prevent you from rerenting (blacklist or not). Your credit rating and history could adversely affect your ability to get a credit card or a loan. So don't rent above your means.

Have you filled out the worksheets and gone through the checklist in this chapter yet? Do it now so you won't have to stop later.

Requirements Checklist

Space and Living Arrangements

Live with roommates or otherwise share? ☐ Yes ☐ No

How many adults will live in unit? 1 2 3 4 5 6

How many young children? 1 2 3 4 5 6 7

Square feet? 200 300 400 500 600 700 800 900 1,000

How many bedrooms? At what sizes? 1 2 3 4 5   Size _____

How many closets? 1 2 per bedroom plus 1 2 3 4

How many bathrooms? Full: 1 2 3 Half: 1 2 3

Do you need a separate living room? ☐

Do you need a dining room? ☐   Must it be separate? ☐

Do you need a separate den? ☐

Do you need a separate office? ☐

What size kitchen do you need? Tiny Small Medium Grand Gross

Do you have specially sized furniture or space needs? Large beds Water-filled furniture Piano Long couch Table Desk Cabinet Rugs Washer/Dryer Exercise equipment

Needs and Expectations

Security system? ☐

24-hour front-door guard? ☐

Intercom system? ☐

Elevator? ☐

Extrawide doors? ☐

Disabled-accessible amenities? ☐

Cab stand? ☐

Inside parking? ☐

Cable TV? ☐

Maid services, food services? ☐

Building complex with stores, services? ☐

Activities, pool, games, groups? ☐

Lots of students, parties? ☐

Peace and calm? ☐

Total privacy and quiet? ☐

Day care? ☐

Kid proofing? ☐

Special kitchen appliances? What? _____

Air conditioning? ☐

Special heating or control over heating? ☐

Special window or daylight requirements? ☐

Special outlet or power requirements? ☐

Special Considerations

Oral month-to-month or week-to-week lease? ☐

Furnished unit? ☐

Short-term lease, maybe even a sublet or assignment? ☐

Very cheap rents/very cheap unit? ☐   Limit? $ _____

Multiyear lease with renewals? ☐

Option to buy? ☐

Credit Qualifier Worksheet

Ability To Pay

Monthly gross income (earnings, interest, other):

Lease signer #1	$ _____
Lease signer #2	$ _____
Lease signer #3	$ _____
Lease signer #4	$ _____
Total Income	$ _____

Qualifying Test #1

Total income $_____ × 30% (.30) = $ _____

Landlord will require that your rent equal no more than 30 percent of your *gross income* to qualify.

Recurring Obligations

Car loans	$ _____
Student loans	$ _____
Other loans	$ _____
Tuition	$ _____
Memberships and dues	$ _____
Judgments, fines, penalties	$ _____
Alimony, maintenance, support	$ _____
Medical insurance and payments	$ _____
Car insurance (monthly proration)	$ _____
Property taxes (proration)	$ _____
Other recurring expenditures	$ _____
Payroll taxes	$ _____

Other Monthly Expenses

Monthly credit-card payments	$ _____
Food	$ _____
Charity	$ _____
Entertainment	$ _____
Insurance (all other types)	$ _____
Clothing (other than charges)	$ _____
Travel (other than charges)	$ _____

Vehicle expenses and repairs	$ _____
Local transportation and parking	$ _____
Work-related costs (lunches, etc.)	$ _____
Laundry and cleaning	$ _____
Savings and investments	$ _____
School books, etc.	$ _____
Other monthly expenses	$ _____
Total Monthly Obligations	$ _____

Qualifying Test #2

Subtract total monthly income from total monthly obligations to determine what is left for the gross rent.

Total monthly income	$ _____
Total monthly obligations	$ _____
Maximum Available for Gross Rents	$ _____

Net Rent/Gross Rent Worksheet

For apartment at: _____

Management and phone: _____

Net Rent Components

Rent on lease $ _____

Extras owed monthly to landlord $ _____

Additional Rent Components

Electricity $ _____

Gas (hot water, heat, cooking) $ _____

Fuel oil $ _____

Air conditioning (landlord add-on) $ _____

Water and sewer $ _____

"Assessments" $ _____

Taxes $ _____

Telephone (local and long-distance) $ _____

Cable TV $ _____

Security service $ _____

Scavenger service $ _____

Elevator, dock, receiving services $ _____

Pet fees $ _____

Regular cleaning and/or lawn services $ _____

Decorating fees (prorated) $ _____

Carpet cleaning fees (prorated) $ _____

Furniture/appliance rentals $ _____

Repairs/maintenance $ _____

Storage $ _____

Pool, club $ _____

Parking $ _____

Other: _____ $ _____

Other: _____ $ _____

Total Gross Monthly Rents $ _____

2

Finding a Place To Live with Confidence

> ***Location Needs***
> - Local Services
> - Community Amenities
> - Access to Transportation
> - Proximity to Job, Friends, Family
> - Safety Issues

Location

Why would you choose to live in Bayside as opposed to Unity Park? Is there any difference between living a stone's throw from the MTA Green Line or the I-5 corridor? Yes, yes, yes! Deciding on the location of your apartment is based on what local services and amenities the immediate community provides; access to transportation; proximity to job, friends and family; and safety issues. These are your location needs.

This is really the easy part of apartment hunting because you can tick off what you need. Assume you are a first-time renter and new to town. Where should you start? First, define your location needs. Next, ask your co-workers or personnel department, fellow students or housing office, and local friends and family for recommendations. If you don't have a car, you'll want to live within walking distance of work or school or be close to convenient public transportation. If you have a car, there is more leeway, but you still want to live close to roadways that can conveniently take you where you want to go. Buses that run once an hour or freeways that jam from 6:00 A.M. to 6:00 P.M. weekdays are probably not convenient. If you do a lot of out-of-town travel, consider access to the airport, train station or ferry docks as you evaluate location.

Location also relates to the local scene. Food, clothes, sports access, the beach, bars and rave action are life-style location considerations. If you bike a lot, maybe the Hillcrest or Canyon Drive part of town is not for you.

Familiarizing yourself with a new town requires time. In addition to asking people where is a good place to live, you can find help in the form of newcomer information from the local chamber of commerce or library. Book, grocery and hardware stores sell local maps. In some cases, local real estate agents can help, but I recommend a more independent search method. In large cities there may be local books on history, layout, neighborhoods or ethnicity. These can be very helpful. Sadly, the issue of personal safety is also a consideration. Talk to a community relations officer at the police department to check on which areas have less crime and which areas have more. Will you feel safe walking down a certain street at night alone? Will you feel safe *during the day?*

Define your needs considering your life-style, work situation and location, transportation resources and short-term or long-term strategy.

Examples: You're into the art scene and work Near North. You don't own a car. A location near work and the galleries could be very appealing. If your building was close to a public transportation line or cab stand, it might be ideal. So you might start your search close to work, balancing the price for rent against convenience.

You and your family are just moving to town. You may stay for a year or five years. You may want to "test" a community by renting before you buy. What are your considerations? If you have a car, you consider the routes, both urban and suburban, that will take you to work quickly. You explore the areas near the spokes and grid lines these roads make on the map. If public transportation is also available, you follow those lines. You check with your boss or personnel department about van pooling. You next consider basic family needs: proximity to stores, malls, parks, doctors and hospitals, schools, cultural attractions, religious institutions, friends and family.

There are other location questions to consider. Is there a certain part of town in which you would be more comfortable because of the customs or language spoken there? Or conversely, is there someplace you would feel uncomfortable because of language or ethnic differences? Would the noise that comes with living under an airport flight path bother you? Some people have problems with living on busy streets or near fire stations and hospitals because of the heavy traffic and sirens.

Drive-bys

By now you probably have a general idea of where you want to rent. Visit the areas. If you drive, cruise both the main and side streets. If you use public transportation, ride the bus or train from your work, school or place of activity to the areas you are considering. If you have the money, take a cab. Maybe the cabby will fill you in! What you are looking for are the basics you require such as grocery stores, shops, schools, hospitals and entertainment. You'll also observe the general conditions of the community.

If the main drags meet with your approval or interest, walk or drive down the side streets. There you will see how your potential neighbors live. You'll see the type and condition of buildings, yards and vehicles. You might even see "For Rent" signs.

Using the "Location Checklist" and "Area Worksheet" found at the end of this chapter, score each part of town you visit. Learn the principal zip-code number, telephone exchange prefixes and area name(s) so that you can later match newspaper ads to your desired location.

Resources

The worksheets and checklists in chapters 1 and 2 should have created usable profiles. You have a lot of organized information about yourself and what you need, as well as enough information about potential locations, so you are ready to go rental hunting in earnest. How do you actually find what is available? Through classified ads in the newspapers—but not just the daily newspaper. Most communities have weekly or twice-weekly papers that cater to specific areas. You can find some of the best deals from these local papers, and you know that you will probably deal with somebody from the immediate vicinity. Most newspapers will also list real estate agencies, apartment management companies and apartment finder services. Some companies also advertise on television or cable channels. Call them to see what they've got. Although not as fruitful, you can get agency names in the Yellow Pages under apartments, apartment finders and real estate management. Choose companies that are in your selected area. Most areas also have rental guides that advertise lists of units by categories.

Hint: If you can, go back into your selected area(s) and look for the "For Rent" signs on the various buildings. Also go into the laundromats and check the bulletin boards for rental notices. Ask your friends and co-workers about availabilities.

Hint: Start with the "For Rent" signs and classified ads. These give you the freshest listings and the most variety. Management companies and finder services have limited stocks, as a rule. The one exception is house rentals that may be more easily located through a regular real estate agent.

Reading the Ads

The weekend edition of any paper is likely to be the best place to start. Some big-city newspapers run the Sunday classifieds on Friday, Saturday and Sunday. Some papers run ads by geographic zone, so you must have the north county edition if you want to find the north county listings.

Trying to understand the classified ads can be a minor challenge. Everything is coded. Learn the language first and save a lot of time later. To appreciate the complexity involved, try this one: "Lrg 4rm (1bd) wf ac oc-vu hst dst in newer elv bldg, lndry, pkg." Translated at the first level, it reads: "a large four-room apartment (one bedroom), with wood floors, air conditioning, ocean view [is for rent]. The apartment is in a historical district, in a newer building with elevator, laundry and parking facilities." Sounds great, but between the lines the ad might really be saying that the unit is a smallish apartment (living–dining room combination, a narrow "pullman" [as in train car] kitchen the size of a gym locker and a bathroom and bedroom, which equals four rooms) located in a 20-year-old, ticky-tacky building in the wharf district (straddling a geologic fault zone) with a freight elevator, a couple of struggling washing machines and parking for half the tenants (i.e., get on the waiting list for the next space).

Be suspicious about the glowing descriptions. If the apartment is that *good*, there will be a waiting list! Later, when checking out your selections by phone, ask your second question: "What type of building is it in?" (Your first question is "Is the apartment still available?") Don't waste time with buildings that don't appeal to you.

There are many abbreviations used in the ads to save space and money. Generally speaking, it does not take a genius to understand them. If U CN RD THS, U CN RD AN APT AD. The following glossary of newspaper jargon will help you interpret the ads.

a/c or **a/c'd:** with air conditioning. This could mean central air, window units in each room or an old wheezer dripping water onto the living room floor.

ampl or **ample:** plenty of parking, closet space or whatever. Old buildings seldom have enough closet space, and parking may either cost a fortune or will be available on the street as you find it.

apls or **appls:** appliances. Are they new, working or in the basement? Is it traditional in your city to rent a unit with a stove and a refrigerator supplied by the landlord? Find out!

apt: apartment.

blc: balcony (sometimes for real and sometimes a back porch or fire escape).

bldg: building.

bs: a brownstone building. Usually a smaller, older, more elegant structure.

ch: See **coach house.**

cnvrt or **cnvrtbl:** convertible. This is a very small apartment, usually one room, where the main room "converts" from living room–dining room–den into bedroom when you pull down a foldaway bed (Castro or Murphy) out of the wall.

coach house: A coach house is a converted garage, stable or small barn. The coach house sits at the rear of the property on the alley, behind the main house. Sometimes the living area uses both first and second floors; sometimes it uses only the converted hayloft or attic. Often the first floor of a coach house is still used as a garage with all the attendant engine sounds, gasoline and exhaust smells and garage doors opening and closing at all hours.

crptg: carpeting. This may be new, old, clean or dirty. There may be an additional security or damage deposit requirement. (You may also see **w/w crptg:** wall-to-wall carpeting.)

ct: ceramic-tiled bathroom. This might mean the shower wall, all the walls and/or the floor.

dbl plm: double plumbing. This could mean many risers (pipes) for hot and cold water so that water pressure is not affected by flushing toilets, or it could mean only hot and cold running water.

dd or **dam dep:** damage deposit. This is an extra advance payment made when you move in to cover the costs of damages you may cause during the lease. It is returnable to you when you move out provided there are no damages. See **sec.**

dec: See **nly dec.**

dep: See **dd** and **sec.**

dlx: deluxe. (Beauty is in the eye of the beholder.)

dplx: duplex. It usually means a two-story, two-unit building, but it can also mean a two-floor apartment unit.

ef or **effncy:** efficiency. See **cnvrt.** Also see **studio.**

el or **elv:** elevator. (**Frt elv** means freight elevator.)

English apt: See **garden apt.**

f/a: forced air. This usually indicates a modern heating (and cooling) system. Assume that the tenant can directly control the thermostat and will pay the heating/cooling utilities. See **tenant htd.**

f/lmr: first and last months' rent. You must pay the first and last months' rent in advance of moving in. Sometimes this relieves you of paying a security deposit. See **sec.**

fpl or **wbf (wbfpl):** fireplace or wood-burning fireplace. When it doesn't say burning, don't expect it to work. (It will leak water or gas, maybe, but not burn wood.)

free rent: Santa Claus, bridges over the Sahara and the second coming. Sometimes this means that you can use your security deposit for your last month's rent; sometimes it means the rent has been increased to cover the cost of the freebie; other times it means the place needs extra enticements to gain tenants (what's the problem?). Do not make free rent an inducement or reason for taking an apartment.

garden or **garden apt:** garden apartment. A garden apartment is an apartment at or below ground level. Garden apartments are sometimes damp, cold, moldy, dark and short on air circulation.

gs: graystone building. See **bs.**

htd: heated. This has a variety of meanings. In most parts of the country, full-service heat is needed during the winter (and fall and spring). Many states and municipalities have laws about how much heat and when to heat. So this can mean (1) there is a heater of some sort in the unit or (2) central heat is provided. This needs to be clarified with the agent since paying extra for heat adds a lot to the gross rent.

key fee: Not seen everywhere, a key fee is a gratuity, payment or bribe required by an agent or previous tenant to rent an apartment. The money is sometimes to compensate a tenant for improvements made to the unit. More often it is the grease that allows a rent-controlled apartment to change hands.

lk: lake.

lndry: laundry facilities.

loft or **lft:** loft. A loft is an apartment, usually one large room, in a converted factory or the like. Some lofts can be elegant; others may be garrets.

lrg: large. It's hard to judge what "large" really means.

mod bth: modern bathroom (newly rehabilitated, newly painted or merely one with a flush toilet and an old four-legged tub with no shower).

mod, mod ap or **mod kit:** modern, modern appliances or modern kitchen. Sometimes this means a new kitchen; other times is means an electric refrigerator, running water and a non-wood-burning cook stove.

mstr bdrm: master bedroom (one large [?] bedroom, sometimes with a connecting bathroom).

nly dec: newly or nicely decorated. It could mean tastefully repainted and wallpapered with refinished floors and woodwork, or it could mean when they slopped the paint this time, they managed to paint the windows shut and the wall outlets closed for good. It could also mean they painted a couple of years ago (before the last tenants moved in), and the walls still look more white then grime grey.

oc-vu: ocean view. Can you see the ocean, really? Some rental agents call this a "peekaview." Cute.

pkg: parking (where and what to be determined).

pnty: pantry or walk-in kitchen storage area. This could mean that there are no regular kitchen cabinets, shelves or counters.

ri or **riv:** river.

sec: security deposit. This is an amount equal to one to two months' rent as an advance deposit required before you can move in. It is used in case the tenant causes damage or fails to pay rent. It is not the same as first-month/last-month rents, which are usually additional. Is the security deposit refundable when you move out (oh, yeah? Maybe!)? In many states and towns, this deposit earns interest due the tenant on a yearly basis and when the lease ends. There are also other regulations regarding the use and return of security deposits. See **dd.**

sm: small (microscopic).

spcs: spacious (big enough to swing your arms around).

studio: A studio is a single-room apartment with a kitchen in the corner and a separate bathroom. Also see **cnvrt** or **cnvrtbl** and **ef** or **effncy.**

tenant htd: tenant pays the heating bill for the apartment.

vic: This means "in the vicinity of" or can occasionally mean a Victorian-style building. See **bs** and **gs.**

vu: view. View of what? **Lk vu** or **lk-vu** means there is a view of the lake. **Ri vu** or **ri-vu** means there is a view of the river. **Sea vu** and **Bay vu** should be obvious. See **oc-vu.**

wbfpl: See **fpl.**

wf or **hdwd fl:** wooden floors or hardwood floors (not tiled, carpeted, concrete or exposed decking but may be painted or not refinished).

Plan of Attack

Do a scan of the ads, paying particular attention to four factors: (1) location, (2) size, (3) starting date and (4) rent. Mark each ad with a highlighter or red ink so that on the second pass all you have to do is find your marks, instead of re-reading the whole section. Do this scan uncritically; that is, don't worry about amenities or other details. You will be winnowing on the following pass.

Next, cut out the marked ads. Check the back side of each ad to make sure you don't destroy another marked entry. Tape each ad to a separate three-by-five-inch card. Mark the date and source of each listing. Similarly, write up each nonpaper ad on a separate three-by-five-inch card. Later, you can put information from the best ads into a computer data base.

Study these ads and discard those that on second look are not appealing. Then separate and organize the remaining ads by some system that makes sense to you (perhaps all those available on a certain date; all those that meet your price, building type or number of rooms; those that include parking; or organized by street address, bus route or whatever). Just be sure to have a plan of attack.

Phone First

Then start calling. Some of the offerings are from private owners, and they are likely to be around on Sunday to answer the phone. Some management companies might also be open on Sundays. Make the calls, using the checklist below. Make notes on the cards. Have a calendar handy to book appointments and cross-record the address and phone numbers, just in case you later misplace a card. Keep calling until you make contact. Use the "Telephone Checklist" at the back of this chapter.

Try to put yourself in one area or "zone" of town in the same time period on a given day to kill as many birds as possible with one trip. Don't crowd appointments, because it may take you longer at any one place than you had planned since an agent may be late or may wait until several bidders show up so that all can go at once.

No more than two appointments (two units) in 90 minutes are advised when you are driving or one every 90 minutes when you're on foot or using public transportation. Sometimes one phone call will turn out to offer three or four possible places. Stay with the agent for this grand tour and plan other appointments accordingly. When in doubt, consult your map or the local street guide. Be aware that some agents may want to make you miss your next appointment, so don't crowd your time.

Shopping the zone-system way saves a lot of time and a lot of bus and cab fares. It is possible to log 50 miles in a day while looking at eight apartments in two adjoining zones!

The Functions and Business of Rental Agents

In the slippery business of renting, there is the renter—that's you on one side—and all the other guys on the opposite side. In chapter 1, I defined the landlord as all those other guys lumped together, but really it is not so simple. There can be many different entities involved in the rental process. It is important to understand that landlords are primarily interested in filling rental units with paying tenants and keeping those units occupied at a minimum cost to themselves. Essentially, landlording is more the business of money (as in banking) than it is service (as in housing). Property values, tax policy, interest rates and profits drive the rental market. So when dealing with "those guys," remember what their real business is.

In this context, please note that anybody offering you an apartment has a legal obligation (the law of agency) to the owner to be the owner's representative, not yours. Furthermore, with the exception of the actual owner, real estate personnel representing the owner and offering rental units customarily receive a commission, typically one month's rent, upon the execution of the application or lease. Thus, you as a renter represent income based upon signing up. Anything that can induce or encourage you to take a particular apartment is to the benefit of the agent. This is how the system works, and indeed there are rules and customs that promote and govern this system. By the way, the laws of most states require that any person (with the possible exception of the owner of a few units) engaged in the practice of real estate, including property management and apartment finding, must be licensed by the state real estate regulatory department.

The Landlord and the Agents

You may have contact with a variety of people offering apartments to you. You might meet directly with the owner. In this case, there is no question—he or she is the landlord. The owner will show you properties that he or she owns. By dint of ownership, this person is responsible for everything. After a lease is signed, it is difficult for the owner to deny responsibility, although it may be very hard to make that person do what is required.

Often the owner either does not wish personally to show units, or the business is too large for the owner to show units. Sometimes a corporation owns the property. The owner then hires a manager or retains the services of one or more real estate companies specializing in property management.

Rental Agents

Rental agents work for the ownership directly, through a property management organization or as independent contractors. The agent is primarily a salesperson who finds tenants for available units. Who the agent works for will give you a clue about how helpful that person can be to you as you look for your dwelling unit.

Agent of the Owner

The owner's agent will usually be an on-premises employee. The agent may be the building manager or perhaps the janitor. The advantage of this arrangement is that the agent knows the units and also is in a position to negotiate some parts of the lease. Such an agent can probably find and speak directly to the landlord if needed. Also he or she will probably know about other units that may soon be available. The disadvantage is that the agent can only show you what the landlord owns.

Property Management Companies

These companies usually provide full services for the owners. They act as buffers between tenants and landlords. Management companies receive monthly fees from the landlords, approximately 10 percent of the monthly take. For this fee, they keep the building and grounds clean, order maintenance and repairs, collect the rents and fees, prosecute the evictions, keep the books, check tenants in and out, return deposits, advertise and show apartments, qualify applicants and sign leases. The advantage of finding an apartment through a management company is that it represents multiple owners and multiple buildings so it has a larger selection than the single owner. The disadvantage is that it acts as an absolute barrier between you and the owner. With a management company, you may never know who owns your building, nor can you complain about a problem *or* about the management company. Negotiating lease terms can be difficult because the company has its rules and procedures, one of which invariably is not to bother the owner.

Apartment Finder Services

Professional apartment finders offer a service to both tenants and landlords. They find tenants for landlords with units to rent. They generally are independent agents not employed by any one landlord. They move the tenant another step away from those ultimately responsible.

Using a finder service is seductive for the tenant because tenants believe that somebody else will go to the trouble of looking at all those ads and picking out the few good units. This is not true. As a rule, these services only show apartments for which they will receive compensation, usually by prior arrangement. Finders are retained by specific owners and even management companies to advertise and show specific units, qualify prospects, obtain application and lease signatures and collect first and last months' rent and fees. For these services, apartment finders collect a typical commission of one month's rent.

For some prospective tenants, these services are a boon. A salesperson can quickly organize a list of units that meet the renter's needs. The agent will make the appointments and chauffeur the prospect from location to location. If you are new to town or don't have a car, this can be very useful. Since the finder represents a limited number of clients, the service can only offer a limited number of units. Apartment finder services are no substitute for reading the classified ads. Another drawback is that the salespeople are not as familiar with the units, the buildings, the neighborhoods or the management. Specific information is harder to obtain, and negotiating lease terms is either very cumbersome or out of the question. Since the finder service will not have to deal with you or your apartment problems later, its principal activity is a quick sale now, so it may make promises that cannot be kept.

In some states, apartment finders cannot collect the security or damage deposit because by law it must be held separately and used only for damages. By collecting *rent* in advance, a service may be able to keep that money if you change your mind after you sign the application but before you sign the lease. (There is more information about this in chapter 4.)

As a general rule, apartment finder services are run like real estate offices. That is, the "house" splits the commission it receives with the salesperson doing the showing. The salespeople are usually on a commission-only basis, so they are anxious to close deals. Once the application fees are given over, it is very hard to get them back.

Since finder services receive commissions from landlords, challenge a service that wants to charge you for anything else besides a nominal fee for a credit check. From time to time, certain less-than-professional operations have tried schemes like selling a list of "guaranteed" apartments or your money back. Well, you can read a newspaper as well they can. Another scheme is to take an application fee (usually one month's rent) from a prospect with a promise to call when a unit comes up. The apartments are sometimes dumps, sometimes rented and sometimes come-ons for bait and switch. With this scam you'll seldom find what you want. Under no circumstances will you get your money back until the county prosecutor threatens an indictment. Use care.

Telephone Checklist

Put Apartment Ad Information Here

_____

_____

_____

---

1. Is the apartment still available? ☐ Yes ☐ No
2. What is the type of building? ☐ ( )-flat ☐ Low rise ☐ High rise
   ☐ Row house ☐ Town house ☐ Freestanding
3. What is the address? _____
   _____
4. How many units are there in the building, and how old is the building?
   Units: _____ Age: _____
5. How many rooms are in the unit? _____ Is it ☐ large or
   ☐ small? What floor is it on? _____ ☐ Elevator?
6. How much is the rent, how much is the deposit and are there any other costs
   or fees?
   Rent: $ _____
   Deposit: $ _____
   Extra fees: $ _____
7. What kind of heat does the apartment have? ☐ Steam ☐ Hot water
   ☐ Forced air ☐ Space heater ☐ Gas ☐ Electric ☐ Air conditioning
8. Who pays for heat, air conditioning, hot water, and how much does it cost?
   ☐ Tenant ☐ Landlord $ _____
9. Is the unit a ☐ condominium or a ☐ co-op?
10. Who is offering the unit? ☐ Management company ☐ Owner
    ☐ Finder service ☐ Tenant trying to sublet
    Name of person/company offering unit: _____
    _____
11. (If this applies) Are ☐ children accepted? ☐ Pets? (By the way, it is illegal
    to refuse rental housing on the basis of children.)
12. (If this applies) ☐ Is parking available? How much does it cost to rent a
    space? $ _____ ☐ Indoor ☐ Outdoor
13. What is the term of the lease? From _____ to _____.
    When is the unit available? _____
14. Are there any other apartments (which meet your specifications) beside the
    one(s) advertised? ☐ Yes ☐ No

15. When can the apartment(s) be seen?   Date and time: _____
    _____

16. Are there any amenities? List them here.
    (1) _____
    (2) _____
    (3) _____
    (4) _____

Notes

_____

_____

_____

_____

_____

_____

_____

_____

Location Checklist and Area Worksheet

> ## Put Apartment Ad/Area Information Here
>
> _____
>
> _____
>
> _____

Scoring: 1 Very close/short mile or 5 minutes
2 Quick 1 to 2 miles or less than 10 minutes
3 Good 3 to 6 miles or under 20 minutes
4 Reasonable 7 to 10 miles or under 30 minutes
5 Commute 10 to 15 miles or under 45 minutes
6 Ridiculous 20 to 40 miles or over an hour

Distance from apartment to work or classes?   1 2 3 4 5 6   _____

Time to travel from apartment to work or classes?   1 2 3 4 5 6   _____

Proximity to freeways and expressways?   1 2 3 4 5 6   _____

Proximity to main streets?   1 2 3 4 5 6   _____

Proximity to public transportation?   1 2 3 4 5 6   _____

Proximity to airport, rail station, docks?   1 2 3 4 5 6   _____

Proximity to friends and relatives?   1 2 3 4 5 6   _____

Proximity to city center, attractions?   1 2 3 4 5 6   _____

Section Score (the lower, the better)   _____

Area

Scoring: Circle your observations and rank the area from 1 to 6 with 1 being the highest score.

Area Flavors

New   Old

Ritzy   Yuppie   Staid   Middle Class   Working Class   Mixed   Poor   Slum

Residential   Commercial

Smooth   Rough   Unsavory (not safe)

Ethnic mix: Bland   Exciting   Not your taste

Traffic: Heavy   Light   Quiet

Parking on street: Yes   Some   Not really

Broken glass/dereliction

People hanging on the block: Yes   No
Graffiti/gangs: Yes   No
Section Score (the lower, the better)   _____

Commerce and Industry (Score from 1 to 6 as above.)
 Close to grocery store?   1 2 3 4 5 6   _____
 Specialty food shops?   1 2 3 4 5 6   _____
 Specialty clothing, children's, toy shops?   1 2 3 4 5 6   _____
 Close to book stores?   1 2 3 4 5 6   _____
 Close to hardware store?   1 2 3 4 5 6   _____
 Close to shopping centers?   1 2 3 4 5 6   _____
 Close to services such as:
  Cleaners?   1 2 3 4 5 6   _____
  Shoe repair?   1 2 3 4 5 6   _____
  Gas station?   1 2 3 4 5 6   _____
  Drugstore?   1 2 3 4 5 6   _____
 Close to movies?   1 2 3 4 5 6   _____
 Close to video rental store?   1 2 3 4 5 6   _____
 Close to pollution sources?   6 5 4 3 2 1   _____
 Close to restaurants?   1 2 3 4 5 6   _____
 Close to bars and clubs?   1 2 3 4 5 6   _____
 Close to beaches, pools?   1 2 3 4 5 6   _____
 Close to other entertainment?   1 2 3 4 5 6   _____
Section Score (the lower, the better)   _____

Services
 Hospital?   1 2 3 4 5 6   _____
 Doctor?   1 2 3 4 5 6   _____
 Schools?   1 2 3 4 5 6   _____
 Parks?   1 2 3 4 5 6   _____
 Museums?   1 2 3 4 5 6   _____
 Zoo?   1 2 3 4 5 6   _____
 Police?   1 2 3 4 5 6   _____
 Fire department?   1 2 3 4 5 6   _____
 Governmental services and agencies?   1 2 3 4 5 6   _____
Section Score (the lower, the better)   _____
Total Score (the lower, the better)   _____

Comments

Pass? Fail? Convenient? Safe?

Of the areas you have seen, how do you rank this area?
(first choice to last)   1 2 3 4 5 6 7 8 9 10

Notes

_____

_____

_____

_____

_____

_____

_____

_____

Inspecting and Choosing Your New Place

> **Check It Out**
> - Area Services
> - Street Decay
> - Building Conditions
> - Common Areas
> - Apartment Interior
> - Amenities, Utilities, Services
> - Code Violations

Choosing your living space is a combination of art and craft. You practice the craft of finding a place primarily by asking questions. The results are compiled on the worksheets and checklists. By the end of this chapter, you will also be able to practice the art of rental-space hunting. The art, by the way, is the ability to quickly size up a situation and make a decision with confidence.

Do yourself a favor—read this chapter. Yes, it is detailed; and yes, apartment shopping can be a drudge. Keep clear what you are about: confidently renting a safe place to live in comfort. Prepare yourself for the inspection process while remembering that the rental agent is a salesperson who is trying to hustle a product as quickly as possible at the highest price. Gin-su knives or used cars anyone?

When you do rent, you will rent the unit "as is." That means you accept what you see. If you don't inspect well, you could get a lot less than you expect or require.

The inspection process is one of logic, patience and curiosity. It certainly is one of practicality. The detail of the inspection process should be viewed not as forbidding but as the same type of common-sense shopping you would exercise anytime you commit from $3,000 to $14,000 of your annual income. There is nothing very technical about the process. Learning what to look for and noting what you find can make all the difference between a year of comfort and a year of hell. The rest of this chapter will walk you through the inspection process. In Appendix A, there is a very detailed checklist for initial inspections. Make copies of this checklist so you can use a new one for each unit you inspect.

Tools of the Trade

When you go to your appointments, take your file cards with the ads pasted on, the worksheets you have already filled out regarding needs and location, blank inspection worksheets and a notebook. Also bring a Polaroid or automatic camera, if you have one, with spare film, small flash unit and spare batteries (if needed). Strange as it sounds, you should also take along a simple tool kit that includes the following: flat blade and Phillips-head screwdrivers, a 25-foot measuring tape, a medium-sized Vise-grips or pliers, a $1.99 neon glow AC tube circuit tester (Radio Shack #22-102), a flashlight, a box of long wooden matches (to find drafts and test smoke detectors), a box of toothpicks and a boom box (portable radio) to check sound transmission. For the full treatment, keep reading.

Local Laws

Almost every local governmental corporation—village, town, city and county—enforces a building and a zoning code. Furthermore, local and state governments may have special statues regarding rules for residential rental housing, ranging from safety to rental control to tenants' rights. By calling the village hall or the county building, you can usually obtain pamphlets or other information regarding these laws. As a person shopping for a rental unit, you will want to know about security devices, smoke detectors, fire safety requirements, heating and cooling minimums/maximums, rental price controls and deposit regulations. Information can come from the building department, city manager or mayor's office, community relations office or even a landlord-tenant office. City attorneys and county and state prosecutors' offices also may have information. Most large towns have tenants' rights group that also can help.

Practice and Etiquette

Although chapter 4 covers applications and leases, a few words are helpful right now. Don't sign anything for the privilege of being shown an apartment. Don't pay a fee for looking! There is no exclusive arrangement between you and the agent, and you have no obligation to the agent to get your apartment from him or her. The more sources of supply and variety, the better it will be for you. Don't confide any information to the agent that might affect your bargaining power regarding price, length of stay or special conditions (including your being desperate to find a place before noon tomorrow). Don't rent the first place you see.

Confirm your appointments by phone before you go out. Be on time. Don't try to impress the agent. (That's what the credit check is all about.) There is no reason to be nervous. Go about your business confidently. Using the "Truth-in-Renting Worksheet" at the back of chapter 4, ask the agent as many questions about the area, building, unit, lease and ownership as you think necessary. If you need to use the circuit tester, screwdrivers, flashlight or pliers, do so without apology. Know your requirements and be prepared to walk away from a unit as soon as you are sure it doesn't meet your needs.

Now start your engine. . . .

The Inspection Process

Assessing the Community

Could you live in this part of town? Do you like the area? Does it have the stores, entertainment, schools and transportation you require? Can you feel safe? You should find the area convenient and feel comfortable about the community.

Assessing the Neighborhood

Walk or drive around the block where your potential unit is located. Look at the general conditions. Do the buildings and houses appear to be in good shape? Are the streets clean or full of junk? Study the age and appearance of the cars. Do you see derelict cars and broken glass? Is parking an issue? Are there gang markings? Are there beggars and loiterers hanging on the corner? Can you comfortably walk to and from public transportation? Will your friends or family be afraid to visit? While you are looking around, check out the alley for gang signs, trash and other forms of urban decay.

Assessing the Exterior

The exterior of the building is a strong selling point for the landlord. If the outside looks good, it attracts tenants and makes a promise that the complex is well managed and maintained. If the outside is shoddy, think about how responsive management will be to your problems. If the outside is lacking, what about the heat, pipes and wires on the inside?

Outside Appearance

Look at the house, complex or building critically as you approach it. How would you describe the conditions? If there is landscaping or a lawn, is it well cared for, clean and free of trash? If there is no lawn, why not? Is the building front in good shape? Is it well painted? Are the wood, stones, bricks and mortar intact and clean? Look at the door and window trim. Is it solid, loose or are there pieces missing? Do you see dirty, broken or boarded windows? If appropriate, do you see combination storm and screen windows? Look down at the sidewalks and steps. Are they safe and solid or chipped, cracked and loose? If it is winter, are ice and snow cleared?

Outside Doors

Examine the exterior front and rear doors. Are they in good shape or in disrepair? Do they automatically close and lock? Is there an intercom and/or doorkeeper? Will the doorway be well lit at night? Do you see a plaque or sign clearly posted that announces the owner or management's name and a 24-hour emergency phone number? Many municipalities require this notice in case of fire or police emergency. The name and number should reassure you that somebody is stating their responsibility for the property and is reachable after hours.

Walk around the entire building if practical. Is there a gangway? Does it smell of urine or contain garbage? Is there evidence of homeless people or gang signs? At the rear, how do the back doors appear? If there are there rear exterior stairways, porches or fire escapes, are they in good shape? Are they clean, and do they appear safe? If there is a backyard, parking area, service area or alley, is there trash scattered around, graffiti, abandoned refrigerators or junked cars? Can a burglar jump from another building or from the ground to get into the building from the rear?

Assessing the Common Areas

The common areas consist of the inside parts of the building that offer public or tenant access. The purpose of inspection is twofold: (1) to ensure you are getting what you need and (2) to establish the level of care and commitment from the landlord (don't expect better service inside your unit than outside of it). Common areas should be clean, with no signs of obvious wear, and they should not be smelly. They include the entrances and lobbies; storage and laundry facilities; and mailboxes, stairways, hallways and elevators.

Entrances

You look for areas to be clean, well lit and obviously well maintained. Check entrances for secure inner doors with door closers and automatic locks. Make sure the intercom and the electronic opener really work, or you'll discover later that tenants either buzz anybody in or just prop the door open permanently. Is this building begging for burglars to walk through the front door? What about mailbox security? Are the boxes intact, or does it look like they've been peeled open? Will your UPS packages be safe?

Lobby

If there is a waiting area or lobby, is the seating arrangement respectable, or is seating torn, stained and tottering? Do you see loitering? Is the lobby clean, and does it smell fresh? Are the walls painted, and is the carpet not torn or worn out?

Halls and Stairs

Hallways and stairwells should be lit 24 hours a day. Most building codes require fire protection, and you should expect it, code or not. For safety's sake, there should be a fire extinguisher on each landing and hall end as well as smoke detectors on the ceiling of each landing and at the center of each hallway (and ends of long hallways). Even if you are renting a house, make sure of the smoke detectors! Floors should be solid, with no loose tiles, planks or nails. Carpeting must not be torn, worn or loose. Stair railings should be strong and tight to the wall. Look for exit-sign lights pointing to "the other way out." Are there any smells?

Elevators

If the building has elevators, evaluate the one(s) you ride in. Your issues are safety from mugging and crashing, convenience (speed and reliability) and noise (will it wake you up at night?). Is the waiting area well lit and safe? Is there a TV security camera? Is there a panic button nearby? Is there a floor position indicator? Did it take a long time for the elevator to come? Can you see evidence of where an "Out of Order" sign is regularly hung? Can you hear motor noise and door clunking as the elevator car moves along? When the car arrives, does the door open quietly and smoothly? What is the condition of the inside? Is there an emergency phone? When your floor is pushed, does the elevator lurch on takeoff or jerk, dance and bounce on landing? Do you see a current inspection and operating permit?

Assessing the Rental Unit

This inspection process has several purposes of equal importance. One purpose is to assess the condition of the unit. The other is for you to see how you can fit into this particular place. You will want to measure rooms for floor size and evaluate the position of doors, closets, windows and heating units. Will your furniture slide through a door, make the bend in a hallway and fit properly in a room? King-size beds in eight- by ten-foot bedrooms are too tight a squeeze. (See Appendix A, page 181, for bed sizes.) Long couches, tall hutches and dining room tables must be considered. What about rugs and drapes? Bring your furniture measurements with you. Do you have liquid-filled furniture or a water bed? Will these be allowed? If you have appliances, where will they go and will they fit? What type of power, gas, water and drain connections do they need, and can the unit accommodate them?

Whether you're considering an apartment, condo, loft, town house or house, it is all the same. This is where you may live, so this is where you concentrate your energies. Please remember that as far as you are concerned, you will rent the place *as is*. That means that you shouldn't expect anything else to be done, *even if it is in writing!* All the talk about painting, carpet cleaning, repairs and new appliances may be hot air. The landlord or agent can talk a good game and promise you almost anything to get your name on an application and money in the agent's pocket. Later you may be unable to get what was promised, or it is so much trouble that you give up. In chapter 4 I'll discuss how to get promises into the lease and how to protect yourself. My best advice is not to rely on promises but on what you actually see.

Using the worksheet, go through the entire apartment.

Smells and Noise

Start with "disturbances" outside of the apartment itself, namely, smells and noise. As you approach the unit, give the area a sniff test. Listen for street sounds and building sounds. Do you hear doors slamming, elevator noises or mechanical pumps and grinds in the building? Remember, you'll have to sleep through these noises!

What about odors? A building that smells, stinks. Don't waste more time. Odors can come from poor plumbing and broken fixtures, poor tenant housekeeping, poor management upkeep, overcrowding, leaky gas pipes and appliances, faulty heating systems, poor garbage disposal systems, bad ventilation, mold and mildew, mice and rats, fire, flooding, etc. Such conditions can make you sick and might kill you. Your nose can tell you about the attitudes of management regarding how they select and treat other tenants and about cleaning, maintenance and building problems. Don't expect you and yours to be treated any better. Get the picture? If it stinks, walk away from it now.

Entry Doors

What about door security? Examine both the front and rear doors. Look for scratches, gouges and pry marks on the outside door edge and adjacent door frame. See that the door frame itself is not cracked. Look at the condition of the door strike. (That's the part the door latches into.) Most burglars who go through doors use a flat pry bar or large screwdriver to break away the frame. The trim and wood behind it splinter and crack, the strike is ripped out and the door opens. It takes two or three grunting whacks, and it's all over. Once the frame (and door) is compromised, it should be replaced, not patched up. The door should close tightly and fit snugly to the frame. When locked, it should not rattle. A loose door is easy to break down. If the door has a window, could a burglar reach through the broken opening and unlock the door from the inside?

Determine that the door itself feels heavy and solid when you swing it and knock on it. Some hollow-core doors, or doors filled with plasterboard or styrofoam, are so weak that a hammer blow will crack them wide open! A so-called steel door is usually a styrofoam core door with a thin sheet-metal exterior that is easily punctured. If there are enough solid blows to the door knob, the mechanism will fall out.

Locks

Beside the lock in the knob, many municipalities require an extra single-cylinder deadbolt lock, where the key locks only from the outside and a small knob operates the lock from the inside. They also may require a see-through or peephole, so you know who's knocking.

If the doors don't give you the safety and security you need, walk away from the unit. Once a place has been broken into and the necessary repairs and new safety precautions have not been made, it is ripe for a revisit. Be good to yourself and your loved ones. Go to your next appointment.

Windows

Windows, windows, windows. Poorly insulated, drafty windows account for up to 25 percent of heat loss in an apartment. Check the glass for cracks and shake the windows for loose panes (caulking). If the windows rattle, they are leakers and require weather stripping or refitting. When closed, will they seal against outside weather, including drafts, dust and water? If the frames are metal, are they insulated? Metal frames are notorious for conducting cold into rooms and "sweating." Look for plaster disintegration and water and rust stains on and around these frames, including the floor. Check for leaking frames and trim by observing dirt streaks that come out of the frames like ant trails. In the winter, that's where the cold air leaks in.

Make sure that all windows open and close easily. If windows are the sash type (most windows are of this type, which slides up to open and down to close), they should have intact counterbalance chains, cords or strips. This keeps them level and easy to move. If the window is mechanical, the crank or push rod should be present and easy to operate. Window hardware should include handles and latches. If a window is close to the ground or easily accessible from a porch, fire escape or nearby building, an additional window movement limiter or security lock is highly recommended. Some localities require extra window security if the windows are within 20 feet of the ground or are otherwise at risk. New York City requires protective window bars in high-rise apartments when occupied by children under ten years of age. These may include wrought-iron bars, reenforced glass, glass block and special rods or blocking devices to prevent sliding doors and windows from opening (johnny bars).

Do the windows have screens? In many towns screens must be supplied from late spring through early fall. Are there storm windows or thermal-pane or "low E" windows to cut down heat loss in winter (and cooling loss in summer)? Find out if storms are a code requirement in your town. (Call the building department at city hall.) If you pay for the heat, you'll want storms.

Comment: Where I live, windows are a big problem. The high-price decorators many landlords hire usually paint the windows shut. Our landlords typically ignored requests to fix the windows (before our local laws changed, which I will discuss in chapters 7 and 8). When you, the tenant, try to get fresh air, the window won't open without a lot of work and then may permanently stick open. Finally, in frustration, the tenant applies available instruments of war such as a screwdriver and hammer to the stuck window. It's a game of glazer's roulette: the window frees up; the window doesn't move; the window is broken. If the window moves this time, it will stick next time. If it stays stuck, somebody sets off a smoke bomb or it rains or snows. If it is broken, your landlord will charge you the cost of replacement. Thus, don't shrug your shoulders if the windows won't work during the inspection.

Walls

Is there exposed brick on any of the outside walls? These walls may be lovely, but they do not insulate at all. In cold weather they will suck vast amounts of heat out of your apartment, raising your heating bill by 15 percent. If you use humidifiers or even boil water for tea, these walls "sweat" when it is very cold outside. Water oozes down the wall to the floor, ruining things mounted on the wall and lifting floor tiles or staining rugs. Wet walls give the place a clammy feeling. If an outside closet wall is bare, water can condense during the winter, permanently staining and mildewing whatever is touched.

Paint and Lead Paint

On conventional plaster walls, does it look as if the wallpaper underneath is about to roll up like a shade? Are there any problems with peeling paint? Good. Are the walls clean? Is the paint job decent? Is the paint tight to the wall without bleeding? In older places, hazardous and now illegal lead-based paint usually is under the new paint. If the paint flakes and falls into food or into the reach of small children, permanent illness can result. Ingested lead causes brain damage (retardation) in children and liver and brain damage in adults.

Plasterwork

Good paint can do only so much. How about the plaster? Bad plaster appears as a wall with tons of crow's-foot wrinkles, a general and continuing unevenness and evidence of a lot of patching. This can become a bad problem if you want to hang pictures or a wall system, etc., on the wall. Unless hung carefully (and sometimes not even then), the wall can develop an ever-widening-and-traveling crack. Ultimately, a piece of plaster from the size of an egg to the size of a basketball can fall out of the wall with whatever is hung. It can cost a fortune when you move out to repair the damage, not to mention damage to your property and person. Earthquakes can also shake bad plaster off walls. Decaying plaster is dangerous because of possible asbestos fibers. This type of plaster dust can cause lung diseases if inhaled or ingested. Inspection of walls goes beyond aesthetic considerations.

Privacy

Can these walls keep a secret? Turn on your boom box and see how sound travels between rooms. Is it judicious to have the kids sleep next to the parents' bedroom? Will the stereo or TV provide entertainment for the whole house while on low volume? Can you hear somebody in the bathroom clearing his or her throat? Ah, the things we ponder!

Ceilings and Water Leaks

Do the ceilings look clean and unstained? Stains mean moisture, and that means water, which stands for trouble. One of the most common complaints I receive is about water leaks that ruined thousands of dollars of clothes, rugs, furniture or stereo equipment. How did it happen, and what is to be done?

Check by looking for the signs: Can you see stains running down the walls or blotches on the ceiling? Do you see peeling paint, particularly in the ceilings and outer walls? Look for large repair patches in the ceilings. Look at the ceilings directly over steam or hot water radiators. In the bathrooms and kitchens, check the ceiling straight above the fixtures (sink, shower, toilet) to see stains, cracks, sags or patches in the plaster. If the ceiling has been dropped (lowered), lift up the tiles and check the real ceiling with your flashlight. All these are signs of leaks. Find out what the cause was and if and when it was repaired.

I am aware of multiple examples where the agent says to the tenant, "That's an old leak" or "We've just had the roof repaired. Don't worry." Sorry folks, do worry! Such a repair is twofold: find and fix the leak, and then repair the ceiling damage. Chances are that if the stain is still present, the problem remains. Beware! Later, when the same problem reemerges, the landlord or a lawyer will remind you about the "as is" aspect of your lease. It is even worse when you renew a lease without getting a written agreement to fix the leak. Although you have certain specific rights regarding such conditions, invoking those rights can be burdensome and prolonged. (See chapter 7 for a discussion about the "Warranty of Habitability" and the other tenants' rights.)

Floors

Floors and floor trim should be checked. Does the flooring snuggle up tightly to the walls and trim, or is there room for floor drafts, mice and rats to come into the apartment? Building smells, cigarette smoke, dirt, roaches and other undesirables can easily leak into your place through bad floors. You do need tight wall-to-wall flooring for your health and safety.

If the floors are bare wood, are loose boards or nails sticking out? Is the wood newly refinished or badly gouged or scratched? When you move out, will you be charged for somebody else's floor damage?

Are the floors tiled? Is the tile over a concrete slab (as in most high rises)? If the concrete slab exists, will you be standing for long periods on these superhard floors? Concrete is also very cold in the winter, despite the interior location of the slab. Are rugs or carpets required by the landlord to keep the sound down (or are they necessary for your own peace or warm feet)? Regardless of floor underlayment, is the tile tight to the floor? Who needs to stub toes and break shoe heels? This is especially important in the bathroom and kitchen, where water can lift tiles and cause damage, particularly to your security deposit.

Are the floors level, or do they rock and roll, lean to the center or do something bizarre that will make it impossible to keep tables or chairs from being tipsy?

If carpet is provided, is it clean and in good shape? Is there a special extra "cleaning deposit" required for the carpeting?

Inside Doors

Make sure all the interior doors shut tight. This reduces drafts and keeps the place quieter. It lets you run an air conditioner or dehumidifier more efficiently. It also provides privacy for whatever you wish to keep private.

Rooms in General

It is a good idea to keep in mind what furniture you have and how those pieces might be used in the prospective apartment. You might want to measure the rooms and sketch a layout of the new place, assuming you are close to making a decision. Otherwise, you should make some estimates.

I am amazed at the unique layouts that can be found in rental units. Pie-shaped rooms or those with curved walls. Doors in the middle of a wall or that hinge open from the wrong side. Radiators that get in the way of a long couch or force a bed this way only and no other. How about that beautiful decorator fireplace that sticks three feet out into the room?

If you have rugs or carpets, will they fit well? When you have large dressers, tables, couches, dining-room pieces, wardrobes, wall systems, bookcases, piano, etc., make sure they can fit in the room and also that they can get into the building, up the steps (or into the elevator), around the corners, down the hall and into the room. Remember to bring the measurements. There are also the usual questions about curtains and shades or blinds. These usually need to be tailored for each window. When evaluating the rooms, make sure, for instance, that your bedroom window is not located downwind from a restaurant or bar exhaust system and that your living room receives enough light to keep your prize green jungle of plants alive.

Smoke Detectors

This is now such an obvious issue that it needs little discussion. Smoke detectors save lives. Most municipalities have a smoke detector ordinance that requires their use in all residential buildings—houses, apartments, hotels, dormitories—wherever people normally live and sleep. Check with your local city building department.

A smoke detector must be located within 15 feet of the sleeping area inside each apartment. In a large apartment, there should also be one in the front hallway or living room. When there is more than one floor in your unit, there should be at least one detector per floor. If the stairway is enclosed, there must also be a detector at the top of the stairway.

Check to make sure the detectors are where they are supposed to be. Push the test buttons to see if the batteries are charged. Now test each for smoke. Stand directly below each detector as you do this test. Using a long wooden match from your inspection tool kit, light it and hold it up toward the unit. Let it burn about halfway down and gently blow it out. Hold it high again for 30 seconds as the smoke curls into the detector. The alarm should sound. Do not do this with central system units or on sprinkler heads! Make sure the landlord agrees to install detectors if they are missing, and replace batteries or units that malfunction *before* you sign the lease and *before* you move in!

Bedrooms

Make sure your bed will fit and can go where you want it. Find out about water-bed restrictions, if this applies to you. Is there a closet? Is there room for a wardrobe, dresser, night table? Will the light of dawn shine in your eyes? Will you be so close to the street, freeway, train or flight path that you will be disturbed by the noises? Can you get fresh air from you bedroom window? Can you install a room air conditioner in the window? Will it fit? Is the power adequate and the outlet close enough?

Closets

Does the place have enough closets for clothes, linens, and "stuff"? Are the closets where you need them? Is there a hall or guest closet? Are the closets big enough? Are there storage shelves in the closets? Are the hanger rods strong enough? Is there a hanger rod for each closet? Are there hooks in the closets?

Will you have to buy a wardrobe or closet system to make things work? Do the closets have regular doors that close (and lock)? If the closets use metal track doors (bifold, accordion or sliding), do they slide easily? Do the doors stay in the tracks? Could you retrack a door if it came off the track or fell out of place? Could the metal door slip off the track and cut your foot?

Bathrooms

The bathroom is the most consistently used area in the apartment. The fixtures should work well. Because of the nature of bathrooms, it is imperative that they be sanitary. Chipped fixtures are unhealthful, and most building codes require that chips be repaired or that the fixture be replaced by the landlord before an apartment is rented. It is obvious that the toilet must work—and it should not leak sewerage onto the floor.

Floor Leaks Check the floor around the tub for sagging or flabbiness when you step on certain spots. See if floor tiles are lifting off near the tub, sinks or toilet. Flush the toilet and see if water can be detected oozing around the base.

Water Temperature and Pressure Run the hot and cold water in each fixture: tub, shower and sink. Do the faucets turn off easily or drip? How is the temperature of the hot water? Most codes require it to be at least 120°F. What about water flow (pressure)? The sink (*lavatory basin* or *washstand* in technical lingo) should deliver water at a minimum of one and one-half gallons per minute.

You can easily identify water pressure problems by watching what happens when you run hot and cold water together in the washstand and simultaneously flush the toilet. If there is a violent change from warm to hot as the toilet fills, you've got underplumbing. The same will happen in the shower when somebody in another apartment flushes the toilet.

Drains Do the sink and tub drain properly and quickly without strange glubs and bubbles? Check where the pipes come out of the wall. Make sure there are seals of some sort to keep the mice and roaches out of the bathroom.

Washstand   The bathroom sink should be made of porcelain with no cracks or scratches. The fancy fake marble (powdered marble and plastic glue) washstands scratch very easily and are hard to clean. They also are reactive to some common household chemicals. Medicines, cosmetics and dyes can permanently stain them. Dropping a bottle or some other moderately dense object can crack a plastic sink, and the sink will melt if exposed to the high heat of a hair dryer or cigarette. One that I had emitted a persistent strange odor.

Shower and Tub   How does the shower head perform? Could you rinse off soap and shampoo in normal time? Most codes require the shower head to deliver one and one-half to two and one-half gallons of water per minute. The same is true for the tub spigot. Fill the tub. If it takes more than five minutes to get to an acceptable level (ten gallons), there is a plumbing problem that will only get worse. When checking water pressure and hot water temperature, keep in mind the time of day. Heaviest use will be the morning shower time and evening dishwashing time. If pressure or heat is weak in the middle of the day, watch out!

The bathtub should drain rapidly and should not let water seep out of the floor trap (a four-inch round plate in the floor of older bathrooms near the tub that is used by a plumber to clean out gunk). The tub/shower walls should be tiled and grouted. Look for hints of mold, mildew, loose tiles or missing grout. These can cause problems, such as floor leaks, wall disintegration, strange odors, roaches, silverfish and mice.

There should be towel racks and a shower rod. (The curtain is your job.)

Toilet   To check the toilet, shake the bowl gently or sit on it and see if the whole assembly, not just the seat, wobbles. If it is loose, it can make a mess on the floor, emit sewer gas or even fall over! Toilets need to fit tightly to the waste-line fittings. Inspect the bowl for chips or cracks. Cracks can be found outside along the base and sides. These leak and expand with time. The bowl may no longer be fixed tight to the waste line and can start leaking. Chips and mars make the bowl hard to clean and keep sanitary. Chipped toilets are generally not legal for use in apartments.

Float a couple of toothpicks (from your inspection kit) in the toilet bowl and flush. Do the toothpicks easily get sucked down the tubes, or do they just barely or not quite make it on the first flush? Don't move into a place with a double- or triple-flush toilet. Can you see evidence of floor rot or stains from a leaky toilet bowl? Does the toilet tank fill back up right away? (It should take less than three minutes.) Does the toilet shut off, or can you hear slow drizzling and dripping? Sometimes malfunctioning toilets make a fascinating wheezing, moaning sound, sure to make the hairs on the back of your neck stand up at 4:00 o'clock in the morning.

Pull off the lid of the toilet tank. Is the rubber stopper at the bottom sticky and gucky? Can you see or hear any mechanism leaking or not shutting off? Is the fill mechanism corroded and stained or clean? Look at the tank bottom. Is it full of rusty, sandy deposits, or is it clean? Accumulated crud indicates the relative condition of the pipes. The worse the mess, the more likely you will encounter both toilet and more general plumbing problems.

Medicine Cabinet   The medicine cabinet should be clean, not rusted and gunky. The door should stay closed or stay open, as you wish. The glass shelves should have smooth, polished (swiped) edges and should fit well. The mirror should be usable for shaving, make-up and hair brushing. If the medicine cabinet has lights or outlets, make sure you don't see exposed wiring. Exposed wires or wiring shorted to the metal medicine cabinet are common. The jolt you get in the morning should be from your mouthwash, not the cabinet. Most electrical codes require the installation of a special circuit breaker either in or for the bathroom when rewiring is done and in new construction after 1980. It is called a *ground fault circuit interrupter (GFCI)*. It prevents electrocutions when using hair dryers, curling irons, razors, radios and the like. If it is in the bathroom, it is in the outlet box where you plug in the dryer. It has a red test button, a switch and an outlet. If you don't see the GFCI breaker, ask about it and the wiring in general.

Ventilation   There is the problem of ventilation in the bathroom. Most codes provide that there must be an openable window to the outside or a working ventilation fan or ventilation system that vents to the outside. An unvented bathroom will mildew and smell. A place should be rejected if the bathroom suffers from ventilation problems.

Kitchen

The kitchen is perhaps the second most important place in the apartment. Don't take an apartment with a poor kitchen. Everything should work. Is the kitchen big enough for your kitchen table and chairs or for you to turn around in? If you have your own major appliances, where will you put them, and will they fit? Are there proper electrical, gas and plumbing hookups available? Will you have to pay extra for hookups? Will management approve the use of your own freezer and washer and dryer?

Floor   How about the floor? Is it clean? Is it cleanable? Are there loose tiles, curling linoleum seams or large spaces between floor planks? If carpeted, is it stained, worn or loose? What happens to the carpet if you spill salad oil or grease on it? Will carpet mites, roaches or mice feast off the crumbs trapped in the pile?

Cabinets   Are there enough working surfaces? Are the counter surfaces scratch resistant? Many security deposits are lost when landlords blame scratch damages on tenants when it is really the fault of the material. Is there an outlet for a microwave and toaster? Is there enough counter space to stack the dishes? Does the sink counter have a back splash and a rolled front lip to keep water from going every which way? What about storage? Is there enough room for your plates and glasses, cookware and foodstuffs? Are the cabinets solidly attached to the walls? Do the cupboard doors stay closed? Are the shelves solid? Underneath the counters, are the storage areas enclosed (not using the wall itself as the back of the cabinet)? How about the drawers? How many drawers are there? Is there enough room for silverware, cutlery and assorted cooking items? Do they open and close easily? Are you afraid they will fall out when extended? Can you keep the doors, drawer fronts and inside surfaces clean? Is there a pantry you can also use? Is it clean? If it has built-in drawers, pull out the bottom drawers and check behind them for roaches and mice—and also for a solid wall/floor seal.

Sink   Look at the sink. Is it clean and cleanable? The old cast-iron/porcelain sinks that are hung from the wall and have legs are wonderfully solid, but they have to be in good shape; with no bad scratches, chips or rust. Like all sinks, they must have a tight drain plug and shouldn't leak from the drain (strainer basket), trap or waste-pipe connections. The old painted steel sink/cabinet combinations usually are rusting out. They tend to leak, and they are hard to clean. The newer counter-top inset sinks are either modern cast iron/porcelain or stainless steel. Stainless steel sinks need to be examined for scratches and dents. The ones used in apartments can be thin and cheap, and they can start to wobble in the cut-out hole, which can cause leaks in the drain system. Since some can be easily dented, take care that you are not socked with a security deposit fee for damage to inferior goods when you move out.

Check that the spigot turns smoothly and water does not leak from the faucet, pivot, spigot or rinser (if there is one). Make sure the faucets operate smoothly, shut off and don't allow dripping and that the rinser does its job (and the rinser hose is new). Look under the sink for signs of leaks and to be sure that the wall is sealed around the incoming pipes to discourage vermin. Look at the drain trap (that j-shaped chrome pipe that runs from the sink to the sewer pipe in the wall) and see if there is corrosion, grease or discoloration at the bottom of the trap. That means there is a rusted trap, a leaky sink drain or water dripping down from where the lip of the sink meets the counter-top cut-out hole. These are three simple jobs for the plumber, or there will be roaches and ruined supplies for you.

While looking under the sink, check for the ground-pepper droppings of roaches and the larger "pencil-lead" pellets of mice. The kitchen sink area is a favorite (along with the evaporating pan of frost-free refrigerators, as well as under the stove) for the little devils.

Refrigerator   It is hard to learn a lot about a refrigerator, but it should be running when an apartment is being shown. There should be solid ice cubes in the freezer. It should look clean and smell clean inside and out, with all the ice trays, racks, glass shelves and drawers properly in place. The main problems with refrigerators are door seals and operating costs. To check the seals, close the door with a dollar bill sticking out between the door and main body. The harder it is to slip the bill out when pulled, the better the seal. Try the test in four spots around the door. If the bill slides out with no resistance or drops inside the box, you could be in for problems. Ask for another refrigerator if all else in the apartment is good or go on to the next place.

The other problem is the operating cost. All refrigerators look alike. A good one is low-cost because it is efficient and well insulated. Most units have an energy efficiency ratio statement (EER) pasted on the back. Without that, unless you call the manufacturer with the model number to ask, there is no good way to find out the operating cost, but it is something to which you should be alerted. It is not unusual to pay $25 to $40 a month to the electric company just for the operation of a frost-free, power-sucking (self-defrosting) model!

If you can, move the refrigerator away from the wall to check for roach and mice droppings and for a proper floor-to-wall trim seal. If you can't get behind the machine, shine the flashlight underneath to see what you can see. The more you see evidence of pests, the less attractive the apartment should become.

Stove The stove is the other critical kitchen element. Do you know how to use the stove that comes with the apartment? Is the range-top clean? Is it in good shape? How about the oven? Clean? Self-cleaning? Gas, electric? Is the stove one of those tiny boxes you'd expect to find in a doll house, or is it up to standard jobs? If it's a gas stove, sniff for leaks from the pilot lights, burners, controls and inside the oven. Do the burners light quickly? Does it "click-click-click" with electronic igniters or use pilot lights? Turn on the oven. Some are designed to take a minute before they light. Be patient. Does the oven work? Look at the broiler. Is it clean? Are all the parts there? Does the oven have two cooking racks? Do clocks, lights and timers function? If it's an electric stove, does the rangetop have standard elements or a flat ceramic surface with pictures of heating elements painted on it? Do all the rangetop and oven-heating elements work? If the stove isn't working ("Sorry, the gas/electricity is off."), base your judgment on newness and cleanness. An old, used or beat-up unit needs a demonstration.

While it might not be advisable to move the stove away from the wall, it is still necessary to peak behind and underneath to check for vermin and holes in the wall. Also perform a sniff test, if you can, behind the stove from the gas valve along the flexible (corrugated) brass gas pipe to where it disappears into the innards. Do you smell gas? Ask to have the valve bubble-checked and the corrugated hookup replaced. Replacing the hookup tube is a common maintenance practice when apartments change hands.

Stoves are so basic that common sense should guide your inspection. If a gas stove doesn't light very well, it might be an inconvenience, or it might blow up. People have sustained severe burns when they inadvertently touched a hot ceramic rangetop. The cost of operating either a gas or an electric stove is relatively comparable. However, the use of the electric self-cleaning function adds expense.

Other Kitchen Appliances The more convenience appliances there are in a rental apartment, the more devices there are to break, not get fixed, but still pay rent for every month. I am suspicious of landlords offering gimmicks of this sort to induce people to rent. You wonder what else must be wrong.

Garbage disposers, dishwashers and trash compactors are nice inducements to move into a place. If the equipment is new, then you get some kitchen bonuses. Most developers and landlords do not put first-rate, top-of-the-line equipment in their rental kitchens. Furthermore, unless this is a high-rise building, getting service may be a problem. Special appliances add complications—for instance, when the disposer gets stuck or clogs, the dishwasher must not be run because it drains into it. If you do not have a double sink, you lose the use of your kitchen. The landlord may delay sending for the expensive repairman. I have seen several rental units where the disposer and/or dishwasher have been disconnected rather than repaired.

Disposers To test the disposer, turn on the cold water and toss in half an apple. (I always carry several apples for this purpose, don't you?) Then flip the switch. If the disposer crunches it up and swallows it quickly, then it works. If it moans and chokes and stalls, forget it.

Compactors Trash compactors have good and bad sides when they work. The good side is you put a lot of trash into a small space, and the garbage is out of sight. The bad side is you now have Buffet Central for the local pests, since you will not empty the compactor as often as you might take out the garbage. And then there is the smell. . . . Another bad surprise is that one little bag of compacted trash can weigh 40 pounds! Since most people end up trying to compact some item (by unknowing error), such as a wine bottle standing straight up instead of sideways, and since that can mess up the compactor's squisher, most people end up using the broken compactor as a tiny garbage can. Guess who pays for the repairs when you move out?

To test the compactor, take 40 pounds of soft garbage and . . . well, you get the picture. Never test when empty!

Dishwashers Most dishwashers require very hot water to work well. Hot means 150°F. If the dishwasher has its own hot water booster, maybe it will work well. As a dishwasher ages, it may start to leak from the motor shaft seal and from the door seals. The shaft leak will attract and feed roaches, until the unit shorts out with a bang one day. The door seals will allow soapy water to leak onto the floor. A constant leak will ruin floor tiles and provide roaches with water.

Kitchen Ventilation Ventilation is important in a kitchen. The windows must open. You should have a door between the kitchen and the rest of the house, if the entranceway is so designed. Otherwise, you need an exhaust system to pull the smells out, or the whole apartment will be made victim. Is there an exhaust fan/hood combination over the stove that really vents to the outside or just recirculates greasy air? Could you easily install a small box fan in a kitchen window to suck out the cooking smells?

Electrical Service

Look at the electrical outlets. Count them to see if there are enough. Are the cover plates painted over so badly that you can't put in a plug? Test a few of them with the little Radio Shack circuit tester from your inspection kit. Are they modern, three-pronged outlets? (These are called *grounded outlets.*) Many modern appliances have three-pronged plugs and need the new outlets. See if and where there are ceiling lights. Ask about the number of circuits in the unit. Four are the modern minimum requirement. If you want to install and/or run window air-conditioning units, better make sure there are special extra circuits, or you could have problems. If you have a computer, better make sure that not everything else runs off the same circuit, or you might fry out your CPU and crash your hard drive when the refrigerator turns off.

Breaker or Fuse Box You need direct, 24-hour access to your fuse or circuit breaker box. Ask to see it (if you are seriously interested in the apartment). If it is in your apartment or just around the corner, lucky you! If it is in the basement, ugh. The top two fuses or breakers will usually have the notation "mains." The fuse-type mains may be inside a pull panel that has a little handle on it. Either way, they control all the electricity into the apartment. They can be rated from 30 amps to 100 amps—the more, the better. The fuses or breakers below the mains are the individual circuits. Hope to see at least four of these. Sometimes you will also have two breakers connected together. These duals are for 240 service to the stove, the furnace or perhaps an air-conditioner circuit. Such circuits using fuses may have pull-out handles similar to the mains fuses. Those 240 circuits are extra and shouldn't be counted as part of the minimum required. You may be very lucky and have six or ten circuits (besides the mains and the 240).

Just in case you blow a fuse (say, on Saturday when the hot-air popcorn popper overheats), you must insist on your direct, 24-hour access to the box. You can't wait until Monday morning when the management office opens up because more often then not, half your lights, the refrigerator and the alarm clock will also be on that circuit. Beware of a rental agent who will not give you a key to your own circuit breaker box.

Heating (and Cooling) Systems

Landlord's Heating

Ask the agent what type of heat is supplied, what the thermostat is set to, what is the heating season and what hours the heat operates.

Generally speaking, any heating system must have clean radiators or registers; quiet fans; steady, even heating; and must be capable of keeping the apartment (legally) comfortable at all times. If the heat is supplied as part of the rent, as is most steam and hot-water heat, then you probably won't have to be concerned with adding heating costs to the monthly gross rent; but you may not have any control over when your apartment gets heat, how hot it gets and how cold it gets. Some communities require minimum heat of 68°F day and evening and 63°F overnight, when the landlord has control of the heat. I lived in one place where the heat sometimes reached 90°F during the day and fell to 53°F at night. Most tenants complain that there is generally never enough heat in low-rise, centrally controlled systems. If you don't have a thermostat in your apartment, you cannot control your heat.

Forced Air

Many larger buildings blow hot air into apartments through ductwork. The air temperature is really not controllable, may be very dry and is usually quite noisy. These systems bring dust and may also blow in microbes and chemicals.

Most sick-building-syndrome diseases are transmitted this way. Since these buildings may also have limited ventilation because windows don't open or won't open very wide, this will be the primary source of fresh air. Newer buildings limit the percentage of fresh air mixed into the supply—with some as low as 15 percent. Ask your agent about fresh-air mix and the location of the fresh-air intake.

Steam Heat

This is old-fashioned or new-fashioned radiator heat. Steam heat comes in two flavors—high pressure and low pressure. High-pressure systems are closed; that is, they don't hiss. They also tend to produce some heating uniformity floor to floor. Low-pressure systems hiss and clank. A low-pressure system is used in buildings of three stories or less and not more than 100 feet from the boiler. Low-pressure systems yield cold first floors, comfortable second floors and hot third floors—provided everything is working. If the thermostat is set to compensate for the third floor (cooler), then floors one and two freeze. If the correction is for the first floor, then floors two and three boil. Find out where the heating controls are if you wish to rent in a centrally heated, low-steam-pressure building.

Look for leaks and stains around the radiators. Low-pressure radiators only have one pipe. Make sure the pipe end is lower than the air vent side, or it will clog during the heating season. Also be sure the floor is not rotting or collapsing under these heavy cast-iron relics.

Hot-Water Heat

Hot-water heat can be through old-fashioned radiators, baseboard radiators, in-the-floor radiant heat or air ventilator systems. As a rule, hot-water heat is quiet and "level." The sequence of heating is the reverse of low-pressure steam—that is, the first floor heats first (and best), and the third floor gets what heat remains. Your first concern is living on the third floor of a old radiator building where the controls are on the first floor. In larger setups, the water is pumped at high pressure and in zones.

The hot-water system is supposed to be closed (no air). Each old-fashioned radiator has a bleeder valve to let trapped air escape. Trapped air prevents the radiator from heating. Ask the agent if a bleeder valve key is provided because you'll eventually need one.

Most other hot-water heating systems pump water through a straight pipe with radiating fins. The heat usually comes from baseboard radiation. In some parts of the country, heating pipes run through the floors. Some large buildings use a power exchanger (univent) system to blow air across the coils and into the apartment. Dust and mold can be a problem with these setups. Regardless of type, you need to check for leaks from the fittings and valves.

Cooling

If air conditioning is part of the landlord's package, make sure it is what you need. Where the power exchange (univent) system is employed, cold water runs through the pipes during the cooling system. At the coils, air is cooled and the humidity is squeezed from it. These systems don't do a great job of cooling or dehumidifying. Furthermore, there can be mold and fungus problems in the coils as a result of condensation. Other central systems blow cool air into units through ducts. (See the previous discussion of forced-air heating.)

Tenant Heating

There are also tenant-controlled heating systems that range from individual boilers to gas space heaters in rooms. Other systems include gas- or oil-fired central forced-air furnaces of various sorts, direct radiation catalytic heaters (which look like gyros grills without the spit) and baseboard or central forced-air electric systems.

Heating Cost Disclosure

Heating (and cooling) can be expensive rent add-ons. If these utilities are extra, you need to determine what those costs will be. Some localities require formal disclosure of these costs if you pay extra for utilities to the power company or to your landlord. Ask the agent for the formal documentation. This information should also be presented if you have to pay for water. Call the local utilities to get the budget payment amounts if a formal statement is not presented.

Set-back Thermostats

Set-back thermostats allow the system to automatically turn the heat up in the morning, down while at work, up again in the evening and down at night. They will save 15 to 20 percent of the typical heating bill. If you pay your own heat, insist that the landlord supply you with a set-back thermostat. (They cost less than $50.)

Space Heaters

In parts of the country where full-time winter heating is a need, space heaters are not desirable. They are the gas-, oil- or wood-fired variations of a Franklin stove. They are very hot to touch, and children and pets can burn themselves. Space heaters tend to be inefficient and generally do not heat more than one room. They are expensive to operate and must be vented to the outside. Sometimes they leak fumes or smoke. They beg for problems. Avoid living in an apartment with space heaters, please.

Catalytic Heaters

Catalytic heaters use gas that burns in the presence of a metal catalyst that is supposed to burn the gas completely and produce a hot radiant plane with no unburned combustion products. This heater does not heat the air (no convection heating) but rather heats objects within line of sight by transmitting radiant energy. The heat is very directional and spotty. Its corollary is a fireplace: there is intense heat on your front side, cold on your back side and the room air does not heat up from the fire. These units are sometimes used in lofts.

Forced-Air Furnaces

A forced air furnace is a "regular" modern furnace. The air is heated in the furnace and blown to each room in the apartment through ductwork. The furnace fan may sound like a DC-3 revving up. The filters may not have been changed for years, and dust allergy might be a constant problem until the landlord agrees to clean out the system. Filters must be changed frequently during the heating season. The tenant usually pays the fuel bill when he or she has and controls a forced-air furnace. When heat is an add-on to the basic rent, it must be figured as part of the gross rent. Heating can add $400 to $1,000 more to the yearly rental expense.

Electric Heating Systems

These heat metal, oil or water in a closed baseboard system, air in an open or forced-air system (see previous discussion) or metal rods in the floor in a radiant system. Electric heat is expensive—four times more than gas, even when the electric company gives you a rate break for electric heating. The only reason to heat electrically is because the rent on your apartment is very low or there is no heating gas available. Otherwise, avoid such apartments; they may not be worth it.

Portable Heaters

A bit of advice: There has been a trend toward using kerosene heaters to augment regular systems. This is unadvisable. It is also unsafe in case of a fuel spill or a tipped-over heater and may be illegal in your state or locality. Most kerosene heaters do not burn the fuel well enough and tend to produce unhealthy levels of unburnt hydrocarbons and carbon monoxide. In addition to the direct health threats, these units produce soot and a smokey smell. Kerosene heaters should be used in open areas only and not in dwelling units. They also are expensive to operate.

Portable electric heaters can be considered only a temporary measure since they draw from 750 to 1,800 watts—a very heavy constant load on an electric system. It costs about the same to operate a portable electric heater as it does to run a room air conditioner. They are not safe to use around small children or pets.

Do not rent an apartment if the agent suggests kerosene or portable electric heaters to supplement the regular heat or offers such heaters with the apartment.

Other Concerns

Drinking Water

While most municipal water supplies are certified to be safe, your unit may not get water from such a supply, or the pipes the water comes thorough may cause contamination. Ask who/what supplies the drinking water to the building.

If it is from a local well or self-run purification system, ask for a certificate of safeness issued by the state, county or city.

Lead is still a serious pollutant in drinking water. It is generally picked up through the water pipes. Lead is a danger to health. (See the previous discussion of lead paint.) In many older cities, lead pipes are used to carry water from the street water main to the building water meter. So even if the water department claims low lead, the building could have dangerous levels. Another source in new buildings is the solder used on copper pipes. How do you find out about lead? Ask the agent if the building pipes are leaded or if lead solder is used on the copper pipes.

Some supplies also have problems with hardness (dissolved calcium), iron (red stain and bloody taste), sulphur compounds (rotten egg smell), certain heavy metal and chemical pollutants and bacteria. Taste and smell the water. For more information, contact the local water department or health department for the latest assay of the municipal water supply.

Hot Water

Hot water is one of the most troublesome aspects of living in many low-rise apartments. Hot water usually is part of the rent. One tank serves all. The standard for hot water is "hot enough" to do what you need to do. This translates to a minimum of 120°F. Technically, an 85-gallon tank firing at 100,000 Btu with a 100-gallon-per-hour recovery ought to handle 6 to 12 units. If you can get to see the hot-water tank (maybe in the basement near the circuit breakers or furnace), read the nomenclature plate. The information is on it. If you live in anything larger than a three-flat and the landlord shows you a 40-gallon, 48,000 Btu tank, you are in big trouble. I lived in one building where the tenants shared the hot-water tank with two restaurants. There was never any hot water from noon until 1:00 A.M.!

If you have an individual hot-water tank, it should have a 40-gallon capacity to ensure constant hot water. Check with your local utility for operating costs (approximately $15 per month for gas). At least you should not have to worry about cold showers.

Pets

The issue of pets is double-sided. If you have a pet now or may acquire one, you'll want a unit that allows pets. Ask the agent what animals are allowed. (See chapter 4 for negotiating pet issues.) If you don't have a pet, you may want to know if pets are allowed so that you are not disturbed by paws scratching across the floor above you, leaking aquaria, loose snakes, meowing cats, barking dogs, screaming monkeys or birds and the various smells and deposits they also produce.

Radon Gas

Radon gas is odorless, colorless, tasteless, but deadly. It causes lung cancer. Radon gas is the natural decay product of radium, which is a natural decay product of uranium. The gas seeps into buildings through the ground-floor slab or basement. The Environmental Protection Agency states that the first three levels of a building are at risk of radon gas infiltration. Ask the agent if a radon gas test has been performed on the building.

Asbestos Fibers

Asbestos is another problem to watch. Asbestos was used as an insulating material in furnaces, water heaters and particularly on heating pipes. Big pipes in the basement or hallways that look like they are encased in a plaster cast are actually covered with asbestos. Asbestos is used to insulate between walls and as the main ingredient in some old ceiling-tiles that absorb sounds. Asbestos is a fiber matrix in old plaster walls.

Asbestos fibers are carcinogenic. As long as the outer shells of the asbestos wrapping are not broken, the place is considered safe. Acoustical ceiling tiles made with asbestos—whether they are the little square type, the two-foot by four-foot type or even the type with a punched metal cover—are not safe. It is also not safe to live in a building undergoing rehabilitation, where the plaster walls are being knocked down. Ask the agent about the use of asbestos insulation. Some banks and federal lending agencies now require an "asbestos-free environment certificate" before they will make a mortgage. Is the building certified? Make sure you don't rent a death trap!

Storage Room

Take a quick look at the storage area, if there is one. Is the area clean, dust-free and ventilated? Storage is very important for those bulky things (snow tires, bicycle, skis, large suitcases, battery charger, college textbooks, the baby crib) that you need but not often. A satisfactory storage facility is one that is easy to access, has 24-hour access, is secure behind locked doors and is dry and temperate. That's probably too much to ask for these days! Most apartment storage is not secure enough or environmentally acceptable—even with rat bait, plastic bags and mothballs. Unless a Brinks guard with rat-killer breath is stationed at the door, don't pay extra for storage and don't store anything of value.

Utility Room

The utilities are probably in the same area as storage. Check out the laundry room for cleanliness and good lighting. It should lock to the outside and smell fresh. See that the machines are in good shape and that it doesn't cost a dollar a minute to dry clothes. This is also the time to see the gas and electric meters, circuit-breaker boxes, the hot-water heater and the building boiler. If these areas are strewn with trash, the floors wet and the walls icky with ooze or white powder, think about the quality of service and care you can expect from the maintenance crew who takes care of things in the basement.

Final Notes

When you see a place you like, take a snapshot or two as reminders or to help plan the furniture layout. Ask to have a sample copy of the application form and lease, including all the extra riders. Leases are not all the same. Just because a lease is preprinted or comes from a stationery store doesn't make it good, right or legal. Some leases are worse than others, and the additional clauses in some may help you decide to accept or reject a particular place. Since a lease is a legal document binding you to pay many thousands of dollars, it is in your vital self-interest to understand it or take it to a lawyer who can explain it to you. (Chapter 4 contains a general discussion of leases.)

An agent should have no problem offering you the samples for study or a lawyer's advice. If there is reluctance, ask yourself what the agent is hiding. A policy of not providing a sample may indicate at what level of arrogance or indifference you will be treated later.

Having Courage

This step-by-step apartment inspection obviously represents a long and detailed study of the place you may have to live for the next one to five years. Now is the time to ask the questions and check things out. After you sign a lease, it may be too late. Remember: The management is renting the apartment *as is*. Even if the management promises you that things will be fixed, added or improved later, it may not be legally obligated to make good on its promises (even if they are in writing). You might not be able to easily break the lease just because management doesn't do what it promised!

Later, you will have the choices of begging to make the promises good, doing some things yourself (perhaps at your own expense), doing without, or in some cases repairing and deducting the cost from your rent, withholding rents, moving out and/or taking the management into court.

Turn to Appendix A for a very detailed apartment inspection checklist.

4

Applications and Leases—Understandings, Negotiations, Qualifications

After seeing your fill of rental units, are you ready to bite the bullet and apply? You still have to keep your guard up.

Start this process slowly. Whatever you do, don't fill out an application for the first apartment you are shown. You need to be able to choose among alternatives. Alternative number one *might* be the best choice, but you can't know until you've seen others. Seldom, if ever, does the good one "get away." Besides, there are always alternatives.

Rental selling is not much different from any other high-ticket retail activity. Thus, the sophisticated sales techniques that apply to other expensive items also apply to rental sales. The agent (or landlord) wants to be your friend and wants you to trust him or her. The agent wants to make a sale. There will be reassurances about your concerns, but without substance. Details may be glossed over or not mentioned. Facts may lie undisturbed. Unlike other retail sales, however, it may not make so much difference later if you are not a happy buyer who wants to become a repeat customer. Sure, it is better if you renew your lease when it comes due, but the rental business is accustomed to turnover. And since it is more difficult to return the product (break your lease), your satisfaction might not be

After you pay the application fee, you have lost your money! After you sign the lease, you have legally committed yourself to pay the rent for the duration of the lease.

that important anyway. And there's always your security deposit and court if you don't pay the rent. In the case of finder services, your dissatisfaction might be to their benefit, since management will go back to them to relet the unit.

You've learned that no place is perfect, but some units raise too many doubts. Avoid being "sold" on an apartment that you know is lacking. Be resolute: No amount of promising will make doubtful conditions change . . . only action does that. If you like a place except for certain things, tell the agent you'll reconsider it as soon as the work is done or the lease is revised.

A Very Short Course in Rental Agent Practices

Practice #1: Now, If You'll Just Fill Out the Application . . .

Whoa, Nellie! In sales parlance, this is called the *close*—closing the deal, getting the signature on the dotted line, hitting home. Isn't this a bit premature? What about your problems with the apartment and your questions about the lease? For the agent, the sooner you bite, the better. For one thing, once you sign the application, it is almost impossible to get out of the deal, and the agent can then hunt for the next pigeon. When you sign, that application check goes into the agent's pocket; that's the commission.

Practice #2: Oh, That's No Problem

Want to make a bet? "Will everything be ready on time?" you ask. "Oh, that's no problem," she says. "I may be transferred to another city next year. Can I work things in the lease so I can move out early?" you inquire. "Oh," he exclaims, "That's no problem!" "My mother (sister, friend, college-student daughter, grandmother) is planning an extended visit with us next summer for several months. Is that okay?" She says, "No problem." "I notice that the front door doesn't lock (or the mailbox is broken)," you say. The agent replies, "Oh, that's no problem." And he or she is correct. It is no problem for them because they will probably not do anything about it. *It will be a problem for you* when you can't move on time, your mail gets ripped off, your friend comes to visit and you get a three-day termination notice or the transfer comes through and you can't break the lease!

Practice #3: Yes, We Can Take Care of That

This is a variation of sharp practice #2. Read this to mean "Yes, we can take care of *you* later!"

Practice #4: Promises, Promises

Do not believe what an agent promises you. Do not fool yourself. Once a lease is signed, the management may be under no legal obligation to comply with agents' promises unless you get them in writing with contingency clauses. (The tenant's performance to pay the rent is contingent upon the landlord's performance to deliver the goods.) What I tell you is true! Even then, enforcing your contract rights is very expensive and can take years in the courts. And even at that, all you could win is actual damages, not pain and suffering. If you want to take an apartment that still needs a lot of work (because it isn't finished or because of your list of things to correct), follow these steps:

First, on the *application*, write something like this:

> Completion of application and execution of Lease shall be contingent upon apartment being completely ready, as to the attached rider of necessary work, and habitable to the satisfaction of Lessee no less than seven (7) days before commencement of Lease. Upon failure to meet the completion date and render the unit habitable, the Lessee shall give immediate notice to the offering agency in person, by phone or by letter. The application shall be canceled, and a full refund of all fees, charges and deposits shall be made at once, upon demand.

That is how you make sure a promise is kept!

Second, *do not sign the lease until after you inspect the completed premises.* Once you sign the lease, you are stuck with it, regardless of what was promised. Why ask for grief? The agent has what lawyers call adequate remedy at law if the place is ready and you back out, but you do not have the same adequacies if the place isn't what you bargained for. So the deal is simple: You apply for a lease. If the apartment is ready when promised, you sign a lease and move in. If the place isn't ready, you get your money back and try again.

Third, *include an attorney's approval contingency clause.* If you have an attorney and the money to pay for a legal consultation, and don't mind extending your approval waiting period, place the following on the face of the application and lease:

> Subject to attorney approval of Applicant/Lessee. Attorney objections to the terms and conditions of this document must be submitted in writing to Lessor within five business days after date of Applicant/Lessee signature(s). Failure to satisfactorily resolve attorney objections renders application and lease null and void, with all prepaid rents, deposits and fees fully and immediately refundable to Applicant/ Lessee.

The point is *Don't be "hot boxed"!*

Example Laurie and Stacey were new in town and shopping for an apartment to share. After the agent rushed them through an apartment, she took them aside and confided that this part of town was "hot" and that the ad for this unit was producing a number of prospects. The agent said that the place would be gone tomorrow if they didn't make up their minds right now. The place wasn't great, and it wasn't a pit. But the roommates had not seen any other apartments. The old saying, "A bird in the hand is worth two in the bush," gnawed at them.

If the roommates called me, I would advise them as follows: Since you don't know what your money will buy elsewhere, you need to look further for comparison's sake. You have some doubts about the unit, as it doesn't meet all of your expectations, so you might not be happy with a hasty decision. I assume you've made other appointments, which means there are other units available in this area, and you will not be left high and dry if you don't take this particular apartment. Lastly, I would be concerned about a landlord who employed high-pressure tactics to sign up tenants. If you are not respected now, can you expect respect later? I would conclude by advising them take a copy of the application and lease to study but to keep looking.

If you get static from the agent, just say good-bye. Do not even consider an application if you can't get decent assurance that a unit will be ready or that the locks will be fixed or whatever. You may have to wait months until the place is livable and pay full rent the whole time. And you may have to warehouse all your belongings. You will have to move twice and pay twice.

Don't be conned, rushed or panicked to apply. Wait until you feel comfortable and *confident*. If it helps, ask to see the unit for a final time. As an excuse, tell the agent you need to measure for furniture. Look into the toilets and peek behind the sink. Do what you want to satisfy yourself. *When you find the right place, you'll know it immediately.*

Signing Documents

Read the documents you receive carefully. Make sure all your agreements are in writing, that the dates are correct and that nothing new has been slipped in. Initial each item that is added (not part of the preprinted form) and each item that is deleted. When you sign the application (and later the lease), keep a copy of it. If you are told "We'll send you a copy when (the authorized person) signs it," request a copy of all documents offered to you at that time. It is not unusual for the landlord to keep your application and lease papers from you. It is a power play. Do not leave without copies of everything, even if the other side will have to send you a completed set later. If documents are mailed to you for signing, make copies of what you sign before returning them.

The Truth-in-Renting Act

No, this isn't another federal law; it's just part of learning about what you may rent and who you are dealing with. If you like the apartment, then this will finish your research. You need to ask the agent some pointed questions, and you expect honest answers. The answers are important to you.

Not only do you want to know more about the unit and building, you want some assurances about safety, what repairs management won't do or expects you to cover, the attitude about repairing and deducting, insurance and special rules.

Legal Disclosures

Did you know that some localities have laws regarding what must be disclosed to you when you make your application? In some towns, much of this information must be disclosed to you as a legal matter of right or the application and/or lease can be terminated by you. You might be able to collect statutory damages and certainly are due *all* monies advanced. Key provisions of most of these laws include giving the tenant officially approved literature regarding local tenants' rights laws; building code violation information; who really holds the security deposit and rents; receipts for payments you make; and information about the additional costs associated with heating, cooling and water. Check with the your local building or housing department, city attorney's office or tenants' rights organization. Turn to the back of this chapter for the "Truth-in-Renting Worksheet."

The Lease Application

The application has multiple functions: it qualifies you financially through credit information; it provides information on where to seize your money or wages if you default on the lease; it states (limits) who will live in the rental unit; through the fee, it ties up your money and probably prevents you from applying elsewhere; and many times it is a contract allowing the agent to take your application money as liquidated damages if you don't sign a lease after approval. The application is typically made part of the lease so that if something is wrong on the application, it is grounds for later terminating the lease (typically for misinformation, business activities in the unit, additional tenants or pets).

How To Qualify

The landlord wants to be sure that you can pay your rent. Remember, the landlord's business is money. *Your monthly gross income must equal at least three times the net rent.* Thus, if you want to rent a $500 condo, you need to show $1,500 in monthly, before-tax income. The "Net Rent/Gross Rent Worksheet" at the end of Chapter 1 should be used to compute what this unit will really cost, and that will help you decide whether the unit qualifies for you. Other qualifying factors will be whether you are employed; who will guarantee or cosign your lease (and if he or she qualifies); and if there are roommates (and if they qualify financially), children and pets.

What do you *have* to tell and what *should* you tell? The agent wants as much information as possible. There may be questions about your marital status; your previous landlords' names; and whether you have ever been evicted, had a money judgment entered against you or declared bankruptcy. There might be questions about your credit cards, checking and savings accounts, other assets, cars, monthly bills, divorce payments and loans. There is always a request for your Social Security number.

Always tell the truth. Most states require anyone signing a lease to provide his or her legal name, place of employment, weekly or monthly income and current and immediately previous addresses. You are also required to list the names of all others living in the apartment, but you don't have to give ages or other information if they do not sign the lease. Some municipalities limit the number of non-related people living together, so in that case you'll have to describe everyone's relationship to each other! Make sure the law requires this before proceeding.

What else you decide to answer is up to you. The more you put down on the application, the more your private life becomes uncontrollably public. If you find questions intrusive or not relevant, ask the agent why they are needed. While you don't want to be uncooperative, you also need your privacy. Did you know that your Social Security number *is not* some sort of national or credit identification number? Did you know that you are required to supply your Social Security number *only* to governmental agencies, employers and financial institutions? You tell all others at your risk. On the other hand, maybe your credit history cannot be found without the number. It's your judgment call.

Credit Check

Your Social Security number, previous address and name are used to run a credit check. In some parts of the country, two checks are conducted: one through a credit bureau and one through an agency that tracks evictions and judgments. When the agent submits your application, whatever information you give is updated on your credit files. Some rental agents will contact previous landlords and current employers, but many do not.

The matter of checking and savings accounts relates more to whether a judgment can be garnished from them than anything else. If you pay your application fee by check, then all the agent has to do is deposit it. If the check clears, you pass that part of the test; and if it doesn't, you don't. At any rate, your checking account number is known. Some banks will confirm that an account exists, and some will tell an inquirer whether there is money to cover a specific check on a specific day. If you won't pay the rent by check, then why does the agent need the information? Savings information is certainly not for the agent.

Most employers will confirm present employment. Some will confirm a job title and/or years of service. Few will confirm your wages; you need to submit a release/request for such information in writing.

When the application part of renting starts feeling like a bank loan request, maybe you should say good-bye to the agent and look elsewhere. When the level of trust has fallen to such a low level, it is questionable how satisfactory the rest of arrangement will be.

Your Credit Rights

If your application is rejected based on a bad credit report, federal law gives you the right to see the report for free and have it explained to you. Immediately (and by law within 30 days) after rejection, ask the agent for copies of the report(s) and also how to contact the reporting bureaus. If there are errors, you have a right to correct the errors (but it may not help you in the immediate situation). If you feel you have been blacklisted by a landlord's reporting bureau, contact a lawyer for a possible defamation action and your local county prosecutor's office.

"Damages" and the Waiting Period

Located someplace on the application in legalese will be words to the effect that if the application is approved, you agree to sign a lease. If you fail to sign the lease, the application fee is forfeited as damages to the agent. There are issues of how many days the management company has to approve the application and how the notification process works. If you are rejected, your deposit should be returned to you. The landlord can change its mind, but you can't change yours without penalty. What a balanced deal! Understand that unless local law provides an out, once you plunk the money down, it is gone.

Make sure that the waiting period is clear. If it isn't, add something like this as a rider to the application:

> Notification will be made before the end of five days counting today, except Sundays and legal holidays, expiring at 11:59 P.M. on the fifth day.

Make sure that the method of notice is precise.

> Notice may be in person or by telephone, but confirmation of acceptance or rejection by rental agency must sent by U.S. mail, certified service, return receipt requested, to be received by applicant within the five-day period, or notice will be deemed not served and the application will expire without penalty. All monies to that point paid or deposited shall be immediately refunded to applicant upon demand.

Rents-in-Advance and Security Deposits

Every city is different when it comes to the subtleties of advance rents and the damage or security deposit. In one town, the agent asks for nothing; in another, the request is for first and last month's rent plus security deposit plus a pint of blood. These will be discussed in more detail in the next section, entitled "The Lease." For the present, I am drawing a distinction between these deposits and the application fee, even though it may be the same money.

Application Deposits and Fees

In a sense, the application form is a distraction. The real action is money changing hands. First there is the wonderful credit check fee. Where else, except in real estate and banking, do you pay *them* for the privilege of qualifying *you* to pay *them* again? Most medium- and large-sized rental businesses do the credit checks through computer. The cost per each inquiry is less then $5. Why, oh why, are they charging you $20 to $50? This fee is generally nonrefundable. Other times it is applied to your rent or damage deposit if you pass the test. Negotiate with the agent regarding this fee.

Next comes Jaws. The agent usually wants a chunk of money, approximately one month's rent, as the application deposit or earnest money. Why? Well, you'll be told that's what it takes to hold the apartment *for you* until you sign the lease. You may be informed that this puts you first on the list or seals the deal. Maybe. You already know that this deposit money is the agent's commission. Once Jaws clamps on to your cash, it's gone!

Sometimes more than one application is taken for a given unit. The applicants all get strung along while the credit checks are "in process." As time goes on, some of those folks can't wait any longer and walk away. The agent keeps those deposits as damages. Perhaps someone higher on the list than you qualifies first and accepts the apartment. Now you're still waiting, only to be told of a mix-up and then offered a different unit. The agent still has your money, is trying to switch you and you've lost valuable time. If a refund *is* offered, you are told it will take a few weeks. Do you take the substitute apartment or keep looking and come up with another application fee elsewhere? It is not wise to apply for more than one lease at a time when you've got a month's rent riding on each transaction. By the way, under federal banking laws, all local bank checks under $5,000 are deemed to have cleared two banking days after deposit, and all out-of-state checks are deemed to have cleared within seven banking days. So don't accept the lame excuse about "waiting for the check to clear." If necessary, check with your bank. Do not put a stop payment order on the application deposit unless you can prove some sort of fraud or you and the agent agree *in writing* to cancel the application and stop payment. You could face criminal and civil penalties!

Strategy Offer the agent a reasonable deposit on your application—say, $50 or $75. This shows your desire to obtain a lease but doesn't prevent you from walking away from the deal if something goes wrong. Agree to bring the deposit amount up to the total requested at the time you sign the lease. The theory is that if you pass the credit check, you're okay. Doesn't the agent trust you? Furthermore, it is an incentive to push the application through the red tape because they don't get theirs until you get yours. You want a place to live, and the agent wants money. Fair exchange, fair bargain.

Many times the agent is angling for advance rents also. Politely decline. Your application has not been approved; there is no lease. See the discussion about rents-in-advance in the next section, entitled "The Lease."

Waiting for Approval

This can be an unnerving time. If you have not put down a month's rent and if the notification period and procedure are clear, be calm. You know what it takes to qualify, and you knew whether you met the requirements before you applied. Be patient; these things take a little time. In the meanwhile, *do not sign another application!* If another agent calls you during the waiting period, tell him or her you are still thinking about that unit but won't make a commitment for five days. Don't blow off any opportunity; just wait.

The Lease

A *lease* is an agreement between you and the landlord. You promise to pay rent, and the landlord promises to give you a place to live. Generally, you promise to pay unconditionally *no matter what,* while the landlord claims the right to break parts of the lease without penalty. Unless your locality or state has tenants' rights laws, you are at the landlord's mercy for the term of your lease. So it is important to know your rights and to understand your prospective lease. (See chapter 7 for a full discussion of your tenants' rights, including lease rights.)

Oral Leases

There are two kinds of leases: (1) written and (2) spoken. They are both equally legally binding. A spoken lease is normally called an *oral* lease. You can enter into an oral lease with a handshake, a wink or a nod. You are usually required to put down the same types of deposits as with a written lease. An oral lease differs from a written lease in a few ways. As a rule, an oral lease is used for week-to-week and month-to-month tenancies. That means that either party can give the other a notice of termination (usually required by local or state law to be in writing) as long as it is given before the start of the last full period of tenancy.

You or the landlord typically must give notice 31 days before the month-to-month lease is to expire. If you pay rent on the first of the month, the notice must be received before the first or it is not valid until the end of the next month. Some states allow a shorter period. For instance, in Washington State only a 20-day notice is required. In a very few instances, 60 days are required. Ask the agent about the local requirement or better, contact a tenants' rights group. Substitute the word "week" for "month" to see how it works for week-to-week arrangements. Notice would then be shortened to eight days before the day of the week you normally pay the rent.

An oral lease does not give the tenant much permanency in the unit since he or she can be dumped with only 31 (20)(8) days of warning. The landlord feels safer if there is a question about the tenant's ability to pay rent or the tenant's life-style or personality. The oral lease also allows the landlord to raise the rents on 31 (20)(8) days notice. Some local laws limit the amount of an increase, but the tenant will have to go through whatever appeals process the town provides to stop the hike. Typically, no reason is needed to cancel or not renew an oral lease. Retaliatory cancellations for sanctioned rent withholding, repairing and deducting, reporting code violations, complaining about the landlord to a governmental agency or community group or forming/joining a tenants' union may be prohibited. (There is more on this subject in the section "Written Leases" and in chapter 7.)

Since the lease is not written, it is hard to hold the landlord to the promises made. Furthermore, agreements about roommates, children, pets, parking, etc., might not be enforceable because they might not be provable. On the other hand, most states have enacted legislation that spells out the terms of an oral lease. Besides fair notice of termination and rent increases, there are definitions regarding habitability, length of term and eviction processes. The only advantage of an oral lease is that it lets the tenant terminate and move quickly. If you are in the process of buying a house or condo, you might want a month-to-month situation. The same is true if you anticipate leaving town soon. There is a sample notice to the landlord of lease cancellation in Appendix C.

Written Leases

A written lease specifies the amount of rent you must pay for a specific period of time. A written residential lease is usually for a year, but it can be any period from a month to as long as perhaps three years. The lease also states who may live in the unit, who is obligated to pay the rent, to whom the rent is paid and when. It also spells out other terms and conditions and rules.

There are textbooks and law school/real estate school courses about written leases. This is not an attempt to add clutter or profundity, nor is it necessary. Since there are scores of lease forms across the country, there is no way to include them in the kit and pick each one apart. You've got to study the lease given to you. Most leases are written for landlords. They are not intended to be fair or balanced. Do not be afraid. Negotiate and modify the lease as you see fit since you'll have to live with its provisions.

The Parties

The landlord is the lessor, and the tenant is the lessee. As a general rule, every tenant who signs the lease is responsible for all the rent. (See "Rents" further on in this chapter.) The landlord *may* be the party signing, *may* be the owner or *may* be a management company. If a problem arises, it might be hard to pin down who is responsible. This makes it difficult when you have complaints or some legal matter. In covered tenants' rights cities, whoever signs the lease or receives the rent for the lessor is deemed to be legally responsible. This makes it easier to get action or sue if necessary. The landlord's business street address, correct legal name and emergency phone number should be on the face of the lease. Where you send the rent should also be noted. I would be leery of a landlord who runs a business out of a post-office box.

Duration

Time provisions specify the first day and the last day of the lease period. One trick with which I am familiar starts and ends the lease in the same month of the same year. It looks like an error, but it isn't. There is a set of written rules but no guarantee for rent stability or longevity. Other leases run for short periods (e.g., six months) and then revert to month-to-month leases. This allows you six months stability followed by nibbling rent increases every few months. The strategy here is to charge you slightly less in increases than it would cost you to move elsewhere. Neat trick, hey? It's a nifty inflation beater for the landlord and a damnable inflation maker for you. Watch those dates!

Rent Controls

Some cities (e.g., New York) have rent control. Various states, such as California, have modified rent control schemes. Under the controls, a unit has a rent ceiling. The amount a rent can increase, from lease to lease (which applies to the same or different tenants), is specified by municipal laws. For some units, an increase is not possible, period. (This is where we see key fees and under-the-table money requests.) For others, a rate of increase is allowed, provided that certain factors relating to code compliance of the unit, property values and other issues are met. It is always a good idea to check with your city government regarding the legal limit of the rent for your unit.

Security or Damage Deposits

Under all circumstances, the deposit remains your money; it belongs to you. Request a receipt for the deposit. Sometimes this is part of the lease; otherwise, you *must* demand a separate receipt stating the amount and purpose of the payment. (See the discussion that follows regarding rents-in-advance.) The deposit is a bond to promise you'll pay for any damages you cause. It is usually also available to pay delinquent rent. Some leases seem to allow the landlord to take money if you "break" a rule, move out early or part your hair on the wrong side. The decision to use the deposit is made solely by the landlord. Some leases state that *you* cannot use the deposit to pay the last month's rent, but the *landlord* can use it to make up any delinquent rent. How nice for management to have its cake and eat it, too!

The amount of the deposit varies. The most standard amount is equal to one month's rent. You may also be asked for an additional deposit for pets, children or some other reason. Some tenants' rights laws limit the amounts that can be held. They also specify that the cash needs to be held in a special account and that interest must be paid on the deposit. The rules vary, but the percentage is at least what a savings account produces. The interest payment is usually due on the anniversary of your lease or when you move out. It can be paid by cash or an offset against that month's rent. Not all landlords must pay interest on security deposits.

The return rules for security deposits vary widely. Some are due upon moving out, period. In other places, there is a waiting period. In Seattle, for example, the deposit is due 14 days after moving out. In Chicago, the time period runs from 45 to 60 days, depending on the landlord's damage claims. Since the money belongs to the tenant, the landlord will have to substantiate with proof (receipts, pictures and witnesses) if the money is not fully refunded. Check you local laws for all the details. There can be sizable penalties against a landlord for abusing the interest and return portions of tenants' rights laws. Some jurisdictions have no set time period, which leaves the tenant with the distasteful options of waiting patiently forever or bringing a small claims lawsuit.

Rents-in-Advance

The lease may specify that first and last months' rent be paid in advance. If you also have to pay an application fee, an application deposit, and maybe more for the security deposit, this is highly burdensome. Be very, very sure you want this lease! The purpose for rents-in-advance is to guarantee that you won't skip out on the lease. There might be certain legal issues as to who "owns" these deposits and where they are. If your landlord sells the building or goes bankrupt, what happens to your deposit monies? Some tenants' rights laws make such deposits exempt from attachment, garnishment or bankruptcy processes involving the landlord since the money remains yours. These laws also specify that all your deposits automatically transfer with the sale of the building (or new management company) to the new principals.

In negotiating your lease, you need a plan.

Strategy When your application is approved, agree to bring the security deposit up to one month's rent when you sign the lease. Agree to sign the lease when all the premove promises have been kept. Agree to pay the first month's rent before you move in. If you have a pet deposit and/or last month's advance rent, make arrangements to pay it off in installments over several months. (Remember, your current landlord is holding on to your other security deposit.) Your new landlord would be making a mistake to make you go broke just to move in.

Rents

Some leases total the rent for a year and then allow you to pay it off monthly. Some only state the amount of monthly rent. The difference is that when you sign a lease with the total amount, that's what you owe, regardless of the payment feature. A lease that states only so much per month may not necessarily obligate you to pay for the whole year. The amount of rent usualy is fixed for the period. Please look for a rent increase sleeper clause that allows for elevations due to property taxes, special assessments, utility rate increases, cost-of-living adjustments, prime-rate fluctuations or phases of the moon. Don't accept a written lease with automatic rent increases. The one exception, however, is a lease for longer than a year, in which you negotiate the yearly increases. (There is more information about this in the section "Hidden Costs" in this chapter and "Rents, Fees and Deposits" in chapter 7.)

As far as money is concerned, somebody agrees to pay and somebody else agrees to receive. *Everybody* who signs the lease as lessee (that's you, the party of second part) is obligated to pay the full amount of the rent. Practically speaking, it means that if two (or three or four) of you, as roommates, lease an apartment, *each* of you promises to pay the *full amount*. As long as you live together, you can have any arrangement between you that you want as long as the rent is paid in full. If one of you leaves, that person is *still* responsible for the full amount. If one of you remains, that party is *also* responsible for all the rent. If the landlord sues for back rents because the remaining tenant can only pay part, all names on the lease will be sued, each for the full amount. The court is supposed to sort out the issue later. Sometimes another person must sign as guarantor. This means the guarantor will pay the rent if the lessees don't and will also be sued if the rent doesn't get paid.

Your rent covers certain items, but it may not cover others that you think are obvious. For instance is heat (and/or air conditioning) included as part of the rent? You might have to supply (or rent from your landlord) the stove and refrigerator. (See the discussions entitled "Appliances" and "Heat and Utilities" later in this chapter for more information.) Remember to keep a running total of the gross rent as you discover all the wonderful ways the landlord is eying your pocketbook.

Late Fee

The rent is typically due on the first of the month, but it can be on any date that is mutually acceptable. If you don't pay on time, there probably is a late fee. Late fees may be governed by a local ordinance or state law. Sometimes they are a set amount, a percentage of the rent or some formula. It is important for you to determine what rights you have regarding late fees. I was recently shown a lease from a large West Coast city. The lease demands a fixed late fee of $50, 12 percent interest on rents later than 30 days, a three-day late period with an automatic cancellation provision and a penalty of one month's rent. If a check bounces, that's another fee of $15. In Chicago, on the other hand, the landlord can only charge a maximum of $10 for up to the first $500 in rent, plus 5 percent of the amount over that. The landlord cannot circumvent the late fee by setting an artificially high rent and offering a rebate or reduction if it is paid by the first of the month. Furthermore, there is a five-day grace period before the rent is considered late.

Changes

A written lease is supposed to last for the duration. All the terms and conditions are not to change except by mutual agreement. That's what you think. Read your lease. It may contain a clause that allows the landlord to change the rules or add or modify terms and conditions! Signing a lease like this is like signing a blank check! If changes are proposed, put them in writing, have all parties sign them and attach the document to the lease. (See "Tenants' Riders" later in this chapter.)

Conditions

This subject is important. Almost all leases say something like the following:

Lessee has inspected the premises and has found it to be in acceptable condition and suitable for the intended use. Lessee accepts the premises *as is*. Lessor makes no warranties as to habitability except to maintain the unit according to building-code standards.

The obvious part is that what you see is what you get. The less obvious meaning is that nothing is going to change *unless* you cut a side agreement, called a *rider*, spelling out all the sweet promises the agent has made. Don't sign the lease until you truly accept things as is and all the necessary work has been done. (See the sections entitled "Possession" and "Tenants' Rider" that follow.)

Possession

You might find the "as is" statement here. This statement grants you permission to use the rental unit for the term of the lease. You accept the unit as is and will return possession of the unit to the landlord at the end of the lease in the (exact) same condition, *normal wear and tear excepted*. This is how you lose your security deposit. The landlord will claim every picture-hanger hole, paint smudge, floor or counter scratch, dust ball, carpet fray, rust stain and burnt-out light bulb as damage.

You need to do an inspection of the unit upon move-in with the agent, understand what normal usage is and agree what the conditions really are. (See chapters 6 and 8 and Appendix B.)

Terminations, Cancellations and Renewals

This can be another of those one-way streets. The lease will list under what circumstances you be can evicted: nonpayment or repeated late payment of rent, breaking a rule, disturbing neighbors or looking cross-eyed. You may be given one warning before eviction or a one-day, three-day, five-day or ten-day notice to vacate with no previous formal notice. With the exception of a near encounter with a thermonuclear device, you don't have similar options. So you can have a roof leak, no water or an unresolved neighbor problem, but you can't break the lease. You might find the lease requires you to pay all costs of your eviction and may take your security deposit as liquidated damages or "just because, so there"! Tenants' rights laws may protect you against this arbitrary treatment. You certainly have a right to make rent protests about conditions without being terminated. Termination under that circumstance can be considered retaliatory and therefore not lawful. You also have the right to be given a fair warning under many tenants' rights ordinances. Furthermore, if your unit is unlivable, you should have the right to leave without penalty. Consult your local tenants' group and the city attorney's office to find out about termination requirements.

Some leases contain within them a notice of termination that says that the lease expires on the date stated on the front and that this is the only notice the tenant will get, and the tenant acknowledges the notice. If your city is "uncovered" (i.e., it has no tenants' rights), the landlord does not have to renew your lease, period. No reason is required. If you are in a covered city, the landlord may have to give you a formal written termination notice 30 to 60 days in advance, may have to offer to renew your lease unless there is a statutory reason not to renew and is required to charge a fair and comparable renewal rent.

Some leases allow that at the landlord's option, the lease will be terminated when it expires, will be renewed for another period at a new rent or will become a month-to-month tenancy at the same or new rent but following all the written rules of the old lease. Read your lease well on this matter. You might have to give your landlord a written notice of termination at the end of the lease to prevent an automatic renewal.

You will occasionally find a lease that contains an early-out cancellation clause. Such leases allow a party to give a 30-, 60- or 90-day written notice to terminate without cause. Make sure that this is mutual for both sides. The down side is that you now only have a lease that is certain within the cancellation period. The up side is that you can move early (presumably without penalty).

Relocation and Humanitarian Terminations

A rare lease allows tenants to cancel without penalty for reasons such as job transfer, job loss, spousal loss, military service and similar humanitarian situations. I advise you to write a relocation clause into your lease. Where relocation clauses exist, they usually specify how many miles you have to move and for what reasons. The IRS allows you to deduct your moving expenses if your employer transfers you more than 60 miles from where you live. If 60 miles is good enough for Uncle Sam, it ought to be good enough for Simon LeGree. You'll need to give your landlord proof in the form of a letter from your employer.

Sublets and Assignments

If your lease doesn't allow outright termination on your part, can you at least sublet the place? Many leases say absolutely not! Why? Well, one reason is that the landlord wants to choose the tenants. For another reason, why not confiscate a security deposit, pick up some fines and sue the current tenant for the balance of the lease *while at the same time* reletting the apartment and picking up double rent? Why not, indeed?

A sublet is an arrangement where the tenant finds another tenant to take over the balance of the lease. The original tenant essentially becomes the successor tenant's landlord. Living in tenants' rights towns, if the sublet provides a comparable tenant who is ready, willing and able to pay the rent, the landlord must accept the new tenant or let the old tenant terminate the lease. In any case, no fees, fines or special expenses can be charged to the original tenant, and nothing more than usual fees and deposits can be required from his or her replacement. (See chapter 7 for more information on sublets and assignments.)

I strongly encourage you to *assign* the lease instead of subletting. An assignment takes your name out of the process and makes the other party directly responsible.

The "Body"

Leases are called contracts of adhesion because you get "stuck" with terms you must accept if you want to rent. This concept conveys the idea that you are not in an equal bargaining position with the landlord (and you are not). The basis is that each clause is independent, meaning you still owe the rent, no matter what. The stickiest part of a lease is that someplace in the boilerplate (standard printed form language) may be a clause that goes something like this:

Rents. Time is of the essence. Lessee agrees and shall pay to Lessor, or to whomever Lessor shall designate, all rents due in the amount specified on the dates specified as shown on the front of this Lease. Payment of rent shall be independent of any duty of the Lessor to perform under this Lease (except if unit is rendered uninhabitable as declared by proper governmental authority). If rents are not tendered as agreed, Lessee agrees to waive all rights to due notice and process and agrees that Lessor has the right without further notice to immediately (regain possession of the premises); maintain an action at law for possession of the unit; obtain judgment against Lessee for all back, present and future rents; and to assess all legal and court costs against Lessee.

What the hell does that mean, anyway? It simply means that you always owe the rent, regardless of whether your landlord breaks any part of the lease. If don't pay your rent on time, you'll be evicted without legal notice or due process of law.

Furthermore, it means that you'll have to pay what you currently owe and might have to pay for the rest of the lease, even if you are tossed out. As insult, you might also have to pay the landlord's lawyer! Often another clause is tossed in, called "confession of judgment," whereby you agree to hire your landlord's lawyer to tell the court that you accept the charges leveled by your landlord! Oh yes, and you also agree to pay you landlord's lawyer for the work!

You may also find language to the effect that you agree not to withhold rents, abate (reduce rents) or deduct rents for repairs (or any other reason) (without written permission in advance from the landlord). These actions are probably illegal because of tenants' rights laws and/or case law, but the landlord might try to evict you anyway. I usually strike the word "independent" and substitute "dependent," which changes the bargain to say "No service, no rents!" (See chapters 7 and 8.)

Here is another clause that could be troublesome:

> **Waiver of Liability.** Lessee agrees to hold harmless Lessor, its agents, employees, servants and heirs without liability for all damages, injuries and losses of whatever nature and whatever cause including willful and negligent acts, including but not limited to fulfillment of lease provisions, casualty fire, natural disaster, failure of essential services, and acts of third parties which may adversely affect Lessee's use of premises. Further, Lessee agrees not to attempt to collect damages of any sort from Lessor, Lessor's insurance carrier, nor file any action-at-law regarding such matters. This agreement constitutes an absolute and irrefutable affirmative defense against any such action.

This gobbledygook simply means you agree not to sue your landlord for anything and in so agreeing, waive your civil rights in the area of liability and your ability to recover damages.

Are you to willing sign an agreement like this? You need to discuss this matter with the agent and explain that you have expectations regarding the landlord and that unbalanced or unfair provisions are not acceptable. Figure out which clauses can be cut and which can be adjusted.

If where you live has tenants' rights laws, you may be protected against the these clauses, as well as many others. As a matter of fact, good tenants' rights laws go a long way toward obviating most of the standard lease items except for duration and rent. Where these laws exist, such clauses are considered *unconscionable,* which means unenforceable. Many ordinances state that anything you are forced to sign that is contrary to the local law is null. You cannot sign away your rights. Some ordinances go as far as allowing a tenant to sue for relief (injunction) and damages (money) if the landlord attempts to enforce illegal clauses.

Insurance

You should buy tenants' insurance, since the landlord will typically not be responsible for your personal property or liability. The most common insurance issues are theft, fire or water damage, and window breakage, followed by general liability (known in the trade as trips-and-falls insurance). Your landlord will be responsible for all damages of any sort if what happens is caused by the landlord's actions (willful) or inactions (negligence) or a combination (willful negligence). I hope you'll never have to find out who pays for what! Make sure that your lease does not force you to release your landlord from all liability. (See the previous section, entitled "Waiver of Liability.")

Boilerplate

The rest of the printed lease usually contains conditions regarding the use of the unit, repairs, maintenance, local laws, landlord's rights about entering your unit and so forth. One lease I've seen contains a clause granting the landlord a first lien on all your personal property (just in case you don't pay the rent). Nonetheless, be aware of the following:

Access

This is when the landlord can enter your unit for the purposes of "inspection, repairs or showing the unit for sale or rent." Do *not* give him or her *carte blanche*. Make sure the days and hours are stated and the method of notice is reasonable. Many tenants' rights laws specify an advance warning in writing of two days, and access is only during daytime hours and not on Sunday. In an emergency the landlord can enter at any time, as a common-sense rule. You are probably required to give the landlord a set of keys (if you change the locks). This makes sense as long as you can trust the janitor or manager. Landlords can use access to harass or punish tenants.

Appliances

Who is supplying the appliances? Does the unit come with a stove, refrigerator, other kitchen appliances, hot-water tank, heating system and/or air-conditioning system? Will the landlord rent these to you as an extra? If so, for how much? Can you rent these appliances from a local company? If you install something, can you remove it later without penalty? Will it be cheaper to buy the items you need? Should you find a unit that rents appliances as part of the deal?

Duties and Responsibilities

There usually are separate clauses for landlord and tenant. The tenant is not supposed "to make waste or leave belongings in the hall," etc. The landlord typically promises little.

Heat and Utilities

This specifies who supplies the heat, hot water, water and sewer, cooking gas, heating fuel, electricity and so forth. Make sure that you have an individual meter if you pay for utilities. Don't accept some sort of prorated deal from the landlord. Many tenants' rights laws require that the landlord disclose the monthly average utility costs for each service. You can find this for yourself by calling the suppliers directly. Watch out for outrageous add-ons based on "excess water usage." Cable TV or master antenna charges can come in this clause. Contact suppliers directly to price these services before you accept the landlord's deal or restrictions. The same is true for telephone services. I have a friend who took a deal from an apartment building that offers ADAS (apartment door annunciator service), where the phone rings when someone downstairs pushes your doorbell. Much to their later horror, they found they had signed up for phone services that charged them 20 cents per phone call—incoming and outgoing—plus time and line charges!

Maintenance and Repairs

This clause can be tricky. Make sure that you don't agree to pay for fixing items that come as part of the rent. The clause might say something like this: "Lessor will use with care, and clean and maintain properly, all kitchen appliances, plumbing fixtures and systems, heating and air-conditioning units, and windows, and provide for service of these items." If you rent a freestanding unit, such as a house, you might find you've agreed to pay for repairs to the roof or foundation as well. As a rule, if you break it, you fix it. If it breaks, wears out or is damaged through no fault of yours, the landlord should be responsible. See that this clause is set right.

Rules

Then there are the "rules." For example, you are not allowed to "bring disrespect upon the building." You must carry your groceries through the back door, use the freight elevator and have all deliveries made to the rear only. Overnight guests (must register, can only stay three nights per year, must keep one foot on the floor at all times, are not allowed). You cannot or must install (shades, curtain rods, carpeting). You cannot be barefoot in the lobby or wear shoes in the pool. One lease I saw prohibits tenants from allowing their friends to park motorcycles within 300 feet (on the public street) of the building! Use of the laundry facilities is governed by your floor and the day of the week. Display of political posters in your windows may be prohibited. One preprinted form I have states that you can't play a TV or stereo after 10:30 P.M. This is where you find standard rules regarding pets, water beds, your own appliances, use of extra heaters and air conditioners. Read them and weep or laugh.

Landlord's Riders

We are not finished with leases. In addition to all the boilerplate, there are the additional clauses, attachments and riders. These may be more important than the lease language, since they are very special extra agreements. They may have to do with condominium or co-op rules, insurance requirements, guests and nonfamily sleepovers, smoking and drinking, phobias or prejudices of the landlord, local laws or special arrangements. These additional clauses can include an alternate payment schedule, credit for doing maintenance or decorating (a *decoration clause*), early termination and sublet conditions, lease renewal or unit purchase options, pet or carpet cleaning rules—you name it. The rider may also state that the tenant acknowledges receiving a set of rules, cash receipts or has inspected and approved the unit as is. As often as not, no such documents are provided, and no such approval is actually given. Since these are additional agreements, a judge will consider that you knew and accepted them and will more than likely enforce the rider if you are dragged into court.

A brief comment is in order concerning carpet and drapery cleaning. Let us examine the logic of charging for this service. *Wear and tear* means normal and intended use. Over time, paint normally fades, walls collect schmutz, wooden floors scuff and carpets collect traffic dirt. Is it fair or reasonable to agree to repaint the landlord's walls or sand and revarnish the landlord's floors? So why is it okay to charge for or agree to professionally clean the carpet? The landlord's rent is assumed to include the costs of upkeep. You should be held to the same standard for carpets as for floors and walls. Draperies have even less logic. If carpets and drapes are a selling point, charge more for units with them; don't deceptively say they are part of the package and then charge extra!

The dreaded *pet rider* is a common addition. It permits you to have a pet under certain circumstances. It may require that only that pet, by name (what do you call your goldfish?), can reside with you. If it makes messes or noise, it's gone. A special pet security deposit is added. I think such a rider is a good arrangement that respects the needs of the tenant, other tenants and the landlord. If you have a pet, try to get a pet rider first, before smuggling Fifi into your apartment.

The *parking rider* is also quite common. If you rent a parking space, you'll want a rider or separate lease for the space. You will note that management takes absolutely no responsibility for your vehicle or contents. Furthermore, you may have to give them a set of keys. If you lock your car when you shouldn't, park in the wrong space or let someone else use your space, the offending vehicle will be towed at your expense and set afire in a public ceremony. Are you sure you need that car? Taxi!

I recently saw a five-page rider that fined the tenant $100 per day per violation! The landlord was demanding money for something having to do with curtain rods. The tenant's question was whether the landlord could take the money from the security deposit and also terminate the lease. My guess is that it will take a good lawyer to convince a judge that the tenant didn't understand the rider, even if local law doesn't allow for "fines." Another rider I was shown charges the tenant $25 each time the landlord sends the tenant a required notice. Many riders will also contain contradictory clauses that conflict with parts of the lease or the other parts of the rider. Study the landlord's riders and strike what you can't tolerate.

Tenants' Riders

Tenants submit lease riders to cover special circumstances and also to make the landlord agree in writing to promises regarding special arrangements, repairs and improvements. For instance, under the Americans with Disabilities Act, a disabled tenant has the right to make physical changes to the landlord's property by, for example, enlarging door openings, installing chair lifts and modifying plumbing. Before such work is undertaken, an agreement should be executed and attached to the lease.

Other understandings relate to extended-period leases, where you agree to renew for two additional years with a 3 percent rent increase each succeeding year. If you are getting married, you might want permission to add your spouse's name to the lease. Or maybe you expect another person to join you during the lease period. You'll want an agreement that allows another person and does not increase the rent. This is a problem when a relative lives away and then comes home (from school, the hospital or another relative).

Appendix D has a complete sample "Tenants' Rider" that spells out the repair and improvement promises you expect from the landlord. This tenants' rider will have to be written to fit the subject, but use the opening and closing form of the sample. You'll always want to put in a clause allowing you to reduce rents, use your rent money to have the work done or terminate the lease if the landlord breaks the agreement.

There is one special rider I find to be helpful and important. I strongly urge you to attach it to the lease, as simply as writing it out by hand at the bottom or on the back of the lease. Both parties need to initial it. It is an agreement to mediate any disagreement or dispute you and the landlord might have *before* the lease is broken or an action at law (eviction, lawsuit, demand for possession) can take place. Here is the rider I suggest:

> In the event of a dispute, the parties agree to a good-faith effort to resolve the issue(s) through the use of mediation with a qualified community mediation service or certified mediation practitioner prior to lease termination or any action at law. The cost, if any, is to be shared mutually by all parties.

I am a great fan of alternative dispute resolution, a process that focuses on mutually beneficial solutions and not on expensive and time-losing legal wranglings. (See chapter 9 for more information on mediation.)

Hidden Costs

These are the sleepers, extras and specials hidden in the lease and the riders. I've discussed carpet cleaning, air-conditioning surcharges, repairs, taxes and assessments, fines, lawyers fees and notice service. Can there be more? Of course. This is the landlord's lease, remember? I've seen a standard rider that states that if the tenant stays less than three years, the cost of repainting the unit will be taken from the security deposit! So much for normal wear and tear. Some buildings charge for use of a freight elevator or loading dock. Look for pool charges, package-receiving charges, broken-window charges, charges for emptying the fuel-oil tank, charges for too much garbage, charges for using too much water or charges for losing your keys. Keep looking.

Condos and Co-ops

When you rent a condo or co-op, you may have special problems. The owner is probably an investor who does not have a lot of experience as a landlord. The owner is responsible for what goes on *inside* the walls of the unit. So when you have a complaint, if you take it to the office of the building, you may be told to talk to the owner. The owner may say that you should deal with the building. You, of course, have nobody to turn to. Also, condo owners may believe they are exempt from most laws governing landlords, and this causes further problems. Know and trust your owner or agent before you rent a condo or co-op.

Signatures

A lease is a legal document, and your signature binds you to the terms. Read over the lease, making sure that everything you've talked about has been handled through additions, deletions and riders. Initial all changes to the preprinted forms. Please insist on keeping copies of all documents presented to you. Most states have case law (court decisions) that rule that if a lease is signed by at least one party, the lease is valid as long as money is offered for rent and accepted. Some states say it is a deceptive act or an act that violates real estate or contract law to fail or refuse to give all signing parties copies of documents such as leases. If you don't have the paper, you don't know what you really agreed to or won't be able to prove your deal. Make copies of everything *you* sign, even if the agent tells you your signed copy will be returned to you later. Take it with you in complete form or copy it. Don't leave without your copies.

By this time, I hope you have a flavor of what the lease contains and appropriate expectations regarding the lease and the landlord. As I discuss leases, I constantly refer to tenants' rights laws. But if there are none to protect you, how do you protect yourself? First, make sure everything in the apartment is the way you want it *before* you sign. Second, only put down substantial amounts of money incrementally, as each step in the rental process is successfully completed. (See the comments in this chapter's "Strategy.") Third, I have included a "Universal Tenants' Rights Rider" in Appendix E, which you may want to attach to your lease if you are not otherwise covered by local law. Take a look at it before you start negotiating.

Truth-in-Renting Worksheet

Put apartment ad information here.

_____

_____

_____

Notes

- Why is the apartment available? How long has it been empty? How full or empty is the building?

- Is the unit a condominium?

- Are there any conditions in the building that require repairs (roof, new plumbing or wiring, replacement of the rear porch, new heating system)?

- Is the building involved in any building-code compliance or housing-court hearings? What is the reason? How long has the building been under official review?

- Are you satisfied with the environmental issues, such as lead paint, lead and other water issues, radon gas and asbestos fibers?

- Are there roach, mice or rat problems in the building? Is there a regularly scheduled extermination service provided?

- Have there been any burglaries in the building in the past two years? What are the details?

- Has the building had any fires in the past several years? What happened?

- Who is the owner of the building (or condo)? Is the building up for sale or condo conversion? (This means a big rent increase or worse when the current lease expires.)

- Are the building and common areas regularly cleaned? How often? By whom (tenant, live-in janitor, management-company personnel)?

- What repairs will management make, and what repairs will the tenant have to take care of?

- How do tenants report maintenance problems? How long does it take for repairs?

- What are the emergency, after-hours phone numbers? Is this an answering machine in the office or a real person?

- Will the management company reimburse tenants for parts and labor if tenants make their own repairs?

- Does the management carry building liability insurance for you and your guests if you are hurt *outside* your apartment while on the premises and in cases of management negligence? What are the details?

- Are there any special conditions for tenancy placed upon residents in the building? (Examples of such special conditions include the following: replace hallway light bulbs or smoke-detector batteries, shovel the snow, no water beds, no pets, no children (illegal in your community?), no automatic dishwasher or clothes washer/dryer, no air conditioner, no extra door locks or maybe even no overnight guests or parties.)

Lease Analysis Worksheet

Address of the unit: _____

Name of the landlord, agent or management company: _____

_____

Address and phone number of the landlord: _____

_____

Place where rent is to be sent: _____

Names of all lease-signing tenants: _____

_____ , _____

Names of all additional tenants: _____

_____

Amount of security deposit: $ _____

Proof of security-deposit payment: ☐ Separate receipt ☐ Receipt is part of lease

Amount of rents-in-advance: $ _____

Proof of advance rents payment: ☐ Separate receipt ☐ Receipt is part of lease

Term of lease: ☐ Weekly ☐ Monthly ☐ Yearly

Starting and ending dates: From _____ To _____

Amount of rent/amount of monthly rent payment: $ _____

Rent control provisions: ☐ Yes ☐ No Ask to see documents.

Monthly due date of rent: _____

Rent grace period: ☐ 1 day ☐ 3 days ☐ 5 days ☐ 7 days ☐ 10 days

Late-rent penalties: $ _____ or _____ %

Special terms written in on the face of the lease: _____

_____

_____

_____

Tenants' rights or other laws: ☐ Protected ☐ Unprotected ☐ Copy received

Use of security deposit for last month's rent: ☐ Yes ☐ No

Use of prepaid rents: _____

Renewal terms and conditions: ☐ Automatic Advance notice time: _____

Heat and utilities:

    Who pays? ☐ Tenant ☐ Landlord

    Who supplies? ☐ Utility companies ☐ Landlord

    What are the monthly average costs for?

        heat: $ _____

        air conditioning: $ _____

electricity: $ _____

hot water: $ _____

water and sewer: $ _____

cooking gas: $ _____

other _____: $ _____

Cancellation/termination provisions:

Warnings first: ☐ Yes ☐ No

Number of days for termination: _____ days

Number of days for cancellation: _____ days

Notice provisions: _____

_____

Mutual early cancellation provisions? How many days written notice: ___ days

Relocation clause: ☐ Yes ☐ No

Humanitarian cancellation clause: ☐ Yes ☐ No

Sublet permission: ☐ Yes ☐ No

Landlord's access: ☐ Does he or she have keys? Hours/notice: _____

Use restrictions: _____

Who supplies the appliances? ☐ Landlord ☐ Tenant ☐ Rentals $ _____

Maintenance and repair responsibilities: ☐ Landlord ☐ Tenant Who pays for what? _____

Insurance requirements: ☐ Tenant insurance ☐ Other _____

Waiver of landlord's liabilities or tenant's civil rights? ☐ Yes ☐ No

Can changes to the lease be made unilaterally by landlord? ☐ Yes ☐ No

Special rules:

Guests: _____

Appliances: _____

Pets: _____

Noise limitations by type and time: _____

Pet rider: ☐ Yes ☐ No   Extra security: $ _____   Extra rent: $ _____

Fuel-oil rider: ☐ Yes ☐ No Duties: _____

Parking rider: ☐ Yes ☐ No Terms: _____

Condo rules attached: ☐ Yes ☐ No

Local laws attached: ☐ Yes ☐ No

Inspection forms attached: ☐ Yes ☐ No

Landlord's rider attached: ☐ Yes ☐ No What does it say? _____

_____

_____

Is the tenant's rider attached? ☐ Yes ☐ No

What is expected from the landlord in terms of promised repairs, decorating, rent payment schedules, added tenants, renewals, etc.? _____

_____

_____

_____

Have you kept and filed copies of everything given to you? ☐ Yes ☐ No

5

Racism, Sexism, Ageism, Gayism, Children and Disabilities

Types of conditions or situations protected by federal laws against housing discrimination.

There are strong laws protecting various classes of people seeking housing in this country. In addition, federal law gives persons with disabilities special rights. Most federal housing rights are gathered under the Fair Housing Act of 1988 (FHAA), which amends the 1968 Civil Rights Act. This law covers almost all rental issues and is the minimum you can expect. Many localities have gone beyond the FHAA to protect more situations. The box at the beginning of this chapter indicates the types of conditions protected by the law.

While most "classes" are obvious, some need an explanation. "Handicap" refers to any physical or mental disability including hearing, mobility and visual impairments; chronic alcoholism; chronic mental illness; AIDS; ARC; and mental retardation. The condition needs to substantially limit one or more major life activities. You are a member of this class if you have a record of the disability or obviously can be regarded as having it. Present drug users and those who pose a threat to the safety or well-being of others are excluded.

Family status goes beyond married with children under 18. It also includes pregnant women, a person who has legal custody (e.g., a guardian) of a child or children, or the formally identified (in writing) designee of a parent. For instance, when Grace sends her daughter MariLou to live with Uncle Bill or Grandma Anne, the relative (in this case) becomes the designee, provided Grace makes a formal declaration that the designated person can act in Grace's stead for most daily and emergency matters regarding the daughter. Sometimes a lawyer will have to draw up this letter.

Under the federal law, all rental housing is included, with the exception of owner-occupied buildings with four or less units, private clubs and for-sale-by-owner single-family housing. So you can expect (demand) fair treatment unless you want to rent and live with the landlord.

What actions are prohibited? Study the following box to see what is covered. A landlord is not allowed to take any of the actions listed in the box based on race, color, national origin, religion, sex, family status or handicap.

An Owner, Agent or Landlord May Not Do The Following to Federally Protected Classes

- Refuse to rent
- Refuse to negotiate for housing
- Make housing unavailable
- Deny a dwelling
- Set different terms, conditions or privileges for the rental of a dwelling
- Provide different housing services or facilities
- Falsely deny that housing is available for inspection or rent
- Blockbust
- Deny anyone access to multiple listing services related to the rental of housing

Federally Prohibited Acts of Rental Discrimination

In addition, it is illegal for anyone (would-be neighbors included) to threaten, coerce, intimidate or interfere with anyone exercising or assisting in the exercise of a fair-housing right.

Where I live, it is no longer socially acceptable to advertise apartments with notices that say "Catholics need not apply," but when I was a kid you might have seen those ads. Nowadays I see ads saying "Adults only" and "No children." All these practices are illegal, since a landlord must rent to anyone who can pay the rent (satisfy standard credit requirements), who is not an obvious threat to the safety and well-being of the property or other tenants and will not overcrowd the unit. Newspapers across the country are being pressured through negotiation or lawsuits to refuse to accept or run restrictive ads. These "pattern and practice" suits come from private fair-housing agencies as well as governmental prosecutors. About the only exception is restricting children in buildings that are exclusively for people over 55 years of age and that are specifically operated for seniors.

How do you identify discrimination? I want to cover the standard prejudices first. Later in this chapter, I'll discuss disability and family discrimination. There is, of course, open hostility and rudeness that is unmistakable: "We don't rent to your kind." "You'd be happier in another part of town." "I don't have anything that is suitable for *you*." But there is more subtle prejudice designed toward the same result. If you travel with an agent and all you see are rentals that fit a certain racial or ethnic stereotype (basically matching yours), assume you are being "steered," which is a polite way of saying you are being segregated. You must be shown all the housing that meets your needs for location, price and size. If you suspect you are being steered, ask the agent about other locations. Subtle variations on this theme include the following: you are only shown units in decrepit buildings; you only see units in bad need of repair; or you are only shown units in basements, in the rear of buildings or next to expressways.

Another common practice is an announcement that the unit has just been rented. You suspect this is untrue because other people are being shown the place, the ad is still running or you make a "blind" call and are told the place is still available. Here are some variations on this theme: "The old tenant decided to stay." "We've decided to do additional decorating." "The building is being sold, and the buyer doesn't want any new leases." Then comes bait-and-switch or "Sorry, we don't have anything else right now." Since you have the right to inspect your credit-check report, it is difficult to refuse you on that basis, so other scams may be tried. You might be told that you need the first and last months' rents, a two-month security deposit, a key deposit, etc. You suspect that others aren't paying this much up front. A variation might be that the rent suddenly escalates because "The newspaper ad was wrong" or "I grabbed the wrong file." Most agents have long lists of available units. If you are denied access to the lists, be suspicious. Watch what notes or symbols an agent places on your papers. It is not uncommon to find a code indicating race or some form of discrimination that affects your rights to obtain rental housing.

Children's issues can run a similar gauntlet, with additional twists. The blatant way is that the landlord announces that he or she doesn't rent to families with children or rents only to families with one child less than you have or not to children under six or over six, cleverly disqualifying you.

There are other ways. For example, you are only shown units with one bedroom, which is a sure way to discourage renting. Insist that you are shown the unit size you require. Ask to see the list, etc. One way to get around renting to families with children (which really translates to a single mother with two or three kids) is to show the perfect apartment and say, "This is the bedroom and over here is the 'den'." You are told that you can't have more than a certain number of people sleep in a given bedroom unit because "it is against the local building code." Do you think for a minute that because an agent gives a room a name, it can only be used to watch TV or crack peanuts? Furthermore, as a rule, building codes specify densities—minimum square footage for bedrooms per person—and make the difference between little people and those over 12. A code seldom requires people to sleep only inside walls called bedrooms.

In addition to all the other scams, persons with disabilities get a special runaround. Those with mobility impairments aren't shown available units on the first floor in nonelevator buildings. A person who needs care or assistance is told that only "independent" persons are allowed. Folks who need an animal for help, such as a seeing-eye dog or a pet that gives therapeutically required companionship to a person with an emotional or mental disability, are told there is a "no pet" policy. Other arguments given in refusal are that the wheelchair can't get through the door, there are steps, the person will cause a disturbance to other tenants and so forth. Sometimes you might be stopped outright (as you move in) when the landlord sees that somebody in the family has a disability.

The federal law extends special housing rights to people with disabilities. For instance, where parking is available, a mobility-disabled person can request (and receive) a parking place for the car near the door. Special arrangements must also be made regarding snow shoveling so that a person can get out of the building and get to work.

Since not all units conform to the new federal guidelines for rental buildings finished after March 13, 1991, regarding access, hallway and doorway widths, and heights and layout of sinks, toilets and light switches, this class of tenant is granted the right to make the changes for themselves. This means that if a disabled tenant finds a place but needs to widen the front door, install a chairlift or replace the toilet, the tenant may do so. The tenant must pay for the changes, agree to restore the premises to the previous condition when he or she leaves and be reasonable about what is done in relationship to the structure of the premises. By federal law, the landlord may not refuse a tenant with disabilities the right to rent or to make the changes. There are other, more easily accomplished accommodations also. The hearing impaired might require a door "bell" that uses flashing lights or a fan. Each member of the protected class will have small but important needs that may not be refused. The issue is always "reasonableness."

If you are reading this chapter, it is because you have sniffed the stench of discrimination. Once you think this has happened, what should you do? Find the local not-for-profit organization that assists in your type of discrimination. For instance, persons with disabilities should look for a local Center for Independent Living. Race discrimination victims should look toward civil rights or housing antidiscrimination groups, so-called "fair housing" organizations. Issues regarding children should be taken to the latter groups, plus groups concentrating on women's and children's issues. If you qualify, you might consider contacting a legal assistance, or community law or legal services agency (which does federally funded legal work for the poor) or a local law school "law clinic." I suggest this route first, because these groups have experience and knowledge that can be very helpful. They can explain, guide and plot strategies. They will reduce the runaround you'll get from the public agencies you may ultimately have to contact. They have attorney resources. In most cases, they will also help with paperwork, follow-up and advocacy.

As a general rule, when we talk about tenants' rights, the laws offer remedies if you don't get your due. While I don't wish to quibble with the lawyers, you really don't have practical remedies with FHAA in that tomorrow you go to the Department of Housing and Urban Development (HUD) or the Department of Justice and all is righted. What you have is a lead-weighted club that will ring the skull of a landlord dumb enough not to cooperate. Unfortunately for you, the whacking can take upwards of two years. In the end, if you are successful, you'll get money damages and whatever compliance the judge orders. In the meantime, you've probably moved someplace else or suffered without what you should have under the law. Under special and rare circumstances, the Department of Justice might seek an injunction against the landlord, perhaps holding the apartment off the market, until the matter is resolved.

As you might guess, the power of the law is what happens to your landlord if it practices discrimination. The law provides for a minimum fine (paid to the feds) of $10,000 up to a maximum of $50,000 for repeated occurrences of the same discrimination. You will be able to collect money also for your hardship, humiliation, suffering and other damages, plus legal costs. The landlord, of course, will have to pay up and comply with the law. So the incentive to get compliance at the time of a discrimination is what happens eventually if the landlord refuses.

The importance of making your case or getting immediate compliance rests with the skill of the advocacy group with which you work. As soon as you detect discrimination, contact a group. If you cannot find a group, you'll have to go directly to the local, state or federal agency that ultimately takes the case. (This is described in the pages that follow.) Your advocate will study the case and advise a practical plan. It first might contact the landlord and suggest a meeting to explain the landlord's obligations as well as work out a practical plan (particularly if it is disabilities-related arrangements). Or the advocate may decide to first send out "testers." This process pairs several teams that apply for the same or similar housing. Some teams may be white; others may match your conditions or circumstances. With the key exception of race, sex, disability or children, the teams will match. The teams report what happens. What is so often the case is that the able-bodied white teams with no children get offers to rent or are shown the better places, while the protected-class teams are shown the door.

After the testing results are in, a request to negotiate may be made, or a suggestion is made to file a complaint. If you proceed with a complaint, there are some key components. You must file within one year of the alleged violation. A request to complain is made to HUD and/or a more local equivalent agency. (These agencies have names like the Fair Housing Commission, Human Relations Commission or Human Rights Commission.) HUD will refer most complaints to the equivalent agency, but HUD should be contacted at any rate. (You can call HUD toll-free at 1-800-543-8294.) While the initial complaint can be by phone, experience dictates that you should send a follow-up letter setting forth your complaint. You don't have to talk about the testing but only about what happened to you. The reason for the letter is that complaints get misinterpreted and misdirected. This should protect you if you are refused or denied help because of a misunderstanding. Send this letter by certified mail, return receipt requested.

The agency will either send you forms or request that you personally appear to fill out, verify or correct forms based on your call or letter. Although the matter is supposed to be accepted or rejected within 120 days, it can take much longer because of the case load and personnel shortages. Next the case is assigned to an investigator who may ask you more questions and will go to the landlord for information. The investigator will attempt to conciliate the issue by acting as a go-between or sometimes setting up a meeting between the parties. Investigators sometimes decide the "proper" solution on their own and try to force it down the throats of parties. This can prove quite unsatisfactory.

If the matter is not resolved, the investigator recommends the case be dropped or that formal charges be drawn and the landlord prosecuted. If your case is dropped, you can appeal to the HUD Office of Fair Housing and the HUD secretary (and many times that's where your initial letter and statement of facts is helpful).

At any time during the first two years after the discrimination, or until a HUD hearing officer starts to hear the case (whichever happens first), you can, at your own expense, file a federal lawsuit.

The responsibility for enforcing the federal law rests with HUD and the Department of Justice. In the HUD model, cases can be put before a civil administrative law judge (the hearing officer) or referred to federal court. Either party can request a court trial. If that happens, the complainant is represented for free by the Department of Justice. The difference between the administrative procedure and federal court is that damage awards are higher in court and the matter sometimes can go faster in court.

What are the outcomes? Since 1989 federal suits have garnered several million dollars in fines and thousands of dollars in damage awards to individuals. A number of real-estate concerns have either signed court-approved agreements to change discriminatory practices or have been forced to conform to the law.

Additional Classes or Status
Protected by Various State and Local Laws
Marital status
Military status
Age over 40
Sexual orientation
Parental status
Source of income
Affiliation

Where states have equivalent laws, you can avail yourself of the state's procedure, and you can file suit in state court. Many states and localities go beyond federal laws, while employing generally similar enforcement procedures. Filing under a local ordinance may cause things to happen faster. Testing and other investigatory methods are employed, typically by the private not-for-profit agencies previously mentioned.

The most striking local issues relate to rentals to homosexuals and those with nontraditional relationships and life-styles. Affiliation refers to life-style issues such as mixed-race relationships. Source of income goes to refusals to rent to those who receive public assistance, Social Security payments or some sort of alimony or maintenance. I doubt if exclusion for illegal income activities, such as drug dealing, could be successfully challenged if the dealing might take place in the unit.

6

Moving—The Necessary Rituals

> **The Organized Move**
> - Throwing Out the Unneeded
> - Notifying All and Sundry
> - Dealing with a Moving Company
> - Rentals, Boxes
> - Loading and Unloading
> - Staying Organized with a Master Plan
> - Rights and Pitfalls for Movers
> - Security Deposit Return Inspections

Moving is a combination of mindless drudge and last minute detail. While I don't think it can be transformed into "fun," there are a number of things you can do to ease the burden (pun intended) and keep track of the process.

Moving tasks need to be divided into segments. There is the department of physical possessions, the bureau of transportation, the division of budgets, the office of logistical detail, the labor commission and the strategic planning board.

Advance Planning

The first thing to do is to throw out and sell what you don't need any more. There is nothing more frustrating than packing useless stuff, unless it is unpacking the same goods at the other end and wondering why you brought them along. Get rid of that junk! Determine if your old furniture will fit into your new place. Scrap what won't work.

Many charity agencies will pick up your usable/serviceable donated discards. If you have an apartment sale, be sure to obtain a permit if local law requires it. If you are throwing out lots of stuff, you might have to make special arrangements with your current landlord regarding excess trash. Or perhaps you can start early enough and throw out a little each week! Do not trash hazardous chemicals such as paint, thinner, gasoline or the like. Call your local environmental protection office to find out who will take hazardous trash. Sometimes the fire department accepts flammables to use in practice drills. Some towns also have community hazardous disposal groups. If you dump stuff down the drain or sewer, it can explode. For more advance planning information, see "Coordinating Your Move."

Storage

Will you have to make long-term storage arrangements? Maybe your new place comes with appliances you already own? Check out what it costs to store your goods. Small lockers start at $30 to $50 per month. Insurance is extra, and there can be extra access charges. If you miss a rent payment, seizure of your property can happen very quickly. Many storage facilities are not regulated and can make up the rules as they go along. Think about selling what you can't take with you.

Notifications

As soon as you can, notify the post office of your forwarding address and moving date. Three weeks in advance appears to be the minimum safety limit. Use the postal service change-of-address kit to notify your subscriptions and catalogs, credit cards, insurance companies, doctors and dentists, banks and other business relationships, friends and family.

The utilities companies will need to know when to take a final reading; where to send the final bill; where to send your deposit return; and if you are relocating locally, where to continue your service without interruption. The phone company can even let your phone ring at both local locations for a few days if that is convenient. If you are changing phone numbers, the phone company will refer the caller. Give the utilities two weeks warning for continuous service.

If you own a car, have a driver's license or state ID card, have a library card or are registered to vote, you need to submit a change of address to the proper agencies. If you are leaving the state, you might want to set aside your birth certificate, original Social Security card and passport since you may need them to establish identification in your new state.

Are you responsible for professionally cleaning the carpets and draperies? If so, you'd better find a company to come in. Take some bids, since this field has a lot of variables and surprise bills. Maybe you'll want a maid service to clean the whole place. This is the time to get estimates and make an appointment. By the way, it's better to do the cleaning after your boxes are out, if possible.

U-Haul or They Haul?

If your move is local, can you make trips in the back of your car or a friend's four-wheeler? Are you considering a truck or trailer rental? How about Slicky Sam's Midnight Moving and Storage? Your decision is based upon the time available to move, the amount you have to move, the difficulty of the move (big items and impediments, such as stairways), the number of available friends and your budget. Anything you do on your own will require extra hands but should cost much less. So, line up your friends first.

Truck Rentals

If you have the luxury of many days and a big car or small truck, you can make a dozen trips. Strap that ol' couch to the roof and drive on! More viable is a rental. Trucks rent by the hour, partial day, overnight, full day, weekend, week and even month! Expect rates to start at about $40 per period or day and to go higher according to size. Extras or freebies include furniture pads, two-wheel hand trucks, dollies and ramps. Some trucks have lift gates, which can be nice. Check for the right deal for you. There usually are additional charges for mileage and gas. Most rental agencies require a credit card or cash deposit in addition to the driver's licenses of each driver. Insurance is usually extra. Check with your insurance agent before buying unnecessary (and expensive) rental protection.

The truck you rent should fit your needs. If you have an eight-foot-long couch, make sure the truck box is at least nine feet long. If you have to drive under low bridges, through garage doors or must worry about low-strung utility cables, make sure the truck is not too tall or too wide. Measure before you rent.

The capacity of the truck is rated in net weight (maximum cargo weight) and in cubic feet (what the box will hold). To estimate your cargo weight, multiply the number of boxes you have by 35 pounds (for margin of error). For volume, estimate 4 cubic feet (this is a generous formula factor only) times the number of boxes. Measure your furniture and estimate the weight of each piece. (Figure 50 pounds for each person it takes to carry one piece.)

Here's an example of how to figure what you need. You have 40 boxes. Forty boxes times 35 pounds per box equals 1,400 pounds. You also have one bed, two dressers, one couch, three stuffed chairs, a kitchen table with four chairs, two bookcases, two rugs and some other small furniture. I figure it will take 18 person-trips to load the furniture, which equals approximately 900 pounds. (One person-trip equals one person making one completed circuit, either loading from the apartment to the truck and back or unloading from the truck to the apartment and back.) So you've got a total of 2,300 pounds. For the volume calculation, take 40 boxes times 4 cubic feet, which equals 160 cubic feet. Measure the furniture, which comes out to 250 cubic feet (hypothetical). Now add in some space for the plants and fragile things (30 cubic feet), and you know you need a truck with a 2,300-pound cargo weight capacity and a box that holds at least 440 cubic feet if you want to make the move in one trip. Remember to include the length of your longest piece of furniture when ordering the truck. Don't worry about carpets, since they can usually be folded.

The capacities for standard rental trucks are as follows: 10-foot box—1,690 pounds, 368 cubic feet; 14-foot box—3,100 pounds, 669 cubic feet; 17-foot box—3,500 pounds, 849 cubic feet; 24-foot box—7,000 pounds, 1,167 cubic feet. To utilize the full cubic foot capacity, you'd have to squeeze all the air out of the truck—no spaces between anything, top to bottom. You should anticipate a 10 to 20 percent space waste.

Consider whether it would be cheaper and more convenient to make one trip with a larger truck or several trips with a smaller one. Also consider what help you will need to carry everything. If you've got help from friends just for the morning, can you get everything out and in during the time allotted?

If you'd like to hire help, day labor can be found at your local Salvation Army shelter, some mission shelters and from day labor agencies. In some towns you can drive to a specific street corner or shopping-center parking lot and find free-lance help. Wages run from $6 to $10 per hour, cash, plus lunch and sometimes local bus fare home. Day-labor agencies are more expensive, but their people are screened. Don't expect experience, enthusiasm or endurance. You'll need to supervise them. (See more information on loading later in this chapter.)

Trailer Rentals

Trailers are cheaper, especially on a drive-away basis, but they have a much smaller capacity. You might have to pay extra for a hitch and a lighting hookup. Trailers are hard on small car transmissions, especially stick shifts. They tend to be inherently unstable and need to be loaded very carefully, keeping the weight on the bottom and equally distributed between the hitch and the axle. Trailers are also hard to maneuver into loading zones. Highway driving can be hairy, especially in windy or slippery conditions. Then there is the issue of hills, not to mention mountains.

Moving Companies

If you don't have the friends to help you or if you simply have too much to move, your alternative is a moving company. I suggest you get a word-of-mouth reference before hiring one. Locally, almost anybody can hold themselves out as a mover; all they need is a truck and some muscle. Most local movers are totally unregulated, and you may get exactly what you pay for. Each state, usually through its public utilities commission (PUCO), regulates household-goods movers if they transport goods over county lines, so there is an expectation of higher quality. Interstate movers are regulated by the federal Interstate Commerce Commission. "Regulate" is too generous a word because the trucking companies, as a rule, make up many of their own charges and regulations (tariffs), which the various commissions approve and supervise. This is definitely not an area of front-line consumer protection.

A local mover will charge you a flat hourly rate, sometimes augmented by a mileage charge. You'll find that hourly rates range between $65 and $100 per hour for three men and a medium-sized truck. If your four-room apartment is packed and ready, three men (two carrying and one packing) should be able to load completely in less than an hour and a half and unload in 45 minutes. The rest of the time is traffic and delays for stairway and elevator limitations. Add extra time for heavy appliances. A local mover may have no contents insurance or may offer a low payout rate, such as 30¢ per pound per item. So a smashed TV might have a value of $4; a computer, $6; and a 35 millimeter camera, 60¢. Check with your insurance broker or pay for extra insurance (if the trucker offers it).

Rates for intrastate and interstate movers are more complex. They charge on the basis of weight, volume, distance and difficulty factors. Interstate base insurance is 60¢ per pound per item under the "released value" plan! That brings the value of that 20-pound computer up to $12! The standard insurance rate is $1.25 per pound times the total shipment weight, which equals total liability. This means that you could collect up to $2,500 on a 2,000-pound shipment, whether it covered damage for one item (that computer) or the whole shipment (fire, theft or accident). You are charged $5 per $1,000 of liability. You can also declare a value and pay extra. Talk to your own insurance agent.

Regardless of the class of movers, you should deal with them in the same way. Call well in advance for a quote. An estimator will usually come to your apartment to see the job. There are several types of quotes: nonbinding, binding and not-to-exceed quotes. Get the quote in writing. An estimate is clearly just a guess. A nonbinding quote may not be accurate. It means that you can be charged substantially more than the guess. It's legal and you will owe it. On interstate moves, you can't be required to pay more than 110 percent of the nonbinding estimate, *upon delivery*, but will be required to pay the balance within 30 days of the follow-up invoice. A binding quote means that's what the bill will be *except* for special conditions upon arrival (e.g., elevator and stair delays and distance of the truck from the door). You have to pay everything, except the extras upon delivery. A not-to-exceed quote is a firm bid with a cap, no matter what. This is also due in full at delivery. You might have to pay extra for these price guarantees. About the only guarantee from a local carrier is the hourly and mileage rates. Be clear about the insurance issues when you receive the bid, and it is very important that you specify in writing the pickup and delivery dates for your move.

The interstate bid you receive is based upon an approved tariff. That tariff is generally a fat book of numbers, rules and regulations. Any household-goods motor carrier *must* make the tariff book available to you. When you call for a bid, ask the estimator to bring the tariffs to you for examination. In the book you'll see exactly what the rate is for your move and what the extra charges can be. The most common tariff rates are contained in a book called *Household Goods Carriage Bureau Tariff 400H*, published by Joseph M. Harrison, Alexandria, Virginia. Not all carriers use these rates, but all out-of-town carriers must have a rate book to let you study.

Most movers will ask for a nominal deposit upon your acceptance of the bid, which is called an *order for service*. This is not a contract, and you are not obligated to pay the full amount of the estimate. Typically, if you cancel far enough in advance, your deposit should be refunded since no work was performed. When you accept the bid, you can also order boxes to rent or purchase. (See the next section, "Boxes.") If you have no time, or no spirit, most professional moving companies offer a packing service. Ask about the hourly rates and get an estimate as to what it would cost you for this extra. (See "Packing.")

Boxes

You'll need about ten boxes per room. We all know how to scrounge for boxes. The grocery store might have some, but these boxes are mostly cut open, they have no tops and the stores tend to crush them for recycling. My favorite freebie boxes come from liquor stores and bookstores. The partitioned liquor boxes are perfect for glasses, cups and other tall, thin fragiles. Both book boxes and liquor boxes are strong and are the right size for most goods. Small boxes are better than large boxes because you can overfill a big box, making it too heavy to easily move around and carry up and down stairs.

You can also pay for boxes. If you move with a moving company, they will rent or sell boxes. Local truck rental outlets also sell boxes, as do storage-space places and specialty shops catering to people who move. I usually buy what I need from a wholesale or discount office-supply company. I save between 50 percent and 75 percent of the retail price and get the exact sizes I want.

Supplies

You'll need sealing tape. If you buy boxes wholesale, also buy PVC tape and a dispenser. (Estimate 6 to 10 boxes per 60-yard roll.) Plastic bags to line boxes are recommended for boxes that will ship cross-country or be put in storage. Two-by-six-inch self-stick labels are handy to identify ownership/address if shipping cross-country and also to number and indicate the contents of each box (local or cross-country). Pick up a few medium-tip permanent markers and several large-tip markers for label and box marking. Determine if you need to buy plastic peanuts (ecologically correct styrofoam pellets, of course), packing tissue, excelsior and other cushioning materials. Newspaper is good for cushioning but is not good for china or anything else that can be damaged by the transfer of ink.

Box Sizes

Forty percent of your boxes should be in the area of 12″ × 12″ × 12″. These boxes will hold between 20 and 30 pounds of goods, are small enough for one person to easily carry and will stack nicely. Books tend to be the densest and thus belong in these small boxes. The best practice is to put the heaviest items in the smallest boxes you can. The more you can use these small boxes, the better. Another 40 percent of your boxes should be in the 18½″ × 12½″ × 14″ range. These will hold records, your VCR, sound equipment and most everything else. You can use a few 20″ × 20″ × 20″ large cube boxes for pillows and clothes-closet items, including winter coats and other oversize items. Pack your fragiles in these cubes, cushioned by sweaters, towels and blankets. The rest of the boxes will be odd sizes. Moving companies rent wardrobe boxes that have closet bars and protect the clothes you normally hang up.

Coordinating the Move

Keeping track of special details can make all the difference between an easy and a hard move. Keep in contact with the new agent regarding the availability of your new place. You'll be checking to be sure the promised work is being done. If necessary, make arrangements to see the new place five to seven days prior to moving. If you'll have to make alternate plans (motel, storage, another unit), you'll need the warning.

See, if you can get in direct contact with the old tenant. It might be nice to get the lowdown on the management company. If you have to choreograph the move (they out by noon, you in after that), it is helpful and reassuring to work out details between you.

It is also wise to find out who is moving into your old place. Choreography is one reason, but also it's important to establish a relationship so that if the landlord holds back security deposit money, you can confirm (perhaps visit and take pictures) that work was not done or that damage did not exist. (See "Inspections.")

Some buildings (complexes) have special moving rules. You might have to book a freight elevator for a specific time or make arrangements to use the loading dock. I've previously mentioned special charges or deposits for these things. Check on them now. In some towns—for example, New York and Chicago—there are parking restrictions at certain times of the day. Will your truck be able to park near your building when you schedule your arrival? You can keep track of the entire moving process by using the "Moving Planner" at the back of this chapter.

Packing

It's pizza-party packing time. Whoopee! If you can get several friends to help, things *seem* to go much faster. Four people packing can finish a four-room apartment in less than four hours, not counting pizza and beer time. At any rate, here is the routine.

Hold out the things you will need while the move is underway. Pack a suitcase for your necessaries, even if you are only going across town, since unpacking will take several days. Keep your housecleaning and repair tools available. Set aside all the fragiles and valuables to be dealt with separately.

Clear a space in a large room for building up boxes you have purchased. For the prebuilt boxes, reinforce the bottom seams. When all the boxes are "built," this space can become the staging area. Stack boxes against a wall, making sure you don't block any door or passageways.

For the rest, don't make any box heavier than 30 pounds. Pack each box as full as possible, since when they get stacked in a truck, the tops will collapse if you don't. Seal the tops with tape. Packed full and sealed, the stacked weight gets distributed along the sides and protects the contents from scrunching.

Make a general contents list for each box. Number and label the box as to the contents. Indicate on the box top, and on at least two sides, which room the box is to go into in the new apartment. List the box number, contents and destination on the inventory list. Be sure to list all furniture, plants, carpets and *everything else* that gets loaded.

Fragile items, valuables and plants need special attention. Many fragile items can successfully be packed. Cushion them well and mark them "fragile." Mirrors, glass tops and pictures are safely packed by slipping them into flattened boxes. For added security, you can strap flattened boxes on either side of the packed item. Write "glass" on both sides of the item.

Plants transport well in warm weather but not in very hot or cold weather. Before moving them, water them properly and put plastic sheeting over them (dry cleaner's coverings or thin paint tarps). When moving them, keep the plants out of drafts and strong winds. Don't let plants freeze or bake in the back of the truck. Out-of-town moves with plants? Maybe.

Valuables should be packed appropriately and carried with you. If it is replaceable (and insured), ship it. If it is irreplaceable, it's a valuable. Do not ship valuables with your mover. If you cannot carry valuables personally, contact a bonded courier to make the transfer. Valuables include your important papers, photographs and other memorabilia, not just jewelry and coin collections.

Disassemblies

On moving day you'll want to disassemble some of your furniture if you are doing the moving yourself. The legs on many pieces of furniture simply unscrew. Other pieces require the removal of a bolt or screw. Once the legs are off, furniture can store flat and will more easily make the hallway angles, thus reducing the chances of leg breakage. Tape or tie the legs together, put the hardware and a tag identifying where the legs and hardware belong in a plastic bag and tape that to the legs. Keep all these parts in one place, or tape them to the undersides of the furniture from which they came. Put cushions and pillows in large plastic bags, and cover upholstered surfaces with plastic tarps taped in place.

Tape the leaves of tables to the main table. Bed frames come apart easily; head boards unscrew or lift off. Chests of drawers can travel with contents inside as long as the piece can be lifted and carried. If drawers are left in, tape them closed so that they won't open during carrying or transport.

Water beds can be a problem. You should start the draining process in advance of your move. While it might be possible to attach a hose and let gravity pull the water out, you probably will have to rent a small water pump designed to do the job. Discharge the water into a bathtub or floor drain, not a toilet. Measure the distance from the bed to the drain, and make sure you have a hose that will reach! Also make sure you have the proper fittings to connect the water bed to the hose to the pump.

Last-Minute Details

If you used hooks and nails in the walls, patch the holes with latex spackle. Use two putty knives—one to apply and smooth and the other to clean off the first with each pass. Ask someone in a hardware store for the details. Since the patch will shrink as it dries, you'll need to apply it twice, at least four hours apart. Do you need to sand the patch smooth? If so, use a fine-grade sandpaper. Painting is usually a normal wear-and-tear issue. Unless your lease forces you to paint, leave the patches bare, since it will be easier for the painter to prime the patches with the new color.

Clean that stove. So many landlords use a dirty oven as the reason to hold back lots of money from the security deposit. Wash off the smudges from the walls, and scrub the tub and toilet. For dirty toilets, let a quart of bleach sit in the bowl for 20 minutes: it's a miracle! Does your lease require you to wash windows or shades? Now is the time.

Go through the refrigerator. If your move is local, you can pack the contents in coolers or doubled-up boxes filled with ice. This will be the last thing you pack—the last boxes on the truck and the first off. If your move is distant, you are best advised to give away or throw out everything. In all cases, the refrigerator should be empty, washed clean and left running. If you turn off the unit, prop the door open.

Your very last task should be to sweep the apartment clean.

Loading the Truck Yourself

The trick to loading a truck is to load all the boxes first. Have one person stay in the truck and stack them high at the front of the box. Stabilize the stacks. Two porters and one stacker can load 30 boxes in an hour. When you see boxes stacked five and six high, you'll see why they had to be packed full. Load the furniture, carpets and fragiles last. There are some exceptions, however. First, some rental trucks come with a hangover in the very front—you can put your fragiles there. Second, if you have long or square furniture pieces, they will fit in the front corners and allow unlimited stacking. For instance, if a couch will stand on end, stack boxes where the cushions go. Use blankets to cover delicate furniture surfaces if scuff pads don't come with the truck. The bed sets should be the last furniture on because they should be the first furniture off. Carpets can either be rolled and fit in the rear corners, can go under furniture or can be folded and slid on top of the boxes. The carpets come out first.

Load fragiles last (if the truck doesn't have a hangover) or make a special trip. Top-load only the boxes (no stacking). Ship mirrors, glass tops and pictures standing on an edge, not flat. Place plants at the very back of the truck, at the gate.

When the Mover Loads

I always keep plenty of cold water and pop around for movers. This is heavy work, and the more you can accommodate them in these ways, the better. On a day-long move, I'll be sure to have carryout lunch for them, since they probably won't be able to eat otherwise. Do not serve beer or wine. You don't want them to make mistakes that could damage your goods or cause somebody to be hurt.

While you are not an expert, keep an eye on how the move is handled. Are the loaders moving too fast or slow? Feel free to comment if you think your furniture or budget is endangered. Deal with the crew chief and let the information come from that person instead of you.

Check off each box as it goes out of the apartment (or is loaded into the truck). Point out to the crew chief what is fragile, and make sure those items are specially handled. On local moves, watch that things are stacked properly. Make sure the driver knows where to go and when the truck is expected. If possible, lead or follow the truck.

Look over all documents given to you before you sign them. On long-distance moves, you will have inventory sheets of all pieces, a bill of lading (which is the actual contract between you and the moving company) and there may be weight-station tickets and other related documents. Read the bill of lading to be sure the rate is right, the insurance agreement is what you specified, the delivery date is what you want and your new address is correct. You may also want the driver to have your in-transit phone numbers. By the way, you have the right to be present for the truck weigh-ins before and after loading. Sometimes this is done on the other end before and after unloading.

Inspections

You need to conduct a final inspection with the agent. Use the inspection sheet you used when you moved in (if such exists). Compare conditions and make sure you agree on damages. Take pictures of anything that might be questionable. Have a friend go through as a witness—just in case. If there is no move-in sheet, still go through the unit with an inspection form to document the current situation. You'll need this inspection form later to get back your security deposit if claims are disputed. (Use the "Move-in/Move-out Checklist" in Appendix B.)

This same routine is needed at the new place. Go through the apartment as soon as possible with the agent, before the truck arrives if possible. Have the agent sign the inspection sheet. Make any notations on it regarding something that might be a problem later (loose windows that might later fall out, existing scratches, paint problems, dirty oven, stained carpets). If the agent won't make an inspection, you do it anyway, and send him or her a copy. If you think you'll need photos of something, take them now to prove that a condition exists. If your camera provides date stamps, so much the better. Otherwise, save the photo lab receipt as proof of the date.

Unloading

Unloading is a lot faster, unless you are stuck with tricky stairways, odd hall angles or fussy elevators. Put the fragiles in a safe place. Start the refrigerator, wipe it out and put your cold food in it. Meanwhile, carry and lay the carpets first. Then bring in the furniture. The beds come first and should be set up. Then comes the rest. Set the boxes in the proper rooms as they are marked. Watch to make sure the handling is gentle.

It is very important to use your inventory list to check off each piece as it comes into the apartment (or off the truck). Tell the unloading crew if something is missing. Inspect each piece of furniture for damage. You may not be able to make a claim later for scratches, grease marks, tears and cracks since these should be visible at unloading. Even when dealing with a moving company, you can't be expected to note hidden damage inside boxes until unpacking starts.

Discard the packing materials in the method approved by your new landlord.

Paying the Movers and Complaints

If you are using a moving company, you've been told what methods of payment are acceptable. Not every company will take a personal check or a charge card. Most take cash, money orders and certified or cashier's checks. Do not sign the freight bill or pay until after you have thoroughly inspected your furniture for damage and have checked off all the pieces on the inventory list. If you wish, turn on your televisions, computers and other equipment. Write the following on the bill:

> Received in good condition except for the following: missing items—(inventory numbers) not received . . . ; damaged items—(inventory numbers) damaged as follows . . . ; hidden damage not yet determined.

You still can make claims later for hidden damages, including breakage inside boxes.

Protesting your bill and claiming damages takes place after the fact. Make your written claims promptly (within 30 days, if possible, and no later than 120 days) to the moving company offices (not the driver). The Interstate Commerce Commission will give you advice and a booklet (federal publication 1992 322-492 (60317)) but will not help you collect damages. State regulators provide the same level of assistance. The movers are required to tell you who their insurance carrier is, and you may be able to make a claim directly to the carrier. With local firms, you might be completely on your own. In some cases, an attorney will be needed.

Your moving bill, as compared to the estimate, will depend on the type of estimate: nonbinding, binding or not-to-exceed. If you have a nonbinding estimate for an interstate shipment, you'll only be required to pay 110 percent of the estimate, on the spot, but must pay the rest within 30 days. If you have overages on a binding estimate, you have 30 days to pay the balance of the bid but must pay the base bill on delivery. If you didn't get a written estimate, you owe the full amount on delivery. Truckers have the right to haul your stuff off to storage until you pay, and they will charge you for the warehousing.

New Customs and Old Ceremonies

You may have to come up with new deposits if you are changing utility companies. If you've moved out of state, you'll need to retitle your car, get new plates and a new driver's license. Also, find out if you have to license your bicycles or pets. Don't forget to register to vote and obtain a library card. You might need a passport, birth certificate, old license and two pieces of mail addressed to you at your new address for proper identification. Some states will charge you a sales tax differential on recently purchased cars (usually less than six months) and may require pollution control tests and adjustments. Your new city may also require a vehicle window sticker and/or have street parking restrictions. Check it out. And, oh yes, welcome to your new home!

Moving Planner

Premove Planning

Have you

    Notified the post office? ☐

    Sent change of address cards to

        Friends and family? ☐

        Insurance companies? ☐

        Government agencies (including licensing agencies)? ☐

        Banks, charge cards and investments? ☐

        Subscriptions? ☐

    Set aside important papers? ☐

    Called insurance company regarding moving insurance? ☐

    Notified current utilities?

        Telephone ☐

        Gas ☐

        Electricity ☐

        Other ☐

    Made arrangements with new utilities?

        Telephone ☐

        Gas ☐

        Electricity ☐

        Other ☐

    Cleaned out the nooks and crannies?

        Give away? ☐

        Apartment sale? ☐

        Donations? ☐

        Trashing? ☐

        Cleaned the stove? ☐

        Hazardous materials safely disposed? ☐

        Made short-term or long-term storage arrangements? ☐

    Scheduled landlord move-out inspection? When: _____

    Scheduled landlord move-in inspection? When: _____

    Checked buildings and route for traffic/loading problems? ☐

    Booked loading docks and elevators if required? ☐

Prepacking

Have you

Located sources for boxes? _____

Estimated number of supplies required?

    Small boxes: # _____ $ _____

    Medium boxes: # _____ $ _____

    Large boxes: # _____ $ _____

    Wardrobe boxes: # _____ $ _____

    Special boxes: # _____ $ _____

    Rolls of tape (6–8 boxes per roll): # _____ $ _____

    Cushioning materials: _____ $ _____

    Labels: _____

    Markers: _____

    Inventory sheets: _____

Estimated cubic foot requirements? _____

Estimated weight requirements? _____

Decided on number of trips with rental? 1 2 3 4 5

Preloading

Have you

Taken bids on rental trucks, including extras?

What size truck? _____

    Company _____ $ _____ /hour/day/weekend

    Address _____   Phone number _____

    Company _____ $ _____ /hour/day/weekend

    Address _____   Phone number _____

    Company _____ $ _____ /hour/day/weekend

    Address _____   Phone number _____

Taken bids on moving companies? Extras for boxes, packing, insurance, guaranteed rates? Firm pickup and delivery dates?

    Company _____ $ _____

    Address _____   Phone number _____

    Company _____ $ _____

    Address _____   Phone number _____

    Company _____ $ _____

    Address _____   Phone number _____

Are bids firm estimates? ☐ Yes ☐ No

Confirmed reservation? Signed estimate? ☐

Arranged for friends to help pack and/or load? ☐

    Name and number: _____

    Name and number: _____

    Name and number: _____

    Name and number: _____

Scheduled packing party? When? _____

Cleaned carpets if required? ☐

Packing

Have you

Set aside your valuables?

Set aside your fragiles?

Packed an overnight bag?

Explained to your packers how to pack, tape, label and inventory?

Marked all boxes clearly by *room*? ☐

Assembled and stacked boxes to allow for easy removal? ☐

Loading

Have you

Cash, cashier's check, credit card or money order to pay for moving?

Checked that new place is ready for you? ☐

Boarded your pets? ☐

Made a loading plan—first on/last off? ☐

Provided water and soft drinks for crew? ☐

Set aside proper tools to disassemble furniture? ☐

Checked your box and furniture inventory as loaded? ☐

Made arrangements to feed crew if necessary? ☐

Signed moving company bill of lading? ☐

Given driver new address, confirmed route, confirmed arrival time?

Packed or trashed all perishable foodstuffs? ☐

Cleaned the refrigerator and left it on low, or off and propped open?

Done a final sweeping and dusting?

Left unit closed up and locked?

Taken final meter readings to compare against final bills?

    Gas meter: _____

    Electric: _____

    Water: _____

Conducted move-out inspection with landlord? ☐

Turned in keys and gotten receipt for keys? ☐

Told landlord where to forward your security deposit? ☐

Unloading

Have you

    Laid rugs down first? ☐

    Assembled beds before bringing in boxes? ☐

    Made sure boxes go to rooms as marked? ☐

    Confirmed that all items on inventory list have been received? ☐

    Visually inspected box exteriors, furniture and appliances for obvious
        damage? ☐

    Filled rental-truck gas tank before returning? ☐

    Made your moving company release as per this chapter?

Postmove

Have you

    Filled out move-in inspection sheet? ☐

    Made spare copies of new keys?

    Registered to vote, new library card, new driver's license, retitled and
        transferred cars? ☐

    Contacted school system? ☐

    Made formal written damage claims with movers within 30 days? ☐

Are you having fun yet? ☐ Yes ☐ No

7

Tenants' Rights and Assorted Landlord-Tenant Law—A National Overview

Tenants' Rights

- Protection under the Law
- Freedom from Lockout
- Safe from Rip-offs
- Return of Your Security Deposit
- Constructive Eviction
- Lawful Access
- Safe from Retaliation and Harassment
- Peaceful Use and Enjoyment
- Landlord's Duty To Mitigate

My Tenants' Bill of Rights appears at the beginning of this book. Those 20 articles summarize what you should expect in any landlord-tenant relationship. I have previously devoted several chapters to specific aspects of tenants' rights and have sprinkled other examples in my commentaries on various subjects. This chapter will focus on landlord-tenant law operations and basic rights describing how to obtain them.

Alaska	Montana
Arizona	Nebraska
Connecticut	New Mexico
Florida	Oklahoma
Hawaii	Oregon
Iowa	Rhode Island
Kansas	South Carolina
Kentucky	Tennessee
Michigan	Virginia
Mississippi	Washington

**States that have enacted a version of the
Uniform Residential Landlord and Tenant Act.**

There is no national law guaranteeing the rights of tenants. There is, however, the Uniform Residential Landlord and Tenant Act, a model law drafted by the National Conference of Commissioners on Uniform State Laws. (The act is reprinted in Appendix K.) At least 20 states have adopted a version of the act, as well as several cities, including Chicago. In addition, California, Illinois, Louisiana, Massachusetts, Michigan, New Jersey, New York, Ohio, Texas and Wisconsin have statutes of their own. Many municipalities, particularly in California and New Jersey, have local ordinances.

What Arrangements Are Covered?

Most rental situations are included. Some jurisdictions exclude owner-occupied buildings below a certain size or those buildings or complexes containing less than a certain number of units, usually two to six. Single-family dwellings are generally included, but the rules are relaxed about arrangements that can be made about certain maintenance issues. Condos, co-ops and town houses are covered as if they were apartments. Residential hotels and single-room occupancies are typically covered for tenants who stay longer than a certain period—at least a week—and always if they reside more than a month. Furnished apartments are generally treated the same as unfurnished apartments. "Furnished" generally means there is a bed, couch, chair, table—not just a stove and refrigerator. Boarders (roomers) have certain rights but usually not full rights.

What Arrangements Are Not Covered?

As a general rule, "institutional" settings are excluded. Thus, residents of dorms, convents, live-in schools, hospitals, asylums, group homes, orphanages, jails, prisons and halfway houses must rely on other laws. Transient guests are also not covered. That includes residential apartment hotels for short stays, as well as hotels and motels, which are usually covered by innkeeper laws. Owner-occupied buildings usually exclude tenants from their rights, typically where there are only a few total units involved (e.g., two to six). Landlords' employees are excluded, as are most cases where the tenant is in the active process of buying the unit (not an option to buy but a contract for sale).

Who's a What?

A *landlord* is a person or business that rents out a unit and/or collects the rents, benefits directly from the rents, has the right to evict a tenant or owns a unit. For practical purposes (i.e., whom do you complain to/whom do you sue/who can sue you?), the name on the lease as lessor and/or the person who collects the rents is the person or company responsible. A sublessor (one who leases and then releases to another person) is also a landlord!

The *tenant* is the person who takes possession of the unit and/or pays the rent, lives in the unit and signs the lease as lessee. Occupants are generally thought of as tenants. As a general rule, those living in the unit, signing the lease or openly paying the rent will be held responsible for rent and damages. Tenants also have the right to remedies. (They can demand their due and sue.) Also, please see the discussion about roommates in chapter 4.

What's a Rental Unit?

Your rights include everything inside the walls of your space. As a rule, the rights extend to the premises as a whole, meaning the common areas, the structure, essential services and the grounds. A rotting porch or disintegrating front step is usually part of what you rent and what you can complain about. In some places, your rights extend to snow shoveling (safety matters). If you rent a parking space, this probably is *not* covered because you don't live in it. (Check with an attorney if you are having a parking-related problem.)

What's a Lease?

A lease is any deal, oral or written, between the tenant and the landlord that allows the tenant to exclusively "possess" the landlord's property (such as a dwelling unit) for a period of time. Tenants' rights require that the deal be fair, balanced, reasonable and that the terms and conditions be clear and understandable. The most usual components of a lease are the amount of rent to be paid to the landlord for the premises, when the money is due, how long the tenant can stay and what will break the agreement. Most state laws allow a lease to be valid if at least one party signed and there was an exchange of rent money, even if a copy is not given (to the tenant). (See "The Lease" in chapter 4 for a fuller discussion.)

Rights under oral leases depend mostly on laws and court rulings, since it is hard to prove unwritten promises. In many states, however, if your written lease ends and neither you nor the landlord have given notice of termination, that lease *may* be considered to have been renewed for a similar period of time under the same terms and conditions—except rent, if the landlord asked for more at the start of the renewal period. In some states, the landlord has the option to consider the tenant a holdover and charge a daily pro-rata rent with a 100 or 200 percent penalty clause, convert the arrangement to a month-to-month rental or renew the lease—sometimes at double the previous rent! This notice must usually be given during the first month of renewal. Each state is different. You are advised to give written notice of termination if you intend not to renew a written lease. One twist is that when you stay on, hear nothing and keep paying your rent, *you* can decide whether you are month-to-month or yearly renter. Use it to your own advantage to move out on proper notice as you like or to stop the landlord from raising your rent monthly because you believed you had renewed for the year.

The last thing about a lease is what you've agreed to pay. Did you rent for a year and agree to pay $6,000, due periodically (each month) in equal payments of $500 a month? Or did you rent the place for a year and agree to pay $500 a month? This could make a big difference if you get evicted or terminate your lease. Some states allow the landlord to accelerate all the rents due on the former type of lease. By the way, it may be that enforcing acceleration is really the landlord's attempt to impose a penalty, which is an unacceptable action. (See "Duty To Mitigate," later in this chapter.)

Explicit and Implied Changes

Of some concern is that most landlord-tenant laws allow for rules to be made or changed during the course of the lease. The rules need to be in writing for written leases. They must not change things in a way that renders the use of the unit less desirable than before (i.e., they must not change the fundamental bargain), they must not be retaliatory and they must not be an attempt for the landlord to evade his or her legal obligations. Rules usually are made so that they can be enforced against a tenant so that a lease can be broken for "good cause." Something that is unreasonable (prohibiting nonrelated adults from spending the night) probably cannot be enforced.

What happens when the rules—any rule—change? If they change unfairly, you must register a written protest objecting to the change. Even though the change was explicitly in writing, by making no objection and continuing to pay the rent you have given implicit acceptance without signing anything.

When can this work for you? Let's assume you have a written lease with rent due on the first day of the month. For whatever reason, after the third month you start paying the landlord on the tenth. The landlord takes the money and doesn't issue you a demand for rent (notice before eviction) or even a letter. The next month you do this again. The next month you get a notice (depending on your state, it could be a three- or five-day notice) to pay all rents or a notice to terminate (breaking the lease because of nonpayment of rent). You still don't pay until the tenth. By this time the matter is in eviction court. The landlord shows the lease, which says rents are due the first day of the month, but you show a pattern of payments on another day. Since the landlord has implicitly agreed to a change of terms (a new payday) by accepting money without protest, the lease is changed and you, therefore, are not in default, which is your defense. Tenants who receive Social Security, public assistance or other checks on an "odd" day can benefit from this sort of implicit change to the lease.

What's the Difference Between Rents, Fees and Deposits?

Rent, usually in the form of money, is given to the landlord when due. Rent can also be in kind, where you perform services in return for your unit. Rent is usually due at the beginning of the regular rental period. It is supposed to represent the market value of your unit when rented. Under tenants' rights laws, if the value of your unit is diminished, you can diminish the rents. Prepaid rent is for rent in the future, as is last-month's rent. When you pay rent, it becomes the property of the landlord, except when tenants' rights laws allow you to reclaim it for cause. But prepaid rent (for instance, that last month's rent payment) is there to be used for that purpose. Suppose you have a month-to-month lease where you had to put up, amongst other monies, the last month's rent. Suppose that was $500. Suppose that over time, your rent increases to $650. Now suppose the lease is terminated. How much is your last month's rent? It is $500, regardless of what the monthly rent has been raised to. Do you need to "bring up the amount" each time your lease increases? No, unless that was specifically part of the original deal (in writing, I would argue).

What constitutes rent is factored differently in different states in several ways. Where it is possible to accelerate the rents, it means that the total balance is the rent. (In some states, therefore, if you repair and deduct and are allowed to use all the money on rents owing, you could theoretically use *all* remaining rent [many months' worth]). In other states, rent is what is on the monthly payment on the face of the lease. It may *not* include anything else, especially not late fees (although the fees are legal, just not rent). Other states *include* late fees as part of the rent! Check with your local tenants' organization or an attorney.

The issue of what is and isn't rent becomes important if you get behind. As a rule, first money paid goes to first money owed. If late fees get incorporated into rent, you could make all your payments and ultimately still be evicted for late or nonpayment. For instance, your rent is $500, and there is a 5 percent late fee imposed after the third day. You pay the $500 but not the $25. The next month you pay on time. And the next month you pay on time. In month four, you receive an eviction warning or notice because you owe $75 for the former three months. The late fee was compounded because each new month money was applied to what you previously owed, making your present payment short. Legal and nifty, eh?

Deposits are your money. They are *refundable* under normal circumstances. A security deposit is your money, a key deposit is your money, even an application deposit (not fee) is your money (but it's like pulling teeth to recover this money). As a rule, deposits are held to ensure that you do something—e.g., pay the rent on time or not damage the property. If you do your part, that money is due you when you move out.

Deposits are not rent, and most judges will not let you use your security deposit as rent. This gets to be quite curious when one of the reasons for holding the deposit is to ensure that the rent is paid. I don't really advise you to use your security deposit as your last month's rent, although I understand why you might. If your landlord so desires, you could be sued for eviction, even though the money is in the landlord's pocket. Highly curious. (See chapter 9 for methods of recovering your money, and read on regarding your rights.)

Each state, and many localities, have procedures for returning your security deposit. You must generally give your landlord a forwarding address and also a request for refund. Some states won't let you sue if you don't make a written demand first. The return waiting period varies from immediate to 60 days after move-out (or after demand). Thirty days is common. There are also muddy issues such as back rents due, which may disqualify you from claiming damages or even interest.

Almost every jurisdiction requires the landlord to provide a detailed list of what work was done and receipts for the work if money is held back. Chicago, for example, requires a written list of damages and an estimate within 30 days of moving, with all work complete and a refund of the balance within the following 30 days. Some states do not require that written particulars be given to the tenant but do require them if the landlord is sued.

For failure to return the deposit or give the proper notices, the landlord is liable for damages ranging from paying back what was owed to paying back the full deposit, regardless of what damages the tenant caused. Almost all jurisdictions also have penalties that the landlord must pay the tenant. These range from a flat $100 award to triple the amount of the deposit, or actual damages, whichever is greater. Typically, if a tenant sues and wins a security deposit case, court costs and reasonable attorney's fees are also awarded by statute. All this is because of endemic abuse of security deposits by landlords in the past.

Where laws require it, interest must be paid on the security deposit. Some places give the tenant the interest, since it is the tenant's money. Others award it to the landlord! Interest is either a fixed amount, say 5 percent, or the amount paid for a regular savings account. The interest payment to the tenant is usually made once a year on the anniversary of the lease or when the tenant moves out, if less than a year. Penalties for nonpayment range from what is due plus a small award to an amount double the security deposit.

Fees are supposed to be for some specific service—for instance, a credit check. You may have to pay a loading dock or freight elevator fee when you move or get furniture. If you live in New York and can find a rent-controlled apartment or a building going co-op, you may pay thousands of dollars under the table as a key or lease fee. I don't know whether these are recoverable in a court of law, do you? Pool fees, boat-dock fees, greens fees and weight-room privileges are for things you use and pay for. They ought not to be part of your rent. (See previous discussion about rent.)

Fees that are required for other things may not be fees but deposits, and thus they are covered by security deposit laws. Examples of such fees are carpet, cleanup or move-out fees (collected in advance) to cover scrubbing or redecorating your unit. If you leave the unit clean, why should you have to pay to clean it up? Painting is a wear-and-tear issue. Why are you paying to make the place attractive for someone else? It is assumed that the landlord builds the costs associated with renting into the lease already. Such fees will generally be considered as ways to rename a security or damage deposit to avoid accounting, refunds and interest. You can collect the return of the deposit and argue that the landlord's normal wear and tear are not your responsibility. The bank interest on deposits, required by many states to be paid to tenants, is also due.

Some leases contain a clause that allows the landlord to put a *lien* on your personal property. This is an attempt to find a way to increase the security of the lease. A lien means that if you owe the landlord money, your property can be taken and sold. If you didn't strike this clause from the lease outright, you probably have little to worry about. First, there are limits on the type and amount of property that can be taken. (See "Distrain," further on in this chapter.) Second, the property cannot be taken without due process, meaning you would have to be judged to owe money. Third, some states will not allow this type of lien. Fourth, a hearing on just what could be taken would have to held. Fifth, for most of us, the value of what could be taken would be very small and not worth the expense of the procedure. It may also be that if the landlord has a remedy within the lease—a lien—the use of distrain may be prohibited.

Notices and Waivers

You are entitled to proper notice and due process and maybe the rights to civil action (suing the landlord). Some state laws will not allow a lease to (1) deny your rights granted under the law; (2) not deny your rights to notice about violations or terminations; (3) not deny your rights to be served by the sheriff; and (4) not deny your rights to appear in court, demand a jury or defend yourself. Furthermore, the landlord cannot (evade) require you to waive civil liability. Some state laws allow you to waive these rights as part of a written lease. (See "Adhesions.")

As a general rule, the landlord is not supposed to put anything in the lease that relieves the landlord of the duty to maintain or lets the landlord skirt the laws in some other way. For instance, calling a security deposit a "refundable service fee" will not fly when the amount of the deposit is regulated, statutory interest is due on the deposit or there is a statutory method of controlling it.

Notices are almost always supposed to be in writing. Sometimes they can be handed to the other party or posted or tacked to the door. When mailed, some are valid as of the posting date; others are not valid until received. Certified mail with a receipt is accepted as proof of mailing and proof of receipt.

The type of notices you are required to receive vary. In most states, you must be given a 30-day termination notice to end a month-to-month lease. In some states, it is 20 days; in others, it is 10 days. A few localities may require as long as 60 days. Rent-due notices are not required in some states; in others, you have 3 days to pay; and in others, you have 5 days. The notice times vary for breaking the rules: in some states you have 10 to 14 days to "cure" a breach of the lease; in others, you have 3 days to move out!

The types of notices you are required to give also vary. In some cases, they parallel those for a landlord: notice to terminate a month-to-month lease or cure a defect (notice before repair and deduct or rent abatement). But other times, they are special or even have a variable time limit.

Adhesions

Now comes the part of a lease that makes it one-sided (unbalanced), burdensome (unreasonable), gobbledygook (unclear) or just not fair. These are terms of *adhesion*—meaning you are forced to take a bad deal in order to be able to rent. Most tenants' rights laws forbid either inclusion, enforcement or attempted enforcement of the following:

- *Confession of judgment.* This is where you confess (do not contest) if the landlord sues you under the lease. Many times this goes along with waiving rights to notice of nonpayment, notice of termination for nonpayment, demand for possession or notice to vacate and notice of eviction.
- *Landlord's attorney's fees.* This is where you agree to pay your landlord's attorney's fees for any actions the landlord takes against you.
- *Other adhesions.* These may have to do with joining tenants' unions or making complaints, not having overnight company and attempts to have the landlord make you do his or her jobs on maintenance required by building codes or habitability laws.

Warranty of Habitability

Chapter 8 spends considerable time on the implied warranty of habitability. This warranty is at the heart of tenants' rights because it defines what you can expect. Chapter 8 describes what have become common remedies under these rights. These include repair and deduct, rent abatement, rent withholding and lease termination. A tenant has the right to a habitable place, even if he or she stops paying or cannot pay rent! It is the landlord's duty to maintain until the court orders the tenant evicted and the sheriff comes out to do it! That is the law in most places.

Before tenants' rights laws, the only way out was to claim *constructive eviction* under the common law. The principles here are as follows:

- The landlord acts or fails to act in a way that substantially interferes with the use of the apartment.
- The landlord's act results in "permanent" deprivation of the use of the unit.
- The landlord knows, or should know, that by acting this way, the tenant is deprived of the use of the apartment.
- As soon as it is clear that nothing is being fixed, the tenant leaves within a reasonable time.

This is the rationalization for tenant remedies under many modern state laws on landlord-tenant and tenants' rights.

The hierarchy of complaining, repairing and deducting, and rent reducing and rent withholding are related to not having to choose between continued miserable conditions or having to relocate to a similar situation. Under modern laws now, you can terminate your lease for serious breaches of the warranty of habitability or to your lease.

Deprivation of basic or essential services can trigger constructive eviction— e.g., fire, no water, no heat, no electricity, broken toilet. But there are other conditions that interfere with a tenant's use and enjoyment and for which the landlord has responsibility.

As an example, the roof leaks, which soon causes a ceiling to cave in or a room to become unusable. The landlord is told about the leak, but nothing happens. It rains again and you get more of the same. It should be clear to the landlord that you can't live in a place with that type of condition, yet the landlord refuses to remedy it. You "construe" that the landlord's intent is to make you leave (evict you). You give notice, claiming constructive eviction, and leave since nothing is being done or is likely to be done soon.

You can argue that bad neighbor problems or gang activity in the building can lead to constructive eviction. Only the landlord has the right to toss out the bad apples. If the landlord won't do it, then the result is that you are deprived of what you are paying for. When you can't sleep or safely walk into the building, your use is substantially interfered and denied. If it looks like a duck and walks like a duck, it's close enough.

Repair and Deduct

This subject is covered in chapter 8. It should be noted that you need to follow local procedures, and, of course, they're all different. The principle of invocation is that what needs to be repaired is the landlord's duty. When the landlord fails to fix something after notice, you can do it . . . provided. Ah, the rub: provided it doesn't cost more than a statutory limit; provided you haven't used this method more times than allowed; provided you waited long enough or gave enough notices; provided you have a court order. Fear not. In most places, it is a piece of cake (no court order required). Please check with your local tenants' group, county or state legal information resource. When you do use repair and deduct, keep copies of the receipts, not only to give the landlord, but you need another set just in case the matter ends up in court. Always take pictures of conditions before and after repairs.

Abatement

Coming close on the heals of constructive eviction is rent abatement, which is thoroughly discussed in chapter 8. Some states, and certainly most courts, will not let you keep all the money you withhold. *Withholding*, as defined here, is not paying any rent. Various state and local jurisdictions have set up mechanisms to receive and hold protested rents until repairs are completed (or to pay these out in progress payments). In other places, you need to set this money aside yourself. (Remember, the poor person's escrow account is a money order.) Other courts simply do not allow withholding. What ultimately happens if withholding gets into court is that the judge decides how much deprivation, suffering and humiliation you went through and reduces the amount due the landlord. Be prepared to defend your actions with photographs and witnesses.

Rent reduction is less threatening and more justifiable, since you acknowledge you owe something on the rent (just not as much as the landlord wants). Chapter 8 will give you a formula for reduction. I do advise that the balance between full and reduced rent be set aside, since you may have to pay some money back if you overestimated the reduced value.

Establishing reduced value will vary with a judge's temperament, but you'll need to show what the going rents are elsewhere and how you arrived at your reduction. Sometimes a rental agent will have to testify.

Unlawful Entry/Access/Denial of Access

By definition, the tenant is in rightful possession as long as the term of the lease is in effect and the rent is paid. The tenant is in "rightful" possession until the tenant abandons the unit or the sheriff arrives with a court order of eviction.

The first issue I confront on access is "Does the landlord have a right to the keys?" My answer is "I dunno!" Sometimes the answer is in the lease, which states that you can't change the locks without written permission or that you must give your landlord a set of keys if you are allowed to change without permission.

Most landlord-tenant laws are silent regarding keys. The laws generally allow that the landlord has a right of access "during reasonable hours" for certain purposes such as making regular maintenance or emergency repairs, inspecting the premises, and showing the unit to prospective new tenants or buyers. So the secret question is "How does the landlord get in?" Tenants' rights laws answer this question by saying that the landlord must give reasonable advance notice (24 to 48 hours) to the tenant for most visits (in writing, in person and/or by phone, depending on the locality), so one assumes that the tenant can give the landlord keys or be present to open the door on an occasion-by-occasion basis. Showing the unit gets stickier, since this covers a blanket period of 60 to 90 days before the lease expires. Worst of all are emergencies, since you can't call two days in advance.

The real issue here is the personal security of yourself, your family and your belongings. In other words, the issues are trusting the landlord (or janitor, etc., and security against harm, theft, interference and harassment. When does rightful access become illegal entry? For the tenant, illegal entry means returning to the unit after the sheriff has evicted you. It also means squatting. For both landlord and tenant, it also means breaking and entering, civil or criminal trespass and maybe burglary. In addition, for the landlord it can mean breach of peace, criminal harassment and assault.

A person's home is his or her castle by dint of the right of possession. You do not have to let anybody into your apartment without an appointment, unless for an emergency or because the person is an officer of the law, court or peace (including building inspectors). The landlord may not enter willie-nillie, or without a good reason, without your permission (which you may have given for certain purposes as part of the lease, by the way), or repeatedly for the purpose of threatening you (about anything) or harassing you.

When these things happen, you have many rights that can protect you and remedies to stop the behavior. Landlord-tenant laws usually limit the reasons for which a landlord can enter. Tenants' rights laws specify when and how. Thus, if the landlord comes into your place without your permission *once* without following a rights ordinance, the landlord might be subject to a civil penalty (money due you) and your court and legal fees. If you send the landlord a notice to stop unannounced entries and the behavior continues, you can break your lease and move.

Since, by the law, the landlord can only enter for a good cause and since repeated entries are disturbing your peaceful use and enjoyment, you can call the police and complain that you are being harassed or your peace is being breached. If the police won't make an arrest, find out where to go to swear out a complaint. If the landlord threatens you in a way that makes you believe your physical safety is at jeopardy, charge him or her with simple assault. If a weapon (gun, knife, hammer, fist) is used, it becomes aggravated assault. If the landlord enters your apartment without your permission, call the police and charge the landlord with trespass. If the landlord comes into your place while you are gone (and you can prove it—not so easy), charge the landlord with criminal trespass, breaking and entering and/or burglary.

You already know under what circumstances you must let your landlord in and when you can legitimately refuse entry. What about when someone denies *you* access to your own unit? This can happen when you are trying to move in and the old tenant is still there or the landlord won't let you in. Under most landlord-tenant laws, rent stops until you can move in. Now it gets tricky. . . . Tenants' rights laws usually give you the right to immediately cancel your lease and collect any prepaid rents and deposits held by the landlord immediately, upon demand. Some laws go further and allow you to sue for damages such as furniture storage, re-moving expenses, temporary housing and the difference in rents between what the broken lease cost and the new lease costs.

What happens if you want to move in anyway? Under some ordinances, you can sue for "injunctive relief" or "specific performance" to order the landlord to deliver up the unit (or for a holdover tenant to get out). This is an eviction order in reverse, as it were. Whatever your costs and damages are, these are collectable from the parties you sue. Some laws go so far as to say that if the conduct is willful, you can collect an amount equal to twice the damages! This is a great time to stay at The Plaza!

Here are some scenarios.

> You arrive with a full moving van. The landlord tells you that you can't move in. You think it is because you have a disabled child who uses a wheelchair. It is willful and it seems provable. Sue under your local landlord-tenant laws and have the child complain under the Fair Housing Amendments Act. (See chapter 5.)

You arrive only to find the old tenants holding over. Call your lawyer and request an emergency injunction for possession (which means "instanter" [this instant, without delay] an eviction order and a writ of restitution [order of possession] that the sheriff needs to put the tenants out). After you move in, you sue the former tenants for your expenses (and *if* the tenants have any money, maybe you get reimbursed).

You arrive with that moving van, but the landlord says, "I've changed my mind" or "The floor varnish is still wet" or "The painter won't be finished until next week." It would seem, in each case, that the landlord was willfully dispossessing you. If you want to stay, you can force the issue or obtain damages after you move elsewhere.

Check your local rules for the nuances. Now when the elevator breaks . . .

The following are considered to be acts of lockout:

- Padlocking the doors
- Plugging the locks
- Removing the locks from the doors
- Removing the doors
- Nailing the doors shut
- Disconnecting the utilities
- Removing any kitchen appliance
- Removing or disabling the toilet
- Removing windows
- Cutting the phone wires or TV cable

Lockout Actions Are Illegal

There is another form of illegal denial of access that is known as *lockout.* This is where the landlord takes actions that make the use of your apartment impossible. There may be more "creative" actions, but it is all the same. It is clearly illegal everywhere in the country to dispossess a person from his or her dwelling place without a court order and (usually) the sheriff. Most tenants' rights laws provide that all renters are covered (except transients). As a rule, the landlord is subject to arrest. A civil suit for injunctive relief for restitution usually must be filed. Later, a suit for damages, up to three times the monthly rent or actual damages, is allowed.

Lease Breaking, Sublets and Assignments

As a rule, the tenant always has a right to break the lease for "good cause." Good cause can be specifically stated in a lease (for instance, you might have a relocation clause, an unemployment clause or a family or personal hardship/illness clause). Sometimes a lease can be terminated as the result of a material breach.

It usually takes a lawyer to interpret this, since most tenants' rights and landlord-tenant laws don't allow tenants to easily walk on the lease. Thus, it becomes a matter for the courts. There are habitability and constructive eviction issues related to building conditions and code standards that allow for lease termination. (See chapter 8 for all the details.) In some places, going into a nursing home or declaring bankruptcy will terminate a lease. Tenants' rights laws are quite specific and helpful in spelling out how to give notice and leave.

So the question is, How do you lawfully squirm out from under a lease when the lease has no escape clause and nothing else is really wrong? How do you solve the "early-out dilemma"? The answer is to find a new tenant. The right for the tenant to relet has been a hard-fought but successful battle. Most tenants' rights laws clearly spell out that you can replace yourself. In most cases, the costs of replacement are born by the new tenant, since laws generally prohibit the landlord from gouging you with termination fees, sublet fees and the like. Your only duty, from a practical point of view, is to pay to advertise for the substitute. When the landlord tells you that you will have to pay to redecorate, don't listen. As long as you can find a new tenant who will take the place as is, what's the landlord's problem?

Some laws require you to give formal notice of your desire or formal submission of the new tenant, and the landlord has 10 days to approve the idea and 30 days to approve the new tenant. Other laws simply say that the landlord cannot unreasonably refuse the replacement. You may find that a landlord won't accept a substitute during the last three or four months of the lease. This, on the face of it, is unreasonable and you should find a suitable replacement anyway.

The new tenant has to pass a credit check to qualify, and that should be a principal test. What else are reasonable qualifications? I suggest the following: find a tenant who in some way is similar to you. By that I mean, if there are two of you now, look for one or two people to replace you. Try to match to life-style and income. If you don't have pets, avoid a substitute with pets. In other words, try to make the new person transparent to you from a use, income and life-style point of view. Then if the landlord refuses (say, on discrimination grounds, as in chapter 5), he or she is unreasonable and perhaps treading on the wild waters of Lake Prejudice.

If your landlord is cooperative, maybe you can obtain credit and application forms. You'll need to qualify the tenant (see chapter 4) at any rate. Keep all your notes, documents and ads because you may have to prove that you did your part and the landlord was unreasonable. (See "Duty To Mitigate.")

I look at substitute tenants liberally. That is, you have three routes to choose. One route is to sublet. This makes you the junior landlord. It's still your name on the lease, your security deposit sitting in the landlord's bank and you'll be the one to pay if there is a suit for back rents. Under a sublet, at the very least, get a security deposit from your subtenant and make sure it is *you* who receives the rent payment, which you pass along. If you don't verify that the monthly rent is paid, you'll not know until you are sued. Being a sublessor can also put you in the middle if tenants' issues arise. Subletting, by the way, can be great way to rent your place for several months while you travel and then return to take the unit over yourself.

A better route when you want out is to assign the lease. The difference is that you are completely out of the picture. The new tenants' names are written in and your name is scratched out. You get your security deposit back and no longer have to worry. The landlord may be nervous about somebody coming through you, so do a good selecting and selling job. You must have all copies of the lease marked "assigned to (new names)" and signed at that place by you and your landlord. (See Appendix J.)

The best route is to find a tenant who wants a longer lease. This person is ideal for the landlord because rents can usually be raised, a tenant is available to stay for more than a year and the landlord probably has no expense or effort (no ads, no repainting). In this case, you get to take your security deposit and have the landlord write "lease terminated by agreement on (date)," and both you and the landlord sign all copies of the old lease. (See Appendix I.)

What happens when you just walk out? Most laws provide that you are liable for all reasonable costs relating to finding a replacement tenant, such as paying for ads and in some cases redecorating, if the unit is unrentable as is. You'll also be liable for the lost rents until somebody else moves in. If you paid $500 a month and the landlord rerents the unit at $300, theoretically, you'll have to pay the difference until the end of your lease.

Liquidated Damages, "Penalties" and "Fines"

Under most tenants' rights laws, liquidated damages are limited and spelled out up front. Liquidated damages means to compensate a party (always the landlord) with whatever money of yours they have and can convert to themselves (usually the security deposit) because you didn't do something right. So if you walk out on the lease, they might use the deposit as liquidated damages. They may have other or more claims, but the deposit is theirs, period. Liquidated damages are not penalties, since penalties are not allowed in residential leases. Anything that smells like a penalty or a fine, you can fight. Accelerated rents, sublet and assignment fees, lease termination costs and redecorating expenses all smell funny. If the purpose is not to compensate the landlord for actual damages sustained but to punish or get even with you (or make you an example so nobody else will do it), it is not allowed. At the first wisp of a penalty or fine, call your attorney. Most landlord-tenant laws and tenants' rights acts will allow you to recover your actual damages and/or court imposed penalties from the landlord, plus court costs and attorney's fees.

Duty To Mitigate

Both the landlord and the tenant have duties to mitigate. What the heck does that mean? It means a legal requirement to reduce the exposure, costs or damages to the other side. For the tenant, it means reporting repair problems promptly before a $5 fix becomes a $1,000 nightmare. Since tenant rules are usually spelled out in the lease, house rules or laws, just following them should suffice for the most part. It could be considered a duty to pay for the landlord's advertising to find a replacement tenant (and this is covered in most ordinances).

For landlords, state and local laws are direct and special. Almost all laws require the landlord to diligently find a replacement tenant (if you break the lease) and mitigate damages to the former tenant. The reason is that the sooner the apartment is rerented, the less money you owe on the unfulfilled part of your lease. In the good old days, the landlord would simply hold a unit off the market until the lease expired and then sue for the whole rent. (The accelerator clause is just a way of demanding the money sooner.) The only reason for doing this was to punish (penalize) the former tenant. In fact, many times a new tenant would quietly move in, unknown to the previous tenant.

In most jurisdictions this abuse of the court system, not to mention the tenant, has been declared improper. It is the landlord's duty to (1) advertise the abandoned unit with at least the same diligence other units are offered and in the same manner, (2) show the unit along with all other available units, (3) price the unit according to fair market value as determined by rents for comparable units in the area and (4) place the unit on top, not bottom, of the availability list when filling applications.

Proof of mitigation includes newspaper clips of the ads for *all* apartments the landlord advertised during the empty apartment period, copies of applications taken for *all* comparable units the landlord manages (not just in that building) and the vacancy and rent history records for *all* comparables. Your lawyer would examine carefully any claims regarding redecorating or unit undesirability to determine whether *your* rent was too high or the landlord was hyping the court. He or she would also check if the landlord steered tenants away from the old unit.

Suits for rent and costs after termination, if found to be "cooked," can result in fines and the assessment of tenant's costs against the landlord for bringing frivolous nonmeritorious actions. Lawyers who play this game can be sanctioned and fined also.

Retaliation

Retaliation occurs when the landlord gets mad and attempts to get even. Sometimes these are self-help measures, meaning without the permission of a law or the court. Retaliatory acts are quite stressful, which is the intention. Lockout is an act of retaliation. More common is when the landlord punishes you by making new rules for the lease that are unfair and impossible and that probably only apply to you. Retaliation is when, out of the blue, your month-to-month lease is canceled or when you receive rent increases every month or greater increases than other people in your building are getting because of some lawful activity of yours. Retaliation is when the lease doesn't get renewed. Retaliation is when you get no services as a result of complaining to the city inspector, etc. Retaliation is when your landlord sues or threatens to sue you for eviction based on your conduct of protected activities.

Tenants' rights laws almost universally prohibit retaliatory conduct. This is conduct that is presumed to be done as a result of a tenant making a legitimate housing-related complaint to any governmental body, community group or tenants' group, news organization or to the landlord. It also includes testimony in court. The one caveat is that you must complain, blab, join the union and so forth *before* the retaliatory behavior starts. You can't cry about spilled milk after the barn door is opened. Most laws protect your previous activities for a period of six months or a year.

In most cases, when you are punished through increases, eviction or lease termination, tenants' rights ordinances say that the landlord will have to prove that it wasn't your complaining or tenant organizing or demand for your rights that triggered the action. The landlord has what is called a *rebuttable presumption* that the act was retaliatory. Some good cause will have to be presented to rebut the allegation. If you pay your rent on time (or withhold it legally) and are otherwise a good tenant, the landlord will be hard pressed to find good cause. When you win, you can collect anywhere from $100 up to three times the monthly rent, plus costs. If a building tenants' union membership is made victim of retaliation (i.e., there are multiple eviction notices), imagine the landlord's grief!

Distrain

One of the reasons for modern tenants' rights laws is the common law practice of *distrain,* also known as *distress for rent.* This was the landlord's ultimate self-help measure. When the rent was late, the landlord simply seized the tenant's property to hold as hostage or sell for the rent. Most tenants' rights laws ban this process. Even where legal, the landlord must go through a maze of legalities that are much more expensive and complex than eviction. Even if successful, the tenant is still not evicted; he or she is only without some belongings. It is a common rule of law that in matters like this, once the landlord engages in one legal remedy, he or she is prohibited from taking another. To be clear, once eviction proceedings have been filed, the landlord *may not* resort to distrain. One other tidbit: In some states, if you owe money and move out, the landlord can seize your property anywhere it can be found (from your new apartment, for instance)!

Here's how it works, as well as some of the risks to the landlord. You owe rent. You've been given a notice, if your state requires it. The landlord comes to your apartment *while you are away,* gets in (how?) and removes your belongings. An inventory is created and a distress (distrain) warrant is drawn up and filed with the appropriate local court. This is about the same as filing a lawsuit. The sheriff serves the warrant on the tenant. Hearings are scheduled. Finally, either the tenant pays the back rent, or the property is sold to satisfy the debt.

In real life, this isn't so cut-and-dried. Most states exempt *personal* items such as clothes, cooking utensils, basic furniture, the Bible and workers' tools from seizure. Furthermore, a certain dollar-amount floor may be exempted (e.g., the landlord must leave the tenant with $2,500 in property, no matter what it is). The law says you can only take what belongs to the tenant. If the property of another is taken (say, rental furniture or friends' belongings), then a burglary may have occurred. If the distrain seizure is done incorrectly, the landlord could be charged with burglary or possession of stolen property, could be forced to return all the personal items, could be forced to return items valued up to the floor limit and could face a lawsuit from the tenant for damages.

Rent and Deposit Limits and Renewals

Tenants' rights vary on issues like the amount of rent that can be charged, rent increases and limits for deposits and late fees. Rent controls are limited to a few parts of the country—particularly New York City, various towns in California and parts of Ohio. In most other places, rents are set by supply and demand. Rent control policy in New York City is beyond the scope of this book.

As a rule, rent control is not really control as much as it is a way to reward landlords for building code compliance and punish those who won't comply. This modified form of rent control is also known as *fair rent.* In fair-rent cities, all units required to operate under the ordinance (it varies by number of units, owner-occupied, etc.) must register with the rent board. A base rent usually is established according to formula or current market prices. The landlord is allowed to raise the rent by a certain percentage based on formulas ranging from cost of living to property-tax hikes to changes in property values to condition of the building. As long as a building passes the tests, a rent increase will be granted based on the formula. If code violations are cited, no increase, a lower increase or in some cases a decrease may be ordered. Tenants can attend hearings to protest current rents as well as (proposed) raises and bring evidence regarding the fair market value. Consult your local tenants' organizations for information and assistance.

While not all areas limit the amount of a security deposit, some prohibit a deposit in excess of the equivalent of one month's rent. Some landlords try to stick on special fees as well as the last month's rent to evade the restriction. Chicago requires that security deposits be put in special bank accounts that are segregated from the landlord's other money, similar to a lawyer's trust account. (See the discussion on deposits earlier in this chapter.)

Renewing the lease is far from an automatic right in most places. When you think you are not being renewed because of retaliation, you may be able to make a case. (See "Retaliation" and the discussion about rebuttable presumption as well as information about discrimination in chapter 5.) Otherwise, forget it. Some tenants' rights jurisdictions require that the landlord give you a specific written notice regarding when your lease expires. If you don't get the notice, you can automatically renew (in some places) or stay on for a period of time—say, 60 days.

Many leases say the lease expires as stated on the front and no other notice need be given. While it is always a requirement that the landlord give a notice of termination because you broke the lease or a rule, when the lease expires, there is no law requiring it to be renewed, in most places. As you know, an oral lease automatically renews until either side gives a (written) notice.

If you can't find a local tenants' organization, there is one national group that *may* be able to advise you. That source is the Low Income Housing Information Service, 1012 14th Street, NW, Ste. 1200, Washington, DC 20005 (202-662-1530). If you write, send a self-addressed, stamped envelope. If you call, please understand that it is not a help agency or referral service, just a group of good, overworked people who might be able to answer your question. Please don't make them call you back. (They operate on shoe strings.)

Maintenance and Habitability—"I've Paid My Rent, Now You Fix the Toilet!"

Tenants' Remedies
- Enforce the Warranty of Habitability
- The Basic Bargain
- Repair and Deduct
- Withhold or Reduce Rents
- Break the Lease for Good Cause
- Sue the Landlord

Every Home a Castle?

The landlord is very sure that the unit was rented *as is*. There may be a clause to that effect in the lease, or you may be told that nobody forced you to rent the place. "No," the landlord might tell you, "I don't have to fix it. You had your chance to check the place out before you moved in. I don't care what your problem is, you still have to pay the rent!" Your lease may even call for *you* to make all the repairs, but somehow it doesn't seem right.

Well, the landlord is wrong. He or she *must* make basic repairs or you are on strong grounds, in most states, to reduce your rents, withhold your rents or break the lease and leave. When you have tenants' rights protections, you can also make repairs and deduct the costs from your rent. You are advised to find your local tenants' group, or contact a local attorney specializing in tenants' rights before you blindly embark on making tenants' rights demands.

The Implied Warranty of Habitability

Just what is the warranty of habitability and why is it *implied?* It is implied because even though the landlord won't write it out or even tell you, the landlord must deliver to you a decent, safe, healthy, code-compliant dwelling unit with all the requisite essential services. That is the fundamental part of the bargain: You pay for a decent place to live, and the landlord is legally obligated to deliver it and keep it that way. *Habitability* means "fit to live in." This means fit to live in when initially offered for rent and maintained by the landlord to at least the same standards and conditions as long as there are legal occupants. For the duration of your lease (or until you are physically evicted by the sheriff), all building-code and essential service requirements must be met. Where there is no explicit building code, then generally accepted standards of safety and health will be applied.

The principles of habitability are that the water runs; the hot-water tank works; the gas doesn't leak; the wiring doesn't spark; the roof or ceiling doesn't leak; the windows are tight and not cracked; the toilet flushes; the drains all work and don't leak; the heater can keep you "legally" warm (at least 65°F [18°C] during the day in most jurisdictions); there are no dangerous combustion, sewer or stale-air fumes; there are no rats or mice; roaches and ants are not a danger; the doors lock; the structure is not in danger of collapsing; and there are no other hazardous conditions. These are your fundamental rights as a renter. Most states enforce these rights as a result of direct legislation or court decisions (case law).

There is no way for you to know all of the things that could be wrong with your rental unit. You might rent in June, only to find out in October that the furnace doesn't work. It is totally unreasonable for you to (1) believe that the furnace was not serviceable (you are paying rent for it), (2) fix it out of your own pocket (you didn't break it) or (3) continue to pay some or all the rent when your house or apartment is no longer worth full value or is unusable for the purposes you rented it for originally.

The concept of habitability needs to viewed with reasonable perspective. Here are two examples: First, peeling, lead-based paints are dangerous and violate many building codes; thus, the landlord must do something about this. Second, ugly paint and smudged walls do not typically go to the heart of habitability. In the first case, you can reasonably exercise whatever rights you have to ensure your health; but in the second case, there is little to be done (unless you have a specific lease clause or rider regarding decorating). If the toilet breaks, your landlord must immediately repair or replace it, but don't expect a new velvet-plush, electrically heated seat! The daily trifles of dripping faucets, roaches dancing on your cookies and broken door handles may also be habitability issues but of a lesser god.

Whose Job Is It?

It is the landlord's job to fix what needs repair. It is your job to notify the him or her. If the landlord doesn't respond, it may be your job to make the repairs or take other action. In some cases, it may also be your job to notify the proper local authorities and contact your local community or neighborhood action group for advice and assistance. Ordinary wear and tear, stranger or third-party-caused damage, hidden defects in the unit or appliances, essential services (including structural members like pipes and wires) are *all* your landlord's responsibilities. On the other hand, if you negligently break something, let something happen or let somebody else you invite into the building do something, you pay.

There are communities that will send out a housing inspector or community relations officer to inspect a premises for the purpose of determining how much the fair market value has been diminished. They will write up a form that is your absolute defense for rent abatement. Some of these inspectors look for more than minimum standards—for instance, whether the unit and the landlord is in compliance with local tenants' rights requirements. You typically get quick relief under this type of inspection program.

Of course, when routine or customary inspections from most municipalities result in a violation report, it is proof of a violation. However, these type of ordinary inspections can take weeks or months to get corrective results and can still leave you unsatisfied.

You could ultimately wind up on either end of a lawsuit: either as defendant in an eviction action or as a plaintiff trying to recover overpayments of rent, forcing the landlord to do the job or stopping retaliatory action. Even then, if you win, it is still your job to make the landlord do his or her job. How you handle the major and minor problems is described in the next section.

Rights and Remedies

Well, what good are rights if you can't enforce them? That's what remedies are all about. What good is a remedy that costs hundreds or thousands of dollars to pursue and takes longer than the lease to obtain? That's what self-help tenants' rights are all about. While not all rights are given to all tenants and not all remedies are available, most rights and remedies are recognized and possible to enforce.

As a general rule, when you attempt to obtain your rights, you can use one remedy but not all remedies at the same time. As is discussed in the following section, you probably can't make a repair and deduct the cost from your rent while at the same time further reducing your rent and breaking the lease (for the same problem). Please recall that damage you cause, provoke or that is caused by somebody you willingly allowed into your unit will be your responsibility.

Third-party damage (caused by a party other than you or the landlord) by a known person is that person's financial responsibility, but it's probably the landlord's job to fix, since it is the landlord's duty to maintain. Damage caused by unknown third parties is the landlord's duty. A known third party, for example is a former boyfriend who goes nutzo one night and breaks down your door trying to "visit." As long as you did not voluntarily invite him onto the premises (including buzzing him in the lobby), you are not responsible. When a burglar cracks your door, you are not responsible. When some kid sends a baseball or bullet through a window, you are not responsible.

Repairing and Deducting

You need to determine whether your locality or state formally allows for repairing and deducting. Some states require a court order to repair and deduct. Sometimes you may decide to repair and deduct on your own and take a chance with the landlord or judge. The concept is clear: You pay to repair something out of your own pocket and deduct it from the rent. The practice is more complicated.

Where there are regulations, the amount of the repairs will be limited to a certain amount or monthly rent percentage. Sometimes you can only do this a limited number of times per year. As a rule, you must give the landlord a period of time to comply before you can take action. In Chicago, we can deduct up to half a month's rent or $500, whichever is greater, as long as the total for a month doesn't exceed the monthly rent. We can make repairs and take deductions each month. For most minor problems, we have to give the landlord 14 days before taking action. Where there is no regulation, how long you wait needs to be "reasonable," and the amount you spend is up to you and what a judge thinks is fair. That could be nothing or thousands.

As a general rule, use repair and deduct for smaller items that can wait for a time to be fixed and also for economically remedied emergency issues relating to essential services (gas, heat, plumbing, electricity), dangerous structural problems and security issues (nonfunctioning door locks). You must be able to pay somebody for the parts, the labor or the service out a portion of rents you owe, so it can't be too costly regardless of local regulation. The idea is that you have a right to the service or function under the implied warranty of habitability and either the landlord makes it good, or you'll make it better. Be aware that between regulations, case-law interpretations and wily judges, the level required for habitability varies widely, even from courtroom to courtroom.

Here are some of the things tenants do with the repair and deduct concept. When the apartment is frequently (or temporarily) cold, they buy electric room heaters. When the toilet breaks, they hire a plumber. When the roaches and mice get a bit too much, they hire an exterminator. When the building gas, water or electricity is shut off, they pool with fellow residents to pay the utility bills and get service restored. When the landlord makes a promise in the lease and doesn't deliver, the tenants keep the promise for the landlord. Look at the generic "Notice To Cure" letter (further on in this chapter), which walks you through the notice process. Also, see the sample letters in Appendix C, which has the total litany.

When you invoke repair and deduct, you are taking on certain responsibilities and risks. The responsibility is that the work you hire is done properly and you pay for it. The risks are varied. First, you must be able to prove (to your landlord or a judge) that the damage wasn't your fault. Second, you need to prove that the work done (or services or goods purchased) was necessary. Third, you need to establish that what you did solved the problem. Lastly, you'll need to prove that the price was right.

It is reasonable to believe that work was necessary if you complain in writing about a habitability repair issue, obtain quotes for the work and have the work performed. Your landlord can (almost) always do the work more cheaply because he or she has staff, special tradespeople and wholesale accounts. The landlord's people may understand the work better because of familiarity with your unit or building. Too bad. When the landlord fails to act in time, the excess costs are one of the prices paid.

Without a tenants' rights law, I wouldn't repair and deduct without the advice of a tenant group or attorney. (See chapter 7 for more information.)

Abatements: Rent Withholding and Reductions

When a problem is too big, services or conditions change or there is a lease violation, the use of repair and deduct may be inappropriate, ineffective or impractical. Examples of such problems include the following: the noisy neighbor next door, the repeated and annoying visits to your unit at all times of the day and night by the landlord, the refrigerator that melts ice cream, the stove that deserves a decent burial, the lack of heat or air conditioning, the leaking roof, the dripping ceiling from the shower or toilet upstairs, the garbage that never gets collected, the mail room that closed (or shortened hours), the wood-burning fireplace that doesn't, etc.

In all these cases, you are not getting something you paid for, be it peace and quiet or full use and service. Why should you pay full freight for half a load? To *abate* is to stop or reduce the rent. The basic principle of abatement is that the building remains fundamentally safe, and your continued occupancy will not jeopardize your health but it's not worth the rent. You will always have to give advance notice of rent abatement. If you are reducing rents, you can start counting the reduced amount from your time of warning and take more off your rent the first month you abate.

Rent withholding is usually done to force the landlord to do something quickly. The cost is beyond repair and deduct, or the issue doesn't have much to do with repairs in the normal sense. For example, you will refuse to pay any more rent until the leaking roof is repaired. There was a case where after a fire, the elevator in a 12-story building was taken out of service. Repairs were supposed to take three weeks. After a month, the building went on a rent strike. Only then did the repairs get made. (When essential services continuously or repeatedly fail, withholding is a powerful way to force repairs [and/or live for free].) After months of complaints and bad-faith promises, a tenants' union organized a rent strike. A housing court ordered the building vacated but forgave the tenants all four months of withheld rents. When that special something is completed, none, some or all of the withheld rent is paid over to the landlord. This will depend on local laws, your inconvenience, the judge's temperament or the deal you make with the landlord.

Rent reductions are longer lasting, as a rule, but less coercive than total withholding. You might say that since a stove fails to work well, it has devalued the apartment by some amount. You simply pay the reduced amount until you get a new stove or the lease expires. You reduce to reflect the reduction in value and the factor of inconvenience. How you make that calculation is as much art as science. If you can't use a room because of ceiling leaks or bad flooring, you may claim a percentage reduction based on the square-foot percentage lost. (I call this the IRS method.) On the other hand, if it is the bathroom, small but mighty, you might claim much more than a few square feet because of the percentage of use or necessity. (I call this the value-reduced way.) If you have to live with a friend or shower at the office, your inconvenience level goes pretty high, even though you can still use the place to store your belongings.

When you have a noisy neighbor, the peaceful use and enjoyment of your unit has been diminished. That means that *if* you can still stand to live there, the place is worth less than what you are paying. How you value a night's sleep is for your creativity, but I would think it could reduce the unit's value by 25 to 30 percent. If the problem persists after notification, you reduce your rent by an amount you think is proper, prorating it from when the landlord was notified (if it isn't fixed by your deadline). (See the section "Notifying the Landlord" later in this chapter.) A dispute between neighbors can sometimes be resolved through creativity and perhaps mediation. (See chapter 9.)

I know of a case of rent reduction where the only difference between two apartments was a working fireplace. One rented for $100 more per month. The fireplace couldn't be used because of a chimney problem. When the landlord said he couldn't fix it, the tenant reduced the rent. When the landlord threatened to evict, the tenant showed the landlord the ads for both apartments (they happened to be in the same building), and the landlord backed down, permanently lowering the rent. (Thus, it pays to keep records of all transactions regarding renting!)

If your building dismisses the doorman, the value of rent is less because there are fewer services. You still can live there safely, but it is not worth as much as it was. If there is a promise to paint the apartment every other year, but it doesn't happen, give notice and reduce the rents! If the front of the building looks like a pigsty, tell your landlord to clean it up or reduce your rent (and form a tenants' union) until it is cleaned. Remember, you must be able to justify your reduction formula to a judge.

Terminations

If your landlord fails to deliver a habitable unit or fails to keep it habitable, you might consider moving out temporarily or permanently breaking the lease. If you have a tenants' rights law, it will tell you what you can and cannot do. Generally, you make a demand of the landlord requiring enforcement of your lease and riders or correction of a serious problem—be it essential services, structural danger or loss of your use and enjoyment of the unit. If the required action is not satisfactorily completed, you move out until it is (paying no rent *and* charging the landlord for your alternative housing) or you break the lease.

Perhaps there is a serious heating problem. After several weekends of freezing, you notify the landlord that the heat *will* work properly from now on, or you will start spending nights at the Park Plaza at the landlord's expense. Check your local tenant laws first, but if you live in Chicago, for example, you can do this (with restrictions, of course).

Out-and-out lease breaking requires a substantial breach of habitability—no heat, broken plumbing, gangs, structural dangers, loss of essential utilities, compromised security (no working door locks), wild rats, fire, harassment from the landlord. As an example, your landlord repeatedly enters your apartment without valid reason or permission. You warn the landlord to stop or the next time it happens, the lease terminates. (See "Unlawful Entry" in chapter 7.) Another substantial breach would occur if the hot water were nonexistent after 5:00 P.M. daily. This is an essential service; it is a health and sanitation issue. In this case, the landlord should be given five days, or you should terminate the lease and move before the end of the month.

The legitimacy for lease termination comes from several sources. One is basic reasonableness and logic: if the place isn't habitable, you can't continue to live there and thus have the right to move because it violates the basic bargain of renting a safe, decent unit. Another one is legal: by definition, if a dwelling unit is not habitable, it can't be rented for human habitation. Another is the legal concept *constructive eviction*, which comes out of the common law. This means that by the acts and/or omissions of the landlord, it is *construed* that the landlord must be trying to get you to leave (since no one in his or her right mind would pull those kinds of tricks otherwise). So when you ask for the heat and don't get it, it must mean the landlord wants you out. So move, if that is your desire, after giving the proper notice.

Sometimes you can claim breaches of the lease as the reason to terminate, but they must be substantial, must interfere with your use of the unit or must be the things that induced you to sign the lease in the first place. You would be well advised to talk to a lawyer if you want to break your lease on the basis of a breach not relating to habitability. You may have agreed that all clauses are independent, meaning even if one part of the lease is broken, the rest of the lease remains intact. (Read that to mean you must pay rent, no matter what!)

Notifying the Landlord

Each authority may have a special way to notify the landlord. Few have special forms, but most require a written notice. There are hundreds of variations on the notice process, which can only be discovered by contacting your local or state government or local tenants' organization. The biggest difference will be the amount of time allowed for compliance or the amount to spend. The basics will remain the same.

You've got to put the landlord on notice, and the best way is in writing. State as precisely as possible *who* you are, *what* the problem is, what you *want* done, *when* you expect the work to be finished and what you will *do* if the landlord doesn't comply. The issues are habitability and, secondarily, the value of the rent paid. Many tenants' rights laws also let you lump lease breaches in your complaints. If the situation is an emergency, put it in writing after your phone call.

If you have followed my suggestion of putting a mediation clause into your lease, this is the time to contact the local mediation authority. As a rule, all it will want is your landlord's name and address and a brief description of the problem. Be sure to say that you have a mediation clause in your lease. The mediation group will do its part. (See chapter 9 for a full description of mediation.)

The Notice-To-Cure Letter

Construct your own letter, remembering that you should have only one remedy per problem: either repair and deduct *or* reduce rents *or* withhold rents *or* move out temporarily (with reimbursements) *or* break the lease. The option to sue for damages and penalties is also available. Remember the *who, what, want, when* and *do* elements just mentioned.

Notice To Cure

Date

Simon LeGree
LeGree and Associates Management Company (Lessor)
1200 East Belmont Avenue
Chicago, Illinois 60657

Sir:

The *who:*

I live in apartment 13M in the Gouge Building, 1672 East Waveland Avenue, Chicago, Illinois. Your company manages this building, and I pay my rents to you.

The *what:*

There are maintenance problems in my unit and other items that need your prompt attention. Specifically: the roof leaks in the living room. The leak is located five feet from the east window and three feet from the south wall. The bathtub will not drain, and it contains standing water. Also, the refrigerator won't stop running and can't make ice.

Because of the fire in our building on February 30, the apartment was rendered unusable for ten days as a result of structural damage to the building.[1] The apartment is presently only [50 percent] habitable.

---

1. Immediate notice of the fire, the damage and demand for repairs should be made. You should also state that you will seek (or have already sought) alternate housing for the period of time the unit is not habitable and will deduct such costs from your future rents up to an amount equal to one month's rent for each month (according to your local ordinance or what an attorney thinks is defensible) or portion you are unable to live in your apartment, plus demand credit or repayment of the rents already paid for the time the unit is uninhabitable. Send this notice by certified mail and mailgram (because of urgency) with a confirmation copy requested.

The *want, when* and *do* alternatives:

Repair and Deduct Option

Please fix the leak, repair the plaster and repaint the ceiling. Open up the sewer lines so that the bathtub drains properly and repair or replace the refrigerator.

If you have not corrected these problems by [15 days from date of mailing], I will hire people to do the repair work and deduct the costs [$500 or 50 percent of the monthly rent or what local law allows or you calculate] from the next monthly rent due.

Damage Compensation Option

Please refund or credit to me ten days rent as a result of the fire, and pay to me the amount of [$395] for ten days of alternate housing. A copy of the motel receipt is included. If I do not receive such payment or credit from you by [31 days from date of this notice], I shall exercise all legal rights granted me in this regard.

Rent Reduction Option

Since the unit is currently [50 percent] unusable, if repairs are not completed within ten days of today's date, I will reduce my current and future rents by [50 percent] or [$X] commencing from the date of this notice for each day until your repairs are complete.

Withhold All Rents Option

I will withhold all rents due commencing on [date] if you fail to make repairs within five days of this date. I will continue to hold all rents until these repairs are finished.

Break the Lease Option

If repairs are not completed within [ten] days of this date, this is to give you notice that I will terminate my lease on [date].

Break the Lease and Sue for Damages Option

If repair work of the fire damage is not pursued with diligence by [seven days from the date of this letter], I shall demand the return of all prepaid rents from the date of the fire and all of my security deposit. I shall also vacate the premises, terminate the lease and exercise any other legal rights available to me in this regard.

Please make arrangements with me to [do this work, enter my apartment, send me my money]. I am waiting for your phone call or written response.

Respectfully,
Deborah Jean Tenant
(current address)

Always send these letters by certified mail, return receipt requested, as well as by regular mail. Send the letter to the address on your lease or if you have received a notice to send notices elsewhere, send the letter to the alternative address. If you don't have a special address, send it to the address where you pay rent. If you pay the manager or janitor in your building, *send* the notice; don't slip it under the door. If someone comes around to collect rent, hand that person the notice, have a witness present (and maybe call the cops to protect you). All you have to do is make a good faith effort to inform the landlord. If the landlord wants to play hide and seek, that's his or her problem. Remember to fill out a certificate of delivery like the one in Appendix C. Keep a copy of the letter.

How Long, Oh Lord, How Long?

You must give the landlord the time you specified in your letter. Begin counting days from the day after you mail the letter. If the landlord needs access to your unit, make the arrangements. Don't be stubborn or impossible. You asked for the work, so please be cooperative and reasonable about letting the work be done. This includes providing a key or being present during reasonable working hours.

What happens when time runs out and the work is not started, not finished, slipshod or ineffective? *Ineffective* means that extermination was performed, but you still have the roaches or rats. *Slipshod* means the new lock doesn't line up to close or wobbles. *Not finished* means the old window was removed, but the new one hasn't been put in.

The day after time expires, have your own people on the job if you are repairing and deducting. You don't have to give more notices and warnings as long as you can prove you made a good faith effort to notify the landlord in the first place. That's why the certified letter was invented! Be prepared by taking bids and showing the job prior to starting. Remember, you pay and deduct, so what you pay should be what you are allowed (or reasonably expect to be able) to deduct. If this is an abatement issue, calculate how much the rental value has diminished since you sent the notice. Keep subtracting the daily pro rata reduction until the work is complete or until the next monthly rent payment is due (whichever comes first). On the rent date, subtract pro rata reductions for the previous month, and explain this in a letter to the landlord along with a smaller rent check. As long as the work is incomplete, deduct your daily pro rata reductions from each month's rent. Sample letters regarding activation of repair and deduct, reduction, withholding and termination can be found in Appendix C.

If you go into rent withholding, send your landlord a notice instead of the rent check. A good idea is to buy a money order in the amount of the monthly rents and set it aside (a poor person's escrow account) to prove to a judge your intention was to get service, not cheat on the rent. The amount you finally pay when the problem is corrected can be determined by the same pro rata method used for rent reduction. The argument is that for as long as the condition existed, the market value of your unit was reduced. If you paid full rent after the condition arose, you overpaid.

When the landlord fails to do what's necessary and lease termination is the option, send him or her notice stating the date (and time) when you will vacate and where your prepaid rents and security deposit return should be delivered. Prepaid rents refer to the last month's rent and any other rents paid in advance. (For example, rent has been paid in advance if you move on the 25th of the month and rent has been paid through the 31st.) While you still may be eligible for an overpayment claim based on the reduced market value, make this demand later in small claims court by yourself or through an attorney.

9

Pushing and Shoving—Resolution by Police, Law or Mediation

> ### *Problem Solving*
> - Dealing with Neighbors and Landlords
> - Alternatives to Pushing and Shoving
> - How To Use the Courts To Enforce the Building Codes
> - Stopping Drug Dealing
> - Conducting Your Case To Get Your Security Deposit Returned
> - Trying To Solve a Problem Through the Police

At some level, this book is about flourishing in an adversarial circumstance, primarily pitting you against the landlord and the legal system behind it. High on the list of whom you should get along with well should be folks like your landlord and your neighbor. Yet here is a book that cautions you to be careful and provides reams of information about protecting rights and obtaining remedies. What gives?

Our imperfect psyches either encourage or allow for conflict, sometimes in spite of ourselves. I want to describe circumstances of conflict and methods of resolving it. Conflict arises when what you want and what somebody else wants differ enough that an atmosphere of competition or tension is created. The more one party objects to the actions of the other side, the more the parties will disagree, interfere and upset the other side. As a smoldering coal left untended, a flame may break out

> 1. Speaking directly
>   - Writing an informal message
>   - Speaking confrontationally
>   - Making a formal written demand
> 2. Threatening personal harm
>   - Threatening legal harm
>   - Calling the police
>   - Filing a legal claim

Standard Tenant Conflict Management Methods

consuming all it touches. In practical terms, it means intolerable living conditions, evictions and improperly withheld deposits, to name some relevant concerns.

I spend a considerable amount of my time helping people—landlords and tenants being a sizable part of that population—solve their mutual problems. I am convinced that if people would speak to each other in appropriate and effective ways, many small disagreements could be handled to everyone's satisfaction. While not all conflicts easily go away, it never hurts to talk first. Once you start shouting, it is hard to return to constructive conversation.

Negotiating with Neighbors

Let's look at the usual ways of dealing with a tenant-related problem. Here's a list of common problems: babies crying, children running overhead, dogs barking, pets running on bare floors, radio/TV/stereo too loud/wrong music/wrong time, fights, parties, musical instrument practice, roommate disagreements.

Say your neighbor plays the radio too loud. After the third time, you have had it. So you bang on the wall, ceiling or floor; storm down the hall and bang on the door; or write a nasty little note and stuff it under the door. The result may not stop the behavior, and there may be an animosity created so that the next contact might be not so nice.

It would be better to speak directly to the party the *first* time the radio is too loud. As a rule, you're not so upset (as you'll be after repeated disturbances), and the neighbor gets the benefit of the doubt—that is, he or she didn't know you were being disturbed. This soft approach allows you to portray yourself as reasonable. This is important since you may have to confront the issue again, and, if so, you will have to enlist your neighbor's cooperation. You see, only your neighbor can turn down the volume.

Assume the noise continues. The standard approach now would be an escalation by more banging, retaliatory stereo blasting or some sort of threat to call the cops or punch out somebody's lights. The neighbor starts to make complaints to you, taunts at you or threatens some sort of nasty retaliation. You figure out how to turn off the neighbor's power, or pull some other silly prank, and finally call the landlord or the police. This assumes you didn't get into a shouting or fighting match wherein somebody else called for the paddy wagon.

What's a better way to *try?* Request a meeting with the neighbor. Sit down at your place or his or her or find a neutral spot. Try to explain why the noise upsets you. Find out why the music needs to be so loud. Put yourself in the other party's shoes and ask for the same. After all, while you believe he or she is interfering with you, you are doing the very same thing. There has got to be a solution, since you all live together and it is not easy to pull up stakes and move on.

In the case of amplified noise, evaluate what solutions are available and what the price of peace is. With your neighbor, see if you can set times when it is okay to play music. For instance, decide to have quiet after 9:30 P.M. weeknights and 1:00 A.M. Friday and Saturday nights. Can a tolerable level be established by experimenting together on a volume setting? Can the speakers be moved away from your walls, raised off the floor or lowered from the ceiling? Can the "music room" or your bedroom be changed? Have you tried earplugs?

Remember, what you are doing is negotiating a solution. The problem is something you both share. You need to go into this negotiation with a positive attitude. If you don't think a solution can be reached, it will become a self-fulfilling prophecy of defeat. There are negative ramifications for both parties if it is not solved. A good attitude is that the people are not the problem; the issue (noise, repairs, etc.) is the problem. What you offer has to be practical and mutually beneficial for both parties. It means you both win (in that arrangements are made), and it means nobody loses. There must be some give-and-take as to the idea of the solution but not to finding a solution. Further on in this chapter I'll describe the alternatives to negotiating a settlement, which should be considered the price you'll have to pay not to get along.

This is an agreement between
Hank Occupant, Apartment 3D, 6515 Wynotte
and
Mary Tenant, Apartment 3C, 6515 Wynotte

1. Hank Occupant agrees not to play his music system above the "normal" volume setting, as marked on his amplifier by himself and Mary Tenant, whenever Mary Tenant is at home, except at certain times noted below.

2. Mary Tenant will not complain about Hank Occupant's loud music when the loud times are limited to Friday nights and Saturday nights from 7:00 P.M. until 1:30 A.M.

3. Hank Tenant agrees not to play his music system above the "loud" volume setting, as marked on his amplifier by himself and Mary Tenant, whenever Mary Tenant is at home.

4. Mary Tenant agrees to phone Hank Occupant with any problems at Hank's phone, which is 555-2368.

5. Hank Occupant agrees to phone Mary Tenant to make special arrangements or with any problems by calling Mary's number, which is 555-6823.

6. Mary Tenant agrees not to complain to the landlord or police as long as volume levels and times are respected as per this agreement.

Mary Tenant   (Date)   Hank Occupant   (Date)

Sample Neighbor Dispute Resolution Agreement

Whenever possible, I like to put things in writing. In the example presented in the box, I'll call the tenant with the music system Hank and the other tenant Sue. After getting up her courage, Sue knocked on Hank's door to complain about the music. He agreed to turn it down, but later it got loud again. Sue dropped a note to Hank suggesting he call her about meeting to work out a solution. At the meeting, which started in the hallway and moved to the lobby, Hank and Sue agreed on a music timetable. They exchanged phone numbers so that volume levels could be established by testing between the walls and noting the thresholds. They also agreed to exchange phone calls regarding any future problems. These arrangements were reduced to a simple written agreement. The agreement made everything clear and could be referred to later if there was a question. Please note the mutuality of the agreement. Now when the noise gets too loud, Sue calls Hank. Sue also plans to be away when she knows the music is going to blast. Is the arrangement tolerable? Yes, because both parties came up with it, and it met their needs well enough that they signed it.

Recently, I resolved a music-system disturbance dispute partially by suggesting a cheap "walkperson" play-only radio/cassette for the neighbor. The complaining tenant offered to buy it. Peace was worth $40!

Variations abound. For a crying baby, suggest changing the bedroom. For kids' noisy play, suggest locating the toys away from where you are being disturbed. For pets scampering across floors or that woman with the army-boot stomp, suggest carpeting or wearing slippers! What about parties? Suggest limiting them to certain days, certain hours, a certain number of people and a specified number of times per week. Also work on ways to control the noise and rowdiness.

In addition to an immediate solution, it is very important to keep a line of communications open. For instance, when the problem recurs, you should be able to make a phone call and let the other side know they have to put your agreed solution to work. As long as you can remain on speaking terms, you've got a good chance of minimizing, not escalating.

None of these efforts are wasted, because if you and the neighbor can work it out, you've done so at a minimum of distress to yourself.

Negotiating with the Landlord

Yes, it is possible to come to a working arrangement with the landlord, provided both of you want it. The problem in some tenant-landlord situations is that the landlord does not do a good job of evaluating what can be gained or lost. Sometimes landlords, as do other stubborn people, either want to win, regardless of the price, or they are willing to go down making a useless point of principle. This is dumb. It is mutually beneficial to resolve your differences. You in all likelihood will have a continuing relationship, so it is important to be able to get along. Working out the differences is mutually satisfying since you get to stay in a place that (finally) meets your needs and the landlord gets a good tenant, one who might stay on through the next lease. The most important thing here is that the landlord will deal with you in good faith. You can point out to the landlord that by cooperating, the building gets rid of problems and the landlord keeps the rent coming in.

Let's evaluate the nominal positions of each side in this type of negotiation. If the problem qualifies, the tenant has the options of repairing and deducting, reducing rents, withholding the rent or moving. None of these are in the landlord's interest. There is also the possibility of having the landlord arrested. If there is a structural or mechanical problem, the next potential tenant is going to notice the hole in the ceiling, the lack of heat or the busted toilet. Even if this is a slumlord, the next tenant will squeal just as the last did. So if there is any concern for caliber of tenant or for a little peace, the landlord in all likelihood will have to make repairs whether you stay or not. Why not do it while receiving most or all the rent instead of dealing with a nonpaying unit?

Tenant	**Landlord**
• Remain in unit	• Keep rents flowing
• Have repairs made	• Improve property
• Lease is renewed	• Reduce vacancy rate
• Better service in future	• Cooperative tenant
• Better relations with landlord	• Better relations with tenant
• Don't have to spend time with inspectors	• Stay out of violations court
• No courts, lawyers, judgment records	• Avoid lawsuits and evictions
• Protect reputation	• Protect reputation

The Win-Win in Tenant-Landlord Negotiations

Of course, the landlord could also have to deal with the local building inspector. Chances are that you would gladly extend yourself to show the inspector *all* the problems you know about. No building is without them, you know. If you have tenants' rights, you could also sue for rent overpayments or injunctive relief. All those nasty things can be avoided if the parties will talk in good faith. Some of you may decide to wait out an eviction process. If you are in the right court jurisdiction, this could take several months, and the landlord would get no rent—then or ever (not that I encourage you to have an unpaid judgment placed in your credit files). But as you can understand, for a landlord, there can be a price to pay for resting on principle or being stubborn.

Agreements, such as leases, can be changed provided the parties both want it. Isn't it easier to make a mutual exchange (say, a rent reduction in exchange for the paint job that never got done) rather than be sued for specific performance or material breach of the lease? Having an attorney on retainer doesn't mean your landlord will obtain unlimited free legal work on a contract dispute. A lawsuit will cause the landlord a certain amount of expense and extra attention. What happens to the landlord's reputation when other tenants find out about how the landlord responds to tenant needs? Might some people move out at lease end rather than fear dealing with a boor? Might some prospective tenants hear of the reputation? Your landlord is in a public and competitive business, and its reputation is known and has value.

You know how to evaluate your costs and exposures when hassling with the landlord. To avoid lawyers, inspectors and evictions, wouldn't a good-faith attempt at finding a solution be a logical first step before escalation? You've got to sit down with the landlord and spell out what you want. Flexibility, patience and accommodation are signs of intelligence and strength, not weakness. Your agreement needs to be in writing, with all issues clearly and fairly covered. Remember, if the landlord breaks the deal, you have all your options still intact, and a court might find the landlord to have dealt in bad faith. Not good for its case.

Mediation

There are circumstances that may be more than you can handle. You may not feel comfortable cutting a deal, or the issue is complex. Maybe there are many parties involved in the dispute. It is still in your best interest to approach the other side as soon as possible to inform them of the problem. Next, since you don't feel confident to handle it alone, contact your local dispute resolution center.

There are many community-based *free* mediation centers across the country. They go by such names as Neighborhood Justice, Community Mediation Program, Conflict Resolution (and Mediation) Center, Dispute Resolution Center or Service and Mediation Project. The American Bar Association Standing Committee on Dispute Resolution maintains a list. Contact them at 1800 M Street, NW, S-200, Washington, DC 20036. They will accept telephone inquiries at 202-331-2258. There is no charge for the ABA service at this time. Another good source for local mediation centers is Conflict Resolution Center International, 2205 East Carson Street, Pittsburgh, PA 15203. There is a $10 search fee. Their phone number is 412-481-5559. The fax number is 412-481-5601. You can reach the center via E-Mail on ConflictNet through Internet. The CompuServe Go Mail address syntax is >*Internet:crcii@igc.apc.org.* The Federal Trade Commission and the National Institute for Dispute Resolution have jointly produced a booklet that contains an 11-page resource directory. Write the FTC, Division of Marketing Practices, Washington, DC 20580, and ask for a copy of *Road to Resolution: Settling Consumer Disputes.*

These centers practice mediation. You don't need a lawyer to mediate a case. You don't need evidence preparation or even witnesses. All the parties need is a desire to find a workable solution. Mediation is a process where a neutral third party assists the people in dispute to find a peaceful and workable resolution. Mediators do not make decisions, do not take sides and do not tell the parties what to do. They do not act like judges or juries. Mediation allows the parties to negotiate between themselves. Mediators keep the parties on track. If the parties come to an agreement, the mediator can help write it down.

Mediation is sometimes confused with arbitration. With arbitration, one or more arbitrators listen to the arguments, examine the facts, sometimes look at relevant laws and other arbitrators' decisions and then tell the parties what to do. In mediation, the parties decide 100 percent for themselves. And in mediation, there are no sudden surprises or unfortunate decisions. When all parties participate in good faith, between 60 and 80 percent of the sessions result in an agreement.

The mediation center needs your name, address and contact phone number as well as the names, addresses and phone numbers of the other parties. The center will make contact and set up a mutually convenient time for the mediation session. If all parties agree to meet, a mediation practitioner will conduct the session. If the parties do not meet, or if the session is not successful, the parties still have every other remedy available, including calling the police, going to court, hiring a lawyer, filing a lawsuit and invoking tenants' rights. You can't lose by trying.

Other Options

When you can't talk, you can take action. Your actions are the price you pay when you can't peacefully resolve a problem. When the situation calls for it, contact the police. When other tenants are the object, it is usually because of noise, some sort of disturbance, threats, violence against you or your property, fear that someone else is being hurt (spouse abuse, child abuse), theft, guns, dealing or arson. Police are called when landlords threaten or beat up tenants, try to evict them without a court order, enter apartments without permission (burglary, breaking and entering or trespass) or lock out tenants.

The problem with the police is that they are overworked and under incredible stress. This should be *their* problem, not yours. They are also not supposed to *judge* a situation, only assess it. That means they are not to decide when or if the landlord has the right to beat the living you know what out of you because you owe rent. It is the not the duty of the police to take your neighbor around the side of the house and break a rib. Your reason for calling the police is because you need some sort of protective action, whether it be to warn your neighbor about the noise, haul an abuser off to the cooler or disarm some dude in the hallway.

My problem with police and these run-of-the-mill domestic-type disputes is that little is done at the time, even if an arrest is made. Worse, when you tell the police to arrest party B, he or she may be demanding the same thing of you, and you both ride to the station house in the back of a meat wagon, both to be held in the same cell overnight!

The next day, or whenever, whoever was arrested is bailed out and goes back to live next door—or collect your rents. Hearings and trials take months, and what is the result? If the person loses his or her job, bond card or reputation because of a conviction, maybe they work out a deal. (See "Mediation.") If not, they'll just be angry. When was the last time somebody did time or paid a fine for a loud stereo or aggressive collection of the rent? Worse, many times the police won't do anything at all, and you have to go court or a police station to swear out a complaint on your own. There has to be a better way. Wake me when it is invented.

I want to deal with a few myths about the your safety, the police and the courts. Around here people say, "Go to court and get a 'peace bond' on this guy." You might know of this is as a protective order or a "stay-away" order. The idea is that the judge warns the person to stay away . . . or else. You'd probably feel a lot safer if the person moved to another state or was held in jail. What good does the bond or order do? It might stop an individual who has never or seldom comes up against the law, but an experienced meany does not worry so much. If rearrested, all that usually happens is that bond is raised. With our crowded jails and overloaded courtrooms, I wouldn't rely on a piece of paper to protect me. I do believe, because I see it all the time, that mediating this type of dispute is a very good idea.

Civil Actions

On the civil side of things is the lawsuit. Not everybody can see the mutuality of the problem. Sometimes it takes a judge to convince people. When one side is stubborn or makes a policy of abusing the other party (and the courts) by never settling, either you hire my cousins Guido and Schmuel or you go to court.

You should already be familiar with the various remedies available to you regarding tenants' rights, those being injunctive relief, payments to you of penalties and/or actual damages and compensation for your legal expenses.

Law and Equity

If you are going to force your landlord to do something, you will have to go to the court that deals with leases or contracts, known usually as *law* or *contract* court. You might have to go to a special court for injunctions or restraining orders, called a court of equitable relief, known generally as *equity* or *chancery* court. In these cases, you will probably need a lawyer to draw up the complaint, plead the case and follow through all the steps of obtaining evidence from the other side (discovery), arguing the case and perhaps appealing it.

Small Claims

There is a court you might be able to handle on your own. Most court systems have a division to take claims for money too small for the lawyers to bother about. Some courts call these *small claims* and place a top limit of $1,000 to $3,000. The courts I am talking about go beyond just small claims in that the whole system is set up to allow a private individual to bring a money action without the need of an attorney. In San Diego County, California, the court is called *pro per*; here in Cook County, Illinois, it is called *pro se*. It basically means "by yourself." The forms are simpler, the time limits shorter, the judge relaxes the formal atmosphere of the court and the rules are abridged. While the other side has the right to a lawyer, the judge may keep the reins tight. The TV show "People's Court" is a stylized version of the real thing.

The most likely reason to go to small claims court is to get your security deposit and interest. You should call ahead to find out where to file your case and approximately how much it will cost to file and send out the summons by sheriff. You may have to bring cash. When you sue, you sue for only what the law allows. You generally cannot sue for time lost from work to prosecute the suit, the cost of gathering evidence, bus fare, gas money, parking, baby-sitters, pain or suffering. You are limited to the security deposit, the interest and the penalties. When the law allows for other damages, you should consult with a tenants' rights group, lawyer or the small claims clerk to find out what qualifies.

When you go to the courthouse to file your lawsuit, take all your evidence with you, since in some situations you may have to prove to a special small claims clerk that you have a valid case. Write down in a column on a clean piece of paper how much deposit is owed, how much interest is owed, the amount of the penalties you claim, an explanation of other damages and the total. The result should look like a simple bill. Don't worry about the court costs; they will be added in later. Also bring a copy of the law, since if you don't need it to file, you'll need it in court.

To successfully bring your action, you need to know the correct name and address of the landlord. (See "The Landlord and the Agents" in chapter 2 and "Who's a What?" in chapter 7 for the proper definitions.) You should succinctly state your case to the clerk or on the complaint form:

> The Landlord (or Mr. Jones) failed to return (part of) my security deposit (and pay me the interest due). I demand payment of [$1,500] for the deposit, (penalties and interest as provided under [local tenants' rights ordinance or state law]) plus court costs and fees.

Send the suit by sheriff if possible since this makes for the positive way of serving a case for money.

Most "people's courts" have booklets that explain how they operate. The schedule for the case will be on the complaint itself or told to you. The landlord will have to acknowledge that it is the same person being sued through what is known as an appearance. This is usually a form and a fee filed with the clerk of the court, but it just may be showing up on the trial date. The landlord may also have the right or can request leave of court (permission) to file a written response (usually a denial of the charges), called an answer to the complaint. These courts do not allow a lot of dillydallying, so you should be able to bring your action to trial in less than three months.

When you go to court, don't be nervous because your life and freedom are not at stake. When you appear to argue your case, talk to the judge, not your opponent. You are not trying to convince the landlord! Tell the judge you want the deposit back, plus whatever else is due to you. Then conduct your case. Show the judge the receipt for the security deposit. Show the judge what communications you received from the landlord regarding the return and when. Show the judge photographs of your old place and receipts for work you performed (if any). (If you use photos, you must have the photographer, the film negative and the processing receipts in court with you.)

If you have any witnesses, ask permission to call them. After the court swears the witness, ask the name and address. Then ask if the witness was present on (the day you moved out) at (your apartment address). Ask the witness to describe the cleanliness, the physical condition and specifically the items the landlord claims as damage. Show your witness the photos and ask for them to be identified and described. You and the witness may have to answer questions from the judge and the landlord.

Then it will be the landlord's turn. The landlord will claim that you trashed the place, left it a filthy disaster and gouged the walls with your furniture on the way out. The landlord may claim damages to carpets, pipes or appliances. There may be witnesses and even photographs. As for the photos, ask when they were taken and who took them. If taken after you turned in the keys, ask about who else had access after you left. Demand to examine the photographer for the when, where and what details. Ask where the film was processed. Ask for a copy of the receipt. If the photographer is not present, ask the judge to disqualify the photos. If the receipt can't be found, ask that the pictures be disqualified because "they could have been taken any time." If the photos are date-stamped, say that anybody can reset the clock and the only real proof is the receipt and matching negative stub. For the witnesses, ask if they are employees of the landlord (lying to save their jobs?) and when they first saw the damages.

Ask the landlord and the witnesses if they *saw* who did the damage. Spend some time with the landlord inquiring about what is considered reasonable wear and tear. Find out how often units are repainted and how often appliances are replaced. Was the equipment in the apartment purchased new or used? How long has the equipment been there? Ask about the age of the carpet (demand a receipt) and when it was last cleaned. Ask about how tenants are supposed to hang pictures and mirrors.

Ask the witness about how long it takes to patch a picture-hook hole, how long it takes to repaint, how long it takes to clean an oven, etc. Ask the witness what his or her hourly pay rate is. Ask how much extra time it took to (fix the damage) than it usually takes to prepare the unit.

If the issue is a vacant apartment or early move-out, ask to see the ads run, the ad receipts, the list of applicants, the approved applicants and whether applicants took other units offered by the landlord instead.

For whatever the landlord says, your task is to prove that he or she didn't see who did it, is showing the wrong pictures, is claiming damages done by somebody else or is claiming damages for which you are not responsible.

If your suit relates to the failure of the landlord to follow the notice procedures of the law (failed to provide notice and receipts within 30 days, etc.), do not talk about conditions or show pictures. Instead, when you present your case, simply say that the landlord failed to follow the law. When the landlord starts to talk, as soon as the landlord claims damages, turn to the court and say, "Objection, your honor. This action is for statutory damages for failure to give required notice. The landlord's claims for damage after the time limit are barred. The landlord's pleading is irrelevant and not responsive." Get the idea? Don't talk about conditions unless you have to—that is, unless the judge allows the landlord to raise this as a defense.

After the landlord has its day, you can give the judge additional information—more testimony in rebuttal. Conclude by handing the judge a photocopy of your local tenants' rights law with the appropriate sections highlighted. Then repeat your request for your money.

The landlord, by the way, in addition to having a lawyer (even if you can't), can demand a jury trial or file a counterclaim for more money. Evaluate the circumstance, and be prepared to go forward by yourself, ask for mediation if available, try to settle or hire a lawyer. Be assured that a majority of these "people's court" cases stay in peoples court.

A word about *affidavits,* sworn written statements, and letters from witnesses who can't come to court. It is not likely that these documents will be accepted by the other side or admitted into evidence by the judge since you can't ask a piece of paper questions. Conduct your case with live witnesses whenever possible.

If you win, you still might have to go to another court to force collection, but all the extra costs, even if you hire an attorney, are usually covered. By the way, make a note of where your landlord deposits your rent checks, since you can usually then identify where it has a bank account. In the collection process, it is much easier if you know the landlord's bank so that you can garnish the account for the amount due if you don't get paid.

Civil Enforcement

For neighbors, our civil fathers have thoughtfully provided nuisance laws (maybe noise or drug abatement laws), which in most jurisdictions allow enforcement through a right of private action. That means that some states allow private citizens to enforce various laws (building and zoning laws in this case) by going to court when the governmental entity does not do the job. This assumes that the police method regarding the neighbor has proven inconclusive. You will probably need a lawyer. In most cases, if successful, the judge will level a fine (paid to the city) against the neighbor, enjoin them from the activity and maybe, (maybe) award you attorney's fees and court costs. You'll have to file another suit for damages. Believe it or not, the civil process can be much more costly, time-consuming and permanent than the police route. For private civil enforcement of drug laws, please see "Drug Dealing."

In some instances, you can bring actions against your landlord for building-code or other violations through your private right of action. For instance, in Illinois any person can sue a landlord to comply with a code violation if that person owns, lives or rents within 1,200 feet of the offending property. When you do this, you have to pay to file the suit, provide your own expert witnesses (for the city or county, the expert is the building inspector), pay for your own attorney (if needed) and provide whatever other evidence or witnesses needed. In the case of Illinois, if you win, you get you costs back but no damages. Your case usually is much better than the city's (they just don't have time to do a good job on every case), and the other side is usually overwhelmed because matters are typically cut-and-dried and you've done your homework. I've done this and have found it to be direct and effective.

You might sue to become a temporary receiver. A *receiver* is something like a guardian. The receiver is told what to do by the court (e.g., fix up the building to code standards, get rid of the drug dealers, make the place safe, get out the bad tenants, get in good tenants, pay the utility bills, maybe even sell the building, etc.). The receiver collects the rents, receives a percentage of the take (10 percent in Cook County, Illinois) as a fee and spends what's left. Neither the landlord nor the bank generally gets a penny.

In addition to taking a case directly to violations court, you may be able to join with the city or county in prosecuting it by becoming a third party intervener. The reasons for this may be you don't trust the city to do a good job, you have information you want to get to the judge, you wish to show how important this matter is to you (and your fellow tenants) or you want somebody in your group to be appointed temporary receiver for the building.

Drug Dealing

This falls into the neighbor-from-hell category. I've had discussions about how to handle these kinds of situations and conclude that this is not something to knock on somebody's door and talk about. Dealing is a mean business, and the folks that do it turn mean or have mean friends, customers and suppliers.

All morality aside, safety and peace are the issues. You should know, and the landlord should know, that the federal government has a gimmick called *civil forfeiture*, which lets the Department of Justice seize the assets of any person knowingly facilitating drug dealing. This is not limited to taking a dealer's car or helicopter. It is also for landlords who rent to dealers! Under section 28 U.S.C. 881, once a landlord knows what is going on and is clearly benefiting, the feds can take the building. Under many state and local laws, the same thing can happen. States also take aggressive civil action against landlords who simply allow dealing to happen even if the landlord is not part of it.

What do you do, as a tenant? Find your community organization and ask if it participates in any antidrug programs. If it does, have it approach your landlord and give him or her the options of getting rid of the dealers or facing a loss of the building. Let your local group contact the local enforcing agency—be that police, DEA or county attorney—if you can provide it with specific and precise information likely to lead to arrests.

Some groups have successfully brought their own nuisance actions in state drug or housing courts. The courts take control away from the landlord and appoint a receiver, often a group member. The building is purged of the dealers, new tenants are screened, the building is physically cleaned up and repaired (as money allows) and conditions generally are safer.

Request that the landlord add an anti-drug-dealing clause to all new leases:

The selling or offering for sale, or the purchase or attempt to acquire illicite drugs, or allowing such activities on the premises is a violation of this Lease. If tenant continues such activities after written notice, the Lease will be terminated immediately and Lessee agrees to vacate premises within five days of termination or as provided by law.

Would you like help with a building-related drug problem? There is an excellent national program that has affiliate grass-roots, not-for-profit groups across the country. National Training and Information Center runs a Bureau of Justice Assistance (U.S. Department of Justice) funded program called Community in Action To Prevent Drug Abuse. To find a community group in your area working against drugs and crime or to receive training to do it yourself, call 312-243-3035 or write to the Antidrug Program, NTIC, 810 North Milwaukee Avenue, Chicago, IL 60622.

10

Eviction

An *eviction* is a process to dispossess you from your rental unit. It starts when you break a rule, don't pay the rent or the lease expires and ends when three burly guys using cheap plastic trash bags dump all your stuff on the sidewalk.

Eviction is something that takes time, because in most places due process of law is required. Eviction is also a "summary" process because landlords long ago convinced the judges and law makers that there wasn't a second to waste once the tenant stopped paying rent. So while most lawsuits can take months or years, an eviction can take days or weeks. Nonetheless, it requires the process of law.

As far as I can tell, a court order *must* be obtained in every state in the country before you can physically be removed. In most places, the sheriff is involved in the physical removal, but in some jurisdictions the landlord can do the job after obtaining the proper papers. This means the landlord cannot just self-help itself to your ouster or lock you out. (See the discussion of lockouts in chapter 7.)

Just because a landlord tells you to leave, you don't necessarily have to go . . . yet. If you believe an eviction is in your future, talk to your local tenants' rights group, legal services organization or an attorney to understand the process. Read on here to ask the right questions or prepare yourself for court.

Notices and Process

Here is how it works, with local variations. The most common example of eviction is for nonpayment of rent. For some reason you fail to pay your rent. You may just not have the money, or you may be repairing and deducting or withholding. State or local laws and your lease take over. If you have waived your rights to notice, you may not know what is happening until the sheriff arrives. Some state laws provide that once the rent is late, the landlord can file for eviction, which is sometimes called *possession*. Some laws have grace periods or notice periods. The landlord might have to give you a three- or five-day notice demanding all the outstanding rent be paid. (See "What's the Difference Between Rents, Fees and Deposits" in chapter 7.) If you comply with the notice, the process stops. In other states you will be given a notice to terminate or a notice to vacate without a grace period to pay the rent. The vacate notices usually give three days to leave.

Once the initial period has expired, the landlord may go through the local court system to get relief, judgment or a rule to show cause. Most states call this a *forcible entry and detainer* action. Big cities have courts called forcible, eviction, landlord's or housing courts that hear these cases. In a few instances, an administrative law court hears the case instead. (Milwaukee, Wisconsin, has such a system.)

Rent grace period	0 to 10 days
Rent notice grace period	0 to 10 days
Lease or rule breach grace period	0 to 10 days
Breach notice grace period	0 to 10 days
Service requirements	None, personal, tack, post, publish
Court date	24 hours to 21 days
Time to appeal	24 hours to 30 days
Time to vacate	24 hours to 21 days

Eviction Timetable

The time it takes for the case to come to court varies by local and state law regarding how the tenant is called into court. The traditional way of serving a lawsuit is via the sheriff. In some cases, notice can be made by "posting" via the mail (usually certified), by posting or tacking the summons to the tenant's or the courthouse door, by publishing the notice in a newspaper or by reading notice of the suit on the courthouse steps. Times also vary between the time the suit is filed, notice is made and the court date is set. In some cases, this can take place in 24 hours. Other jurisdictions can take up to 21 days. Remember, most of these laws are made by the other side, so don't be surprised when "they" say this is all fair.

On the appointed day you should go to court. You might be required to pay an appearance fee or your case may be defaulted (automatically lost). Your landlord can sue for several things: possession of the unit, back rents, court costs and attorney's fees, future rents and other damages. Eviction actions tend to short-circuit most civil procedures. Depending on the state, you may not have a *right* to either a jury trial or even an attorney. If you plan on defending an abatement, you'll need to make your argument germane or relevant to the question of rent

Court: Smith vs. Jones. (Smith, the landlord, or Smith's lawyer and the tenant, Jones, come up to the bench.)

Court's
clerk: Your Honor, this was properly served by (sheriff, posting, advertising, etc.).

Court: Smith, you are suing for $1,000 and possession of the premises. Is that correct?

Smith: Yes, Your Honor.

Court: Smith, did you serve the proper notice?

Smith: Yes, Your Honor. Here is a copy of the notice.

Court: Smith, who did you give it to?

Smith: I (gave it to the tenant, or somebody living there) (tacked it to the door).

Court: What is the money for?

Smith: For back rents for last month, plus late fees (plus, plus, plus).

Court: Jones, did you receive the notice? (only in states where this is required)

Jones: Your Hon—

Court: Did you pay the money?

Jones: I—

Court: The court enters judgment for the landlord in the amount of $1,000 plus the cost of filing this case (plus $150 attorney's fees). You are ordered to pay this money within 30 days and vacate the premises (within 24 hours to 21 days).

Smith: Thank you, Your Honor. (In a not so subtle aside:) Jones, be gone before sundown or else.

Jones: Your Honor, you didn't give me a chance to spea—

Court: Quiet, or I'll hold you in contempt. This case is over. Clerk, call the next case. Bailiff, see that Jones leaves here now and quietly.

Typical Eviction Hearing Transcript!

because the court judges all this very narrowly. Sleepless nights and pain and suffering may not count for much unless you have a tenants' rights law (and a lawyer). As a general rule, you won't be able to get time to discover what evidence your landlord has, a right you have in most other civil cases.

Where I live, the typical tenant has about 60 seconds before the court orders an eviction! As bleak as all this sounds, you can have your full day in court as long as you can speak up to the judge or hire an attorney. The key is to know what rights you have under your local laws, how to go about enforcing them, keep all the needed records and organize things so that your argument is both germane as well as logical. If you have not done so, please read chapter 7.

If your court rules of civil procedure allow for such things, you might request a continuance for a trial on "date certain." You would ask for this so that all your witnesses could be in court. If you know the judges won't allow continuances in eviction cases, you'll have to have all your ducks in a row prior to court. If you are granted a continuance, you may have to pay what is called *use and occupancy* for the period you remain. That means that you will have to pay a daily rent on your unit. Ask the court if it will accept these payments to hold, rather than giving them to the landlord.

There are other reasons for eviction besides nonpayment of rent. These include lease expiration or lease termination for month-to-month tenants and violation of the rules. What is defensible in an eviction action and what is not? I'll assume basic tenants' rights exist for repair and deduct, rent abatement and no retaliation.

When you are accused of not paying the rent and you have good reasons, you have what are called *affirmative defenses,* which means even if it is true that you didn't pay, you have a legal right not to pay. Therefore, you do not owe any (or a portion of the) rent. This type of affirmative defense is invoked with legitimate repair and deduct actions, fair-market rental value reductions or the landlord's material breaches of the lease. Rent withholding is defensible when a serious problem exists and the landlord has failed to fix it. You also have other specific defenses when stated as part of your applicable tenants' rights law.

Suits for termination arise from rule breaking or other lease violations. In many cases, under tenants' rights laws you must be given notice of the breach and a period of time to correct it. You have several defenses for breach. They are as follows:

- It didn't happen.
- You (and anybody you *allowed* on the premises) didn't do it.
- You never received a notice.
- The problem has been corrected.
- The rule is unreasonable or substantially changes your living situation and is unworkable.
- The rule is an attempt of the landlord to evade its duties.
- The rule is retaliatory because of some protected complaint or action of yours.

The landlord usually is suing you for return of the unit, as well as rent. Suits for possession only, in addition to terminating the lease for cause, usually come at the end of the written lease or after receiving a month-to-month termination notice. In most cases, no reason is required to not renew or to terminate. When you have engaged in a protected activity (complaining about the landlord or conditions), however, there is usually a rebuttable presumption that the landlord is retaliating against you. (See "Retaliation" in chapter 7.) You make this affirmative defense by bringing the letters, reports, complaint forms, other documents and witnesses to court. Your landlord has to both (1) disprove your evidence and/or (2) come up with a good other reason to not renew the lease.

I strongly advice you to seek legal counsel before you stay on (hold over), since there may be another tenant in the wings. If you lose, you could end up paying the landlord and the new tenant substantial damages. It might be best, with the advice of your lawyer, to advise the landlord of your intentions in adequate time so that a new tenant is not signed up. If that happens, the landlord will probably be unreasonable, not you. I've seen holdover battles last a long time, just so you know what you may be getting into.

To Lawyer or Not?

If you owe the rent, for sure, for sure, why hire an attorney? Why not appear, listen to the judge, ask for as much time as possible to vacate and talk to the landlord (or lawyer) about a payment schedule. If you owe some rent but less than you are being sued for, bring your receipts. Respectfully but forcefully deny you owe all that the landlord is demanding, and show and explain the receipts (cancelled checks, money orders, whatever).

Do I think that just anybody can defend themselves in eviction court? No. Why? Because of the complexity of court processes—typically called the rules of civil procedures. Then there are the laws, not just landlord-tenant laws, but others that affect what goes on in eviction court. Then you've got a judge who doesn't have time to fool around with the likes of you and a lawyer on the other side who knows how to manipulate the process.

About the time you start claiming tenants' rights, you'd better think about an attorney. I hope you've done your homework: taken the pictures, kept the letters and written notices of complaint, copied the receipts and have the comparable ads (or the original ad for your place). You must follow the rules outlined in your own particular tenants' rights law before you can successfully defend your actions. (See chapter 7.)

When It's Time To Go

Between 80 and 90 percent of eviction cases probably end up in favor the landlord. This means that the tenant is given 1 to 21 days to leave. Sometimes you can get a longer period to leave. This can be done by telling the judge about your many years in the apartment or your children, your parents or your infirmities. You might be able to file for a rehearing (motion to reconsider, motion to vacate a judgment or order, motion to stay a judgment or execution) by going to the appropriate court office (usually called the motions desk) and filing the right set of forms. A lawyer may have to help with this. As a rule, all this will do is prolong the agony, not reverse the outcome.

At this point, you've got three choices: (1) leave, (2) negotiate an informal extension with the landlord (if possible) or (3) wait for the sheriff. When the day comes by which the judge said you had to vacate and you are still in possession, the landlord goes back to court and obtains a writ. This has many, many names, but they all mean the same thing: writ of restitution, writ of possession, writ of execution, writ of rendition, writ of ejectment. The important thing is that such a writ has been obtained. The landlord has to pay somebody to actually do the removal. In some places only the sheriff (or other peace officer) is allowed to serve or execute the writ. In a few jurisdictions the landlord can move you without the law, once the writ is issued. If you interfere with the eviction, you can be arrested for contempt of court, interfering with a law officer or even trespassing. Don't add grief to injury.

If you stay until the mean ol' boys toss you out, be prepared. At the worst, all of your possessions will be roughhoused from the unit to the curb. Where I live, you have 24 hours to remove your possessions or the trash department comes and hauls them off. Where you live, if your stuff sits out on the street 15 minutes, it might be stolen. Develop a strategy to salvage what you can—that is, pack before the sheriff arrives. Let the landlord pay to move your well-packed belongings down and out to the street! Have a truck or trailer ready, and off you go.

As previously mentioned in chapter 7, once the landlord takes one legal remedy, it cannot take another concurrently. Thus, when you are physically evicted, the landlord cannot take your belongings in distrain for rent. (See "Distrain" in chapter 7.) Your landlord must go through the proper court processes to collect its money.

Sometimes eviction is the last stage of a failed attempt to communicate and collaborate on establishing and maintaining a decent living situation. If you've been reading this chapter because you wonder how eviction works, read chapter 9 to see how eviction just might be avoided.

When All Else Fails—Tenants' Unions

If you are reading this chapter, I assume you've got a bad problem. What follows is intended for the desperate and, indeed, the oppressed. If you're just curious about tenants' unions, you don't hurt enough yet. Only those who suffer need proceed. This would be a good time to check your community for tenants' organizations. Call one of them because they can help you all the way. Read this chapter before you do anything. Pretend you are participating in all the action and glory.

Up to this point, the discussion has been basically what you, as an individual, can do about protecting your rights. But what happens when you've done all that you can and problems remain? What happens after all your careful apartment hunting, lease reading, letter writing, repairing and deducting, even mediating? The battles are tough ones. Alone, the tasks can be overwhelming. If we stand alone, we're out in the cold. We will lose and the landlord will win.

This whole exercise has got to be worth more than the trouble it is causing, and God knows, there's enough trouble to go around. You start on this path because you aren't getting your money's worth and are placed in physical jeopardy as a result of conditions in and around your apartment. You are either ignored or pushed around by your landlord. By now you want to fix what's broken and make sure you don't have to go through this again. Therefore—the tenants' union.

Goals

Your goals in joining a tenants' union are union recognition, a collective rights agreement, repairs, maintenance, fair rents, security-deposit interest and refunds, heat, smoke detectors, security devices, follow-up on your landlord's promises to individual tenants and prevention of retaliatory actions against union members. All of these are tenants' rights given or protected under various local ordinances and state laws. Unless you pursue them, you can't have them.

You will affirmatively and forcefully represent the tenants of the building to the landlord, the city inspectors, the courts and the public. In addition to using the power of people involved—through picketing, petitioning and publicity—the tenants' association also has the power of money (big money).

You Don't Have To Suffer or Fight Alone

The best kind of help for a tenant is the combined help of many tenants. Organizing gives us the strength and mutual support needed to overcome the obstacles, buoy our spirits and stick it out. Organizing pits the wills of all the tenants in a particular building against the limited powers of the management: singly, we are discrete particles and the landlord is a hammer, smashing us to powder. As a unified, collective structure, we become as sintered metal—fused together and harder than hell to crack.

Tenants' Unions Are Legal

There is no particular case law prohibiting tenants unions. They are, in the first place, protected under the federal Bill of Rights, Article I, as citizens' rights to free speech and assembly. Most tenants' rights laws implicitly or explicitly acknowledge and permit union activities. Legally, any group can organize for any lawful purpose. Such an organization can even register with your county or state as an official, legally constituted group (discussed later in this chapter).

The idea is that where one person cannot succeed, a group can. No more little lies, broken promises or threats. All the tenants know what the landlord is saying and doing. Nobody has to feel like a fool or be fearful of reprisals. There is comfort in the strength of a unified membership.

The Basics

A successful tenants' group needs several elements. It needs the dedication of a few people who can keep the spark alive when the going gets tough. It needs good organization, bylaws and a hardworking group of officers. It needs to draw upon the experience of other tenant groups. (There is no sense in reinventing the wheel in every six-flat and high rise in the city.) Most importantly, it needs to have clear-cut goals. There must be strong reasons for formation, and these cannot later be lost or set aside.

Meetings

Meetings must be open to all residents and closed to all management employees. They need to be somewhat regular between crises and frequent during crises. The membership should be kept informed of what is happening via newsletters and posters. An *esprit* needs to be generated and fostered.

Strength Through Unity

Tenants are afraid to organize because they believe the landlord will get them. This fear has always existed. In the past, the landlord was able to focus all his or her resources on a particular tenant, isolating and bullying the tenant. Since tenants' rights were minuscule and not well known, the landlord could impose itself. The effect was obvious and overwhelming. One tenant could not resist—he or she either shut up or was forced out. An effective tenants' union prevents this from happening. The union informs all tenants of their rights, protections and powers. The landlord can no longer deal with only one tenant at a time—thus, no more divide and conquer. The landlord must face all of its "customers."

You don't need hundreds of people to operate a successful tenants' union. All it takes is participation and dedication. My successful union had 6 units and 15 persons (100 percent adult membership). The only rule is the smaller the union, the higher the percentage of tenants as members.

And what is the "magic" that protects the tenants? It is the unity of all the tenants supporting each other through collective action. It is also the tenants' rights laws. The ultimate, most powerful, fearful and successful action is the strike. Rent strikes, repair-and-deduct strikes and rent-reduction strikes are all mutinies of the bankbook!

Tenant Power

It should be clearly understood and accepted that a tenants' organization is stronger than most landlords. Tenants have the power to put landlords out of business—and very quickly. Landlords know this. They played a game of bully and bluff for a long time. But now, with the combination of tenants' rights laws and tenants' unions, we can enforce building codes and lease provisions by controlling the amount and flow of the rents. And we can even break leases and empty buildings. So, as far as landlords are concerned, the jig is up. Just look at the facts.

Money

The rents paid by the tenants in your building every month add up to big bucks. Reductions or denial of rents are legal. Lease breakings are legal. Tenants' organizations are sanctioned. Figure out how many occupied units there are in your building and multiply by the average rent. If there are 24 apartments and each pays on average $500 rent, that's $12,000 per month. Between the mortgage, insurance, property taxes, scavenger and utilities (not to mention staff), your landlord needs most of that money to keep from going broke. Let's say your tenants' association organizes a repair-and-deduct campaign, and each unit withholds $200 the first month. There's a $4,800 hole in the rents. How's the landlord going to make the mortgage and pay its staff? The next month, a claim of reduced fair market value is asserted, and another $2,400 is held back. What does the landlord tell the people he or she still owes? The month after that, there is more of the same. What explanation will the bank accept?

The Law

The landlord has a right to its fair rents and may decide to go into eviction court. This will take time and money. Because the wheels grind slowly, and because you will have an association attorney, it will be well into the next rent period before your cases come into court. You all have legitimate claims, and you have done all the right things, so you've got winning cases. And if the landlord still refuses to clean up its act, you could empty the building *en masse*. One way or the other, you can get your landlord's cooperative attention, or you can persuade the landlord to get into another line of business: it's the landlord's choice.

If you are dealing with a small operator, you can split your costs among you, while the landlord must bear his or her costs alone, plus suffer the loss of income.

Time and Aggravation

Even if the landlord does succeed in evicting individual rent withholders, it will have to spend months trying to collect the back rents (if they are awarded). The landlord will end up hiring a collection lawyer or service and will pay it 25 percent of the rents collected. It can't really afford this, since the building is mostly empty.

Pressure

Remember, if the landlord empties the building, it will take many months to rerent. By the time he or she gets to this, the payments may be four or six months behind. The landlord is better off settling.

Unity

Since with tenants' rights it is illegal to retaliate against a tenant for legitimate acts of complaining, rent withholding or joining a tenants' union, if the landlord picks on one or two tenants, the whole union can bring pressure on the landlord. It can also assist in filing the necessary lawsuits against the landlord. Tenants who win get money, plus the costs of suing.

Are you convinced? You have the power: people, law, money. A tenants' union is the ultimate weapon. The courts will take notice of what you are doing, and as more tenants organize in their own defense across the country, you will have victory at the mere mention of a union. Your landlord knows what I am talking about. Do not be afraid.

Total Organization

This is where we have been heading—organization. Joined together, we are very strong. With organization we can make ourselves heard and felt. We can deal with the landlords, the city and the courts. We can protect our rights and redress the wrongs.

Landlords want to deal only with one tenant at a time. That way they can bully us and make promises: what happens is between just a few people. If a landlord doesn't keep its promises to one tenant, what can that tenant really do? Go it alone against a stubborn or lying landlord? How do you prove that a deal was even made? How many months do you want to repeatedly repair and deduct to get things right, only to find that you can't get a new lease? Do you really want to move out, or do you just want to get something fixed that will make the place livable? If the landlord keeps the security deposit or doesn't pay the interest, it might get away with this, as long as each tenant is isolated from one another. Let one pip make a squeak, and the landlord can use the rents of all to go after the one. As long as the landlord can keep each of us separated from our fellow tenants, he or she has all the power and we have very little.

When we organize, we are at par with the landlord. One person complaining is a small voice in the void; but all the tenants, speaking in union, are a mighty shout. A tenants' organization is real democracy in action. It uses the politics of the street, the power of the people. In defending our tenant rights, the tenants' union is the first step. Organization must come before the courts, before the lawyers and before complaints to the city.

The Power of the Union

A tenants' group can pool the resources of its membership. It can hire a good lawyer and bring pressure on the city to keep the landlord straight. It can make a strong impression on the judge when its membership is present in court. The union can meet *en masse* with the landlord and pressure it into action. The union has many eyes, ears and hands. It can keep track of the landlord. A tenants' group can wield the ultimate weapon: the rents. A tenants' association holding the rents has an unprecedented amount of power over the landlord.

When and How To Organize

The first step in organizing a tenants' union is to decide if there is a need for one. Are there general building problems, or is the landlord giving you, personally, a hard time? In any case, you can assume the need for a union exists. Landlords do not single out particular tenants. If they are nasty to one, they'll be nasty to all, given the opportunity.

Does Your Building Need a Union?

Is your building clean? Are the halls well lit? How about the hot water, heat, water pressure, security system, front and rear door locks and smoke detectors? Do you have fire extinguishers, screens and storm windows? Are there major promises made by the landlord but not kept? Do your repair-and-deduct letters go unheeded? When something goes wrong, does it get fixed right away? Are the rents being raised out of sight? Analyze your own situation. Go through your apartment and take an inventory of physical conditions. Look at your lease and evaluate some of the add-on clauses. Think about the conditions of the building.

If you come up with a list of problems, you can bet everybody else can make a similar list. Are the conditions bad enough to merit a tenants' union? Well, that depends. Rent raises are one good reason to organize. The landlord sits in its office and squeezes the bank accounts of hundreds of families, but what is the landlord giving the tenants in return for high rents? We deserve what we are paying for. If conditions are not up to snuff, if rents are too high or if the landlord harasses us, we need a tenants' union.

Focus the Initial Effort

The immediate reasons for organizing vary. Some of these reasons are as follows: the loss of heat or hot water; a policy of not returning security deposits or paying interest; not delivering on pre-move-in promises for appliances or decorating; run-down conditions; failure to repair and maintain the building, plumbing or electricity; capricious evictions. You get the idea!

The First Steps

If you think you have the necessary ammunition, start the process. Go to as many occupants in your building as you can. Knock on each door and ask if you can speak to the tenant about building conditions (or the rent raise, the poor heat or whatever). Tell the tenant you are upset about this or that and ask if he or she would like to get together with some of the other residents in the building to talk about the problem or any other problems they might have. Mention a preset time and place (your apartment, early evening, during the week). If your building is too large to see everyone, select people on each floor or section. Later, those who attend the first meeting can help recruit others living near them. You will need 10 to 15 residents to have a good foundation to kick off your organization. In small buildings you need all the tenants. It is possible to organize a six- or eight-flat union. I have done it and it works.

If your apartment will hold all the people you recruit, good. If you get an overflow crowd, meet in the lobby or common area. If your building has meeting rooms, reserve or occupy one. During the summer, meet outside on the front steps or in the courtyard. This way you will also get the attention of others you have not contacted. If the management sees what is going on, that's just fine. This is only the start of the psychological warfare that will exist until everybody understands the reasons and purpose of your association.

No Management Employees

If there are employees of the management present at your meeting, invite them to leave. This is your meeting, not your landlord's. As a matter of common sense, your association should not have any employees of the building as members— no janitors, part-timers or superintendents. The reasons are threefold: (1) being a union member might jeopardize their jobs, (2) being an employee and a member is a conflict of interest that may result in attempts to deflect the goals of the group and (3) being an employee could very well mean being a management spy!

First Meeting

The first meeting is a very informal discussion group. You, as organizer, can speak first. Introduce yourself and explain why you have called the meeting: to discuss the common problems of tenants in the building. Tell the group that if enough interest exists, you would like to form a tenants' association. It would be very helpful if you invited an organizer from a tenants' organization. He or she could work with you before the meeting, address the assembly and answer the many questions the tenants will have.

After the *briefest* discussion about organizing, tell your story (how long you've been in the building, what problems you have and what you were promised). Tell your neighbors how management has treated you. Tell them what your rent is and how long your lease runs. Let them know how you feel about the situation—e.g., how angry and frustrated you are. Ask everybody else to introduce themselves and tell their stories. If there is a special crisis, compare notes on that crisis, but also find out what else is going on. You will be amazed to hear similar stories from most of the tenants—complaints about roaches, bad plumbing, flaking paint, unkept promises and rent hikes rising like yeast bread in the oven. If most people agree that something must be done, *organize!*

The Organizational Committee

The next step is to set up an organizational committee to draw up a simple set of rules, select a temporary chair and secretary for the next meeting, contact everybody in the building to come to the next meeting and propose a few alternatives for organization names. The reason for the committee is to get a group of people involved. This helps share the burden of work and distributes the enthusiasm. Your organization must not be run from the top by a few leaders. It needs grass-roots participation and sharing of the leadership roles. This is very, very important.

Feeding the Kitty

At this first meeting, you should collect a few dollars from each person to cover the initial expenses of organizing. Money will be needed for printing or photocopying meeting notices, duplicating the bylaws or making a pamphlet or brochure outlining what problems exist or explaining about a tenants' union. Later you will need to collect dues on a regular basis.

Time Is of the Essence

The organizational committee should meet as soon as possible. The committee shouldn't be larger than seven people; but if you have more talent, divide the committee into sections to use the surplus help. One section should be responsible for rules and the union name; the other, for publicity and contacting the entire building. In a very small building, perhaps fewer folks can work up the bylaws and do the publicity. By taking care of these procedural goals at the beginning, you free your tenants' meetings for discussion of the major goals: problems and actions.

Second Meeting

Call the second general meeting as quickly as possible. Have teams go from door to door in the building. Give residents a meeting notice and tell them that (a given number of) people have gotten together to form a tenants' association. Invite everyone to come to the meeting, air grievances and join. Keep going back until everybody is personally contacted. If your management tries to stop this meeting, ignore them. Meet wherever you must or can. It is your constitutional right to have a meeting. Interfering with your tenants' rights activities may also be a violation of your local tenants' rights laws.

Set the Priorities

At the second meeting, explain to the newcomers what is going on. The chair should lead the discussion. Set priorities. Find out what general things need to be done: stop the rent increases, get maintenance for the building, get the heat working, fix the elevator, etc., and do it soon. Draw up a list of emergency demands. Appoint a negotiating committee of three people to contact the management to ask what they are going to do about the emergency problems. You could call the negotiating committee the *demands committee*. The committee's job is to get as much as is practicable from management. Its task is to force issues when required and make things as easy as possible for management to give up what the tenants need. Yes, dealing may be part of the process, but using the word "negotiate" does not mean giving away your needs or demands. (See chapter 9.)

Housing Survey

It is also a good idea to distribute an apartment conditions survey. (See Appendix F.) This survey will help each tenant make a list of problems in his or her apartment. The group should appoint a housing committee to prepare a report. This report will be shown to the building inspector, the housing court judge and your lawyer if you have to go to court. This report will obviously be the basis of your demands to the landlord.

Elections—Getting to Work

At this second meeting, you should elect a permanent chair, secretary and treasurer. These people can serve for several months, but do not determine length of tenure in advance. You may need to replace someone early or try to have them stay on longer. A board of directors can also be chosen. These directors represent the group as a whole and oversee the executive officers. This helps keep a balance of power away from some elite leadership. Choose a name and hear what else the organizing committee has to report. Dues should again be collected. The amount of dues depends upon how many people join the group and what your anticipated expenses are to be. Make a list of who joins and how much they pay. Later, the permanent treasurer will open a set of books and issue dues receipts and membership cards. If you are going to hire a lawyer, the retainer will be at least $500 to $1,000, so start saving money. Have the membership authorize the officers and directors to make plans and take actions as needed.

Floor or Section Captains

The key to a successful union is keeping the troops well informed and rallied. Now is the time to select people to take responsibility for a whole floor, entrance-way or some other manageable section of the building or complex. This spreads the work among many people and also keeps contacts on a person-to-person basis. For fast communications, this setup also works as a phone tree, where a few phone calls from the union leadership can branch out to the entire membership quickly. With a phone tree, any one person only makes a few phone calls, but these are to specified people who then make phone calls, and those folks then make phone calls. The calls start at the "trunk" of the tree and branch out. The floor captains can take the housing survey around, recruit new members, pass out notices and collect information regarding what the landlord is up to, giving member tenants direct access to the union. Floor captains are the backbone of the union. Do we have any volunteers?

Negotiating Conditions

Your negotiating committee must meet only with someone from management who has the authority to make decisions and carry out actions. This will be either the owner or the "downtown" office manager. Occasionally, this will be the resident manager. A tiny management company or a secretary fronting for the owner is not good enough. If you are presented with an attorney to represent management, ask the attorney to specify, in writing, that he or she is authorized to make decisions and order work and changes to take place, and ask who gave such authorization. If the lawyer is only a decoy, refuse to deal with him or her, since this is an obvious attempt to delay or sidetrack negotiations.

You should appreciate the politics of this approach. The local manager will be both put off and threatened because his or her authority and management skills are being challenged, and you are short-circuiting the customary flow of command. You are doing this because the local manager (or management company) has failed to do the required job—namely, keeping the customers happy and dealing with the problems or crisis. "Downtown" will not be happy because the local manager is supposed to handle these things (but obviously has not). Nonetheless, everybody will try to palm the problem off on someone else and cover his or her own behind, while attempting to ignore you. While this is frustrating, if you don't deal with the real authority, you'll get no enforceable promises and maybe nothing but delays without action.

Incorporating Your Union

If you are going to open a bank account or collect more than pennies for your activities, incorporation of your group is a necessity. The total cost of incorporating under the not-for-profit laws of most states is small. Obtain a copy of the not-for-profit act, the instructions for organizing not-for-profit corporations and the forms from your secretary of state's office. As a rule, these forms are self-explanatory and easy to fill out. Please see Appendix G for a sample tenants' union charter and bylaws, and refer to the sections entitled "Purpose" and "Other Provisions," which you should study when filling out your state's articles of incorporation. Should you have any questions, consult a tenants' organization for referral to the many free legal and accounting programs designed to assist not-for-profit groups.

Request a Form SS-4 from the Internal Revenue Service, 1-800-829-3676. This gets your FEIN or federal employer identification number. Even though you have no employees, you must submit this form to get the number to open a bank account. As soon as you get your corporation charter, you can submit Form SS-4.

Your Union and Taxes

Although your union is not-for-profit, it is, alas, not tax-exempt. The IRS specifically excludes tenants' unions under 501(c)(4), "Civic Leagues and Social Welfare Organizations." The government states that ". . . an organization formed to represent member-tenants of an apartment complex does not qualify, since its activities benefit the member-tenants and not all tenants in the community." Does this mean you must pay taxes on the activities of the union? Probably not. As long as you do not operate a business, you should not have to be concerned. If you wish, you could file an IRS Schedule 1120A, after consulting with a CPA. Regardless, you must keep good accounting books.

The Corporate Advantage

The advantage of official registration is to force the management company to accept your organization's existence when it comes to negotiating and signing agreements. If you incorporate, you may also protect yourself personally from a counterclaim or lawsuit.

Bank Accounts

No matter how you register, you will need to open several bank accounts. A checking account is needed for your operating funds: dues, contributions, bake-sale receipts, special collections. From this account you will pay your bills. Another account is an interest-bearing account to hold rent monies. Into this account can go regular monthly rents (more about this later) and withheld rents. Out of it comes rents paid to the landlord and funds paid out to firms and suppliers whom the group has hired to make repairs to keep the building safe, as well as repairs under repair-and-deduct actions. You are also advised not to reveal the location of your rent-holding account to your landlord. If you are collecting rents and depositing them to an account, you should have two separate banks, just to protect the location of the other.

The Functioning Union

The duties of the officers should be made part of the bylaws. (See the example in Appendix G.) Before the third meeting, each officer should do some homework.

Chair

The chair should call meetings of the executive committee and the board of directors to coordinate the work of recruiting members and publicizing the association. He or she should keep track of the housing committee and their survey and report. The chair will want to keep in touch with other tenants' groups, community organizations and advisors. It would also be a good idea to shop around for a lawyer, too. Perhaps an attorney should be invited to the third meeting.

Secretary

The secretary will be busy getting papers from the state or the county. He or she will also prepare a report for the tenants, which contains the bylaws and any communications to and from the landlord, to be distributed at the third meeting. The secretary's research assignment will take him or her to a title search company or to the county recorder's office to search out ownership information on the property. The records will show who pays the property tax bills, who owns the property, the purchase price of the building and whether there have been judgments or liens placed against the property. If the building is a federal section 8 building or a building funded under D-221 or D-236 federal financing, the secretary may have to contact the nearest Department of Housing and Urban Development (HUD) office.

Treasurer

The treasurer will affiliate with several banks, get the necessary papers and endorsement cards filled out and signed, obtain bankbooks and checks and establish a set of accounting books. A simple computer bookkeeping program might be a great time-saver. The treasurer may shop around for an accountant who will donate services to bless the books. The treasurer will purchase money receipt books for each of the accounts and get membership cards printed.

Keep this in mind regarding bank account access: normally, you should require two signatures to draw out of the operating account and three to draw out of the rent-holding account. I suggest you nominate the executive officers and the chair and vice chair of the board as authorized signatories. That way, there will always be someone to sign checks, but no one can raid the kitty.

The Third Meeting

The real work of the tenants' group will start with the third meeting. The treasurer will have money in the bank. The housing committee will have a report on the general conditions of the building. The secretary should have received the incorporation application from the state and a complete report on building ownership and financing. If my guess is correct, the negotiating committee will report that not much was accomplished.

Notice to the Landlord

Now is the time for action. Draw up a formal list of complaints, requests and demands. The list should be in the form of a letter to the landlord. The letter should list emergency repairs, general repairs, lease changes, grievances, a recognition request for the association, a no-retaliation warning and a collective-bargaining rights request. Under repairs, each apartment should be listed, detailing specific problems (i.e., what in which room needs what). The same is true for the general building: be very specific.

As per your tenants' rights laws, (section by section) tell the landlord what you will do and when if your demands are not met according to law. You should request an immediate written response from the landlord that states the completion dates for each entry on the list. You should also request a meeting for the purpose of negotiating your collective bargaining agreement.

Keep in mind that with tenants' rights laws, the landlord has specific time requirements. If letters were previously sent by individual tenants, the statutory time limits for compliance may have expired. The negotiating committee is in a position of making a deal with the landlord to give it more time or compromise on the degree of work to be performed, provided there is cooperation. The bottom line is that the committee, if ignored, can recommend to the whole union that rents be withheld on the basis of the law or even under a breach of the implied warranty of habitability. More dalliance on the part of the management can find the negotiating committee turning the matter over to the union attorney for legal action.

Details, Details

The type of organizing done so far, and the work involved, may seemed detailed, but you are fighting a tough battle. You must start from a firm basis, and you must be strong. You have to be legally solid, and you must receive the support of the tenants. You've got to know the facts. When your association can demonstrate that it has the ability and the guts to fight for what is right, you will reinforce the attitudes of the membership and be able to recruit more people into the group. Remember, you are in for the long run, and early preparation is important.

Second Negotiating Meeting

Your letter has been received by management. If you do not have a written response within a reasonable amount of time, contact your landlord by phone and set up your next negotiations meeting. You'll offer the landlord a letter of agreement regarding repairs, rent adjustments and the rest of your demands as contained in your previous letter. You will also present a collective bargaining agreement. (See Appendix H.)

Call a general membership meeting as soon as possible after your contact with the landlord. You will either report on your progress or the unresponsiveness of the management. If there is progress (yea and hurray), keep at it. If not, now is the time to call the mass meeting between the landlord and the tenants. Notify the landlord. Set the time and place. This meeting can take place anywhere except the landlord's office.

The letter can be signed by the officers and can contain a list of names of your membership. The letter should also be signed by each tenant whose apartment is listed as needing work. The secretary should prepare the letter and have the board of directors approve it, before it is signed by the tenants and transmitted. A copy of the letter should be sent to each tenant in the building.

If you have some really nasty problems, also invite a representative from the local city housing and legal departments, representatives from other tenants' and community groups and the press, if appropriate.

Showdown #1

The landlord will usually want to calm things down and so appear to spread some sensibility among its customers. It will also want to get a handle on the relative strength and commitment of the tenants. You, of course, will be delighted to get a chance to get your problems solved. These meetings demonstrate to the landlord that the tenants are both unhappy and mean business. The general consensus is that tenants feel a lot of solidarity when such a meeting is held. They get to gripe at the landlord and put it on the spot. However, do not make a revolutionary speech while introducing the landlord. Be courteous. Thank him or her for coming and remind the landlord that the tenants have already stated what is needed, through letters and the negotiation committee. Then ask when the tenants can expect action. Let the landlord speak.

Your landlord will sink or swim on its own words. Landlords seldom deliver on their promises at such meetings, unless a signed agreement is made during the meeting. You already have most of the necessary documents: the letter of demands sent to the landlord, your membership list and your collective bargaining agreement. Just attach a cover letter to the demands and membership lists which says something like the following:

> XYZ Management Company hereby recognizes Tenants' Association as the legitimate representative of its membership as contained on the attached list of members. XYZ Management Company agrees to make the repairs and correct deficiencies noted in the attached letter(s) (list)(s) and satisfactorily complete all such work by (date certain) . Tenants' Association agrees to pay to XYZ Management Company all withheld rent monies it holds for tenant members deposited with it upon completion of such work, provided work is completed on or before the above date. Should work not be satisfactorily completed by the above date, XYZ Management Company agrees to reduce all rents of all affected tenants by [25 percent] effective from the date of original notification of defects, and will continue the decrease until such time as all work is satisfactorily completed. Signed (Landlord) (Date) and (Tenants' Association President) (Date) .

You could also present your landlord with the collective bargaining agreement. By signing the bargaining agreement, you formalize a cooperative method of solving problems. It is a good deal for both sides.

Sometimes you can't get a landlord to meet with you. This may be because it doesn't want to cooperate or can't be found or is advised by a lawyer to stay away. Don't worry: hold a public meeting anywhere. Invite all the tenants, notify the press and request that community leaders and the area politicians attend. Make your case to them and appeal for assistance. A meeting like this is quite embarrassing to the landlord and usually brings more pressure directly from other tenants and the city, plus it alerts the landlord's banks and creditors. Your need is to find solutions, and if the landlord runs away or drags its feet, the public exposure is well merited.

Other Methods of Resolution

If the landlord fails to come to the meeting or refuses to sign, there are other methods, short of a lawsuit, that can encourage cooperation and seek a solution. For one, you can contact your community mediation center, which is set up to deal with this very type of problem, and try to arrange a voluntary dispute dialogue. (See "Mediation" in chapter 9.)

Taking to the Streets

Should the landlord prove recalcitrant, there are effective ways of getting its attention and setting things right. Don't poke the tiger until you have no other way of getting its attention. These all come from the Community Action Program

(CAP)/Saul Alinsky school of communications. In the first place, you can establish a permanent picket line in front of your building. It is perfectly legal. Make up your picket signs and go march. Just stay on the sidewalk, and don't block traffic along the sidewalk, street or in and out of the building. You can pass out literature, but you are responsible for littering, so be sure and collect any pamphlets people discard. You can sing or chant slogans as long as this does not disturb the neighbors. If the police come, be quiet, march in single file on the sidewalk and smile. You will not be arrested if you are orderly, peaceful and obey the law. One person should deal with the police. You generally do not need a permit, but you might want to check with your local city hall or police department.

The picket signs should contain only true statements of fact. If you are timid, just say "ABC Tenants' Union on strike against 1234 Building and XYZ Management Company (or Joe Blow, Landlord [Owner])." If you want to be bolder, specify some of your demands (i.e., "remove cockroaches" or "fix heat" or "stop leaks"). Bolder yet, list your complaints: "Our XYZ Management Company Building has roaches (mice, rats); XYZ Management Company will not negotiate with our tenants' union; XYZ Tower mistreats tenants; Our landlord (name or company) permits building code violations to exist in the building; We have no heat." These statements are not libelous because they contain the truth. If you are concerned about content, check with your association lawyer. Do not call the landlord a slumlord or an SOB (unless that means "servant of bankers").

If the landlord won't come to you, go directly to the landlord. Find out where he or she lives, and visit the neighborhood on a Saturday morning when the neighbors can see what is going on. The Supreme Court allows picketing of solely the landlord's house when there is no local ordinance forbidding it. The court holds that you cannot force a person to listen to something he or she chooses not to hear. Where such an ordinance exists, you can still picket the entire neighborhood since you are directing your free speech expression generally. Leaflet the landlord's neighbors or simply knock on their doors, telling them why you are in the area and asking them to convey your message to their neighbor, your landlord. Tell them what conditions are like where you live. Explain to the neighbors that your landlord isn't fixing things. Do not slander the person; just tell the truth. Try the same thing at your landlord's place of worship, just after services let out. Go to his or her club—or even grocery store. The landlord may call the cops or run to court; but as long as you are peaceful and not breaking a law, the police should leave you alone. If the courts stop you, you've already made your point. Remember, always tell the truth.

Calling in the Heavy Guns

Are we talking yet? Are we solving the problems? Are we having fun? If not, onward!

You must contact the appropriate governmental agencies. Call your complaints to your mayor's office, the alderman's/councilman's/selectman's office and the proper city department. Does the county attorney have a criminal housing management act office? If HUD or the local housing authority are involved, call these agencies. Call the company insuring the building and report safety, liability or building-code problems. In all cases, write a letter detailing your problem and asking for help. Always, always send a copy of your complaint to your state's department of professional regulations, real estate division (whatever agency licenses real estate brokers and landlords), along with a cover letter asking them to investigate the fitness of the landlord to hold a real estate license. As always, speak the truth. Do not call the landlord names and don't lie or exaggerate. You already know your rights and what the laws cover. The landlord will not like or want the visit of the inspectors, the licensing agency or law enforcement investigators.

The Government Agency Shuffle

Do not let an individual who does not know what you are talking about send you on a wild goose chase. Always cite the relevant law by its number. Make sure you are understood. I am continually appalled by the lack of comprehension of some of the people who answer the phone. These agencies practice the "resolution by attrition" principal: they put you off until you give up in frustration. If worse comes to worst, demand to speak to a supervisor.

Press Liaison?

Of course, everybody wants to call the local muckraking newspaper or broadcast journalist. If your landlord is socially prominent, do it. But for the most part, until people get maimed or mass arrests are made, don't request press coverage. All along the way, you can keep the newspapers and broadcast news folks informed. You can fill in the assignment editors or reporters, as background, about what is going on, but don't try to pull the press around on a string. "Using" the press is abusing a precious resource. Keep the pressure directly on the landlord. The press is not your errand boy. When the time comes, it will be obvious, and you will get all the coverage you need.

A "Reflective" Moment

A word about organizing and picketing . . . Keep in mind that you are engaged in a battle. You want something, and your landlord does not want to give it to you. You attempt to pry it lose. After you ask "pretty please," you organize. You take off your velvet glove and pick up your hammer. The landlord also picks up its shield. When you organize, your landlord ignores the group or denies it exists. So you take up actions: picketing, pamphleting, publicity. Your landlord is now publicly exposed. Its necessary strategy is to counter you. Some landlords try reverse publicity, such as bonuses to tenants to leave the union. They sometimes try lockouts or sending punks around to knock heads and collect rents. When you smell a rat, call the cops or your lawyer. They used to evict trouble makers, but this is now illegal and will lead to petty and protracted legal actions. Defeating retaliatory eviction is fairly cut-and-dried. (See chapter 10.)

Guard Against Suable Errors

In this litigious society, we can expect a landlord to try something expensive, outrageous, without merit and in the long run, not likely to succeed. It might try to get the police to arrest picketers. The charges will range from unlawful assembly to trespass, harassment, breach of the peace, threats or physical assault to persons or property. The landlord might sue for something like tortious interference with a contract (actively trying to stop potential tenants from signing a lease) or interfering with a contractor or supplier or some sort of defamation of character (slander—spoken defamation—or libel—written defamation). The landlord will occasionally throw in some sort of property damage claim or claim of damages for personal harassment.

To get ahead, sometimes you have to take risks. Getting sued is a risk that you'll have to calculate. Well, the landlord does have rights, but so do you. Watch your step. Check your moves with your lawyer. Be prepared for such responses; they are the act of defiant stubbornness and obfuscation. That you will countersue with your complaints and damages is without question. That you have adequate affirmative defenses for what you have said is undeniable (as long as you didn't use terms that contain George Carlin's seven nasty words in reference to the landlord).

At the bottom, such actions are pieces for negotiation. You can withdraw your complaint to take away your landlord's license when it gets the repairs finished or drop your suit when the landlord drops its suit, and so forth.

Other Strategies

Rent Collection

Become a funnel for the rents of your membership. Rent collection is tricky, so be ready to consult your lawyer. You start by collecting the cash, checks and money orders intended for the landlord's rent. Your treasurer must issue a receipt as each member turns over the rent to the association. Tenant checks are to be made out normally, that is, to the landlord. All you are doing is proving your power to control the rents and your strength as an organization. When the treasurer or negotiating committee meets with the landlord to tender payment, a receipt for each tenant's rent is required. You can prepare a payment list that the landlord can sign as a receipt.

Rent Withholding

If the landlord still is uncooperative even after you have proven your association's power to collect the rents, you will have to plan for rent reductions, repair and deduct actions and under extreme circumstances, out-and-out rent withholding. Rent money that is held back will now be paid directly to the union, which will deposit it in that second, well-hidden bank account.

Make sure all participating tenants are current with their rents. Under most late rent notice procedures, if you don't pay all the rent demanded but only part, the landlord can still evict. A member who is under a previous notice, or who just owes money, can pull down everyone when it comes time to pay the landlord, depending on how the rent money is credited to which tenants. This is true because the landlord is allowed to apply the monies received to the first monies owed, so maybe it decides to credit Joe Blow for previously late rent. Defending Joe Blow from eviction could prove to be a discouraging sidetrack. Be forewarned and make everybody come clean on this issue.

It is imperative in any rent-withholding action that the money be collected and set aside. It is not good enough that everyone simply withholds the rent money. There are two important reasons. In the first place, if the tenants' association actually has control over the funds, the members know that they have real power and are accomplishing something important. The association can demonstrate power over the landlord, and the association also knows who is supporting the action and who is not. The second reason to make sure the money is actually collected is that eventually it will have to be paid to somebody. There are the contractors who do the work, for instance. The association may be ordered by the court to pay a receiver. There may be an order to pay part or all of the back rents to the landlord or the landlord's creditors to keep the building open, lit, heated or watered. If the association appears in court and cannot produce the rent monies, its whole case could be lost. The biggest crises of rent-withholding actions come when everybody is supposed to come up with four months of back rents and all those people, instead of socking it away or paying the union, spent it! You do not need that kind of publicity and that kind of defeat. Please, collect the rents and keep them safe until they are needed.

Paying the Landlord

To start with, just hand over the cash, checks and money orders made out to the landlord and given the union by the members. If the union is depositing the money and making payment for the membership, the landlord is obligated to take the tenant association money for payment. It cannot refuse because of the source of the money, since anyone can pay rent for anyone else. You could give the landlord cash; that has certain security drawbacks for you, but cash is always king. Presenting a cashier's or certified check automatically guarantees that the money is available; that is the purpose of these instruments. Don't make out third-party checks. If the landlord refuses the rents on same phoney basis (e.g., "We only take money directly from our tenants."), say that its refusal removes any further obligation from people attempting to pay rent for that month.

You Must Have Witnesses

Always present the money by committee; three persons are best since that makes two witnesses plus the presenter to testify as to the landlord's acceptance or refusal. Always present the rents when they are due, before the commencement of any late charges and before a late rent notice can legally be issued.

Even if the rents are refused, be prepared to offer them again if notices are sent. However, insist that the landlord waive late charges and accept the rents as paid in full and state in writing on each receipt "rent paid-in-full for (month)," thus terminating the legitimacy of the notices and stopping the landlord from attempting to evict on the basis of a small late-fee balance.

Cautions and Consultations

If you are actually depositing rents directly and issuing payments, be sure there are sufficient funds in the union account to cover your check if one of your member's checks bounces. Your landlord may come back to all of you with eviction notices—be prepared. It is not the purpose of the association to pay for people who cannot pay their rents, and this is an unfair burden on the group and can destroy it. Please explain this to your membership. Keep in mind that most rent actions will not relieve people from paying rent. They only postpone payment of rent, divert money to repairs or reduce rent by a moderate amount.

Tightening the Financial Rope around the Landlord's Neck

What other work can or should your association do? The primary task is finding out as much about your landlord and its operation as possible. What other buildings does the landlord own or manage? Do an estimate of the landlord's rent collections. Calculate if it can afford to do what you are demanding in repairs and maintenance. Spend enough time down in the local recorder of deed's records room to see the loan documents on the buildings you think the landlord owns. Also, check the property tax bills.

Try to determine what the landlord's monthly costs are for operation, including employees, office rent, utilities and insurance. It takes a bit of digging and some expertise, but your union has talent and a will to win. Make a list of the landlord's major suppliers and lenders. You may want to enlist their aid in persuading the landlord to fix things up before they get worse, someone gets hurt and rents get diverted.

Stay Clean with Your Attorney

Before you embark on this part of the campaign, write a scenario and clear it with your attorney, since you don't want to set yourself up for a *slander per se* defamation suit or a charge of *tortious interference* with a business relationship. Your lawyer will explain what all of this means.

Keep the Screws Tight, Tight, Tight

If you go into rent reductions or withholding, be sure to inform all creditors, suppliers and other owners. They may start putting a credit squeeze on the landlord. They may ask it for cash payments or insist that the landlord bring its accounts up to current date. They are not about to lose money because the landlord doesn't know how to manage its buildings. If you are holding rents and need repair work, you can always deal directly with the suppliers (although you might have to pay cash on delivery).

The Courts or the Pocketbook?

The act of withholding the rents occurs at a branching point. You either go through with it or take another course, typically by filing one or many lawsuits. Sometimes you have to do this anyway. Your lawyer may advise you to take the initiative and try not to withhold rents without court permission. In such cases, the court usually orders the tenants to pay the landlord and orders the landlord to perform repair work to get the money. If the landlord doesn't cooperate, the court occasionally may allow the money to be held or paid to a receiver. Thus, going to court may limit your options, until such time as the case can actually be argued.

The enforcement of court orders against the landlord is really up to your union. It will be your lawyer who will tell the judge about the landlord's progress or lack of it. If the landlord is not cooperating in repairs or negotiations, you can amend your suit to request an immediate and permanent reduction in the rents on top of everything else. If you have not done so before, you could also amend your suit to request that the president of the union be named receiver to the building.

Tracking the Progress

By this time, the landlord may understand that it will be better to cooperate than face a full-fledged rent strike. After all, miracles do happen, especially if the landlord has any sense (although some don't). City inspectors will be task-forcing the landlord's building. The union will be showing them every violation that can be found. The alderman's office is keeping track of things, letting the city departments know of the alderman's continued interest. A large group of tenants is prepared to go to court—be it violations court, circuit court or even eviction court—and fight the landlord on all fronts until repairs are made and general relations normalized.

While all this is going on, your union is holding frequent meetings, sending out reports, posting flyers, collecting rents, talking to everybody in the building, holding permanent open house to every governmental agency that finds it necessary to visit and sending people down to the courthouse. Rest assured that the press is calling *you* for interviews. These are high times, high-pressure times and high-risk times; but you can handle it.

Watch Your Back

A few more bits of general advice: Keep constant contact will all tenants. Start a master file of letters, notices and memoranda. Ask all tenants to keep notes of what they hear and see, as the notes and information may be needed during the course of court cases. Report any type of harassment to everybody and to your lawyer. Hold meetings frequently enough to keep up group spirits but not so often as to wear down or bore everybody. Keep close follow-ups on your lawyer, the city and the landlord.

If retaliations start, give warning to the management to cease or the building will go into court for an emergency order and sanctions. Remember, you have the upper hand: tenants' rights laws are clear, and your right to be safe is guaranteed. At some point, it will be clear to the landlord that it has a building to keep full and a business to run. Fighting with the union will cost dearly, while cooperating will improve both building and business.

In your negotiations with management, collaborate where it is fair and fight like hell where it is not. Your ultimate goal, you will recall, is a negotiated lease based on a collective bargaining agreement and the correction of problems. Keep your goals in mind.

There are bad tenants as well as bad landlords. Your association should attempt to keep its membership in line. There are legitimate reasons for evictions. Evaluate each case on its merits. Fights and brawls, dealing, tricking, property destruction and filth are not the *cause célèbre* of your union. If you get caught up with this type of diversion, the whole credibility of the organization can be lost. It is also very bad to get involved in political campaigns, unless your candidate is a demonstrated champion of tenants' rights. Your goal is to protect the tenants from rip-offs, not save society. Leave politics to the precinct captains and pols.

You, Too, Can Succeed

Do tenants' unions really work? Hell, yes. In New York City, the tenants of an apartment complex called Co-op City struck to the tune of $30 million. They were protesting rent raises and uncompleted construction. The strike lasted two years and the tenants won! In Chicago, a high rise on South Lake Shore Drive was organized after the tenants complained that the place was going to hell. About one-third of the 150 tenants withheld rents for four months. The union held close to $40,000. The owner of the place needed mortgage money. In the end, the owner decided not to evict and signed a long-term collective bargaining agreement, agreed to a grievance procedure, replaced the building manager and promised to work with the residents to solve a number of other problems.

Seventy tenants in a 12-story building in the university section of a large city organized after carbon monoxide poisoning killed one person and injured ten more. They brought about massive changes—new management and then a new owner as well as repairs, decorating, rent stabilization and new security devices. No one was kicked out. During the negotiations, the tenants held thousands of dollars in rent, fought evictions and got a lot of help from other tenants unions.

Here's my own story. All the tenants in our six-flat building formed an association to force the landlord to complete remodeling of our apartments. It took a rent slowdown, paying the rent on the last day of a late notice, three trips to code violations court and three lawsuits. The landlord finally knuckled under and made the repairs. He also paid part of the association's legal bill and made monthly cash payments to us for three years. This landlord left town.

Of course tenants' unions work! If you think about the real alternatives with and without organization, you can see how a tenants' association opens up the choices. Without a union, you have to take it or leave in most instances.

Have a lawyer available for advice, avoid court when you can and make up your own mind about rent strikes. What is legal and what is effective are sometimes very different: you want results, not shiny halos. When all else fails, a tenants' association is a renter's only strength.

Appendixes

Appendix

The Apartment Hunters' Checklist

Make plenty of copies of this checklist and use one for every serious inspection.

Initial Inspection For:

Address: _____ Unit #: _____

Rent: $_____ Utilities: $_____

Parking: $_____ Other: $_____

Application fee:$ _____ Credit fee: $ _____

Security deposit: $ _____ Other: $ _____

Rental agent: _____

_____ _____ _____

Name/Agency   Address   Phone

The Neighborhood

Parking

How crowded is the **street parking?** Can you find the **fire hydrants,** or are they blocked by **illegally parked cars?** Does the **building** provide **parking?** If you invite friends over, can they park within a mile? Do you see a lot of broken glass in the street or **signs of car break-ins?**

Impressions

Are there other signs of **overcrowding? Gang markings?** Do you have **good impressions?** Do you think it is **safe at night?**

Convenience

Are public **transportation** and expressways **convenient?** What about **schools, parks, hospitals, shopping areas?** Will you or the neighborhood have an **ethnic** or language **problem?**

The Exterior

Front

What is the **general appearance** and impression of the building? Is there a **yard? Grass? Mud hole?** Is the area clean or full of **trash?** Are the **sidewalks and steps** in **solid** condition, or are there numerous cracks and chips, worn spots, loose or missing pieces? If it is winter, is the **snow removed?** Are there **ice patches?** Is the **public walk shoveled?**

Structure

Look at the **front of the building.** Is the stone or brick **clean?** Is the **wood painted** or **weathered?** Do you see **cracks** in the stone or

missing mortar between stones or bricks? Can you see cracks in the concrete window ledges or trim?

Windows

Look at the windows. Do you see combination (modern) **storm and screen windows?** Are the window frames painted (if you can see them)? Do you see **dirty, broken** or **boarded-up** windows?

Entranceway

Look at the entrance area. Do you see the **management company name and** their **24-hour emergency number?** Is there a **night-light** outside the door? Is the **door** structurally **sound,** solid, painted, varnished or clean?

Side and Back

Walk to the back. How is the walk or **gangway?** Do you smell urine? Is there **lighting** on the side and back? Is there **trash** and junk all over the rear? What about the **garbage cans or dumpsters?** Are there **enough** of them? Are they **overflowing** or **smelly?** What about the **back door?** Is it well locked, **secure** and **safe** as a back emergency exit? Is it a good back entryway? **Can burglars** climb up the back porches or nearby roofs and **break in at the back of the building?** Walk into the alley. Is there gang **graffiti, junk** or old cars? Does it look **safe?**

Interior Common Areas

Check the **front door.** Look at the **locks.** Are they secure and working? Does the **door automatically close and lock?** Is there an **intercom system?** Does it work? Can the door be **buzzed open** from each apartment?

Is the **lobby** area **clean?** How about the **mailboxes?** Are they **behind a locked door?** Do they appear to be safe from **vandals?** Are there **double-locked** security **doors** between the outside and the inside?

Is the **hallway/stairway** area **clean?** Are the **carpets** not **frayed?** Is there enough **light?** Are there strong, strange, unpleasant **odors, gas** or **sewer smells?** Can you see **smoke detectors** and **fire extinguishers?**

Does the **elevator** work smoothly, quietly and quickly? Does it have a **valid permit?** Are the **waiting areas safe?** Is it an old **wheezer?**

The Apartment Itself

Sounds

Listen to the **sounds of the building** and the neighborhood. Noisy? quiet? Note the time of the inspection. Will the apartment be **quiet enough** when you are at home? When you want **to sleep?**

Entry Doors and Locks

Ground-Floor Location

If the unit is on the ground (first) floor, is it **high enough** off the ground to prevent break-ins by people using small stepladders or standing on each other's shoulders?

Front Door

Is the **front door solid** or hollow? Is it **cracked?** What about the **locks?** Are they **flimsy?** Is there a security **deadbolt?** Is it a Segal, or does it have a long-tongue bolt? Is the **frame solid** or **cracked, marred** or **gouged?** Are the **hinges** in good condition—**tight** to the frame and door? Is the door **loose,** or does it **rattle** when closed and locked? Doors that do not close tightly are very easy to break open. Does the door **automatically lock** when closed? Does the **door** have glass windows through which, when broken out, a **thief could** reach around and **unlock** the door from the inside?

Back Door

Check out the **back door** in the same manner as the front door.

Windows

Are the **windows painted shut?** Can they be **easily opened** and closed? If they are sash windows (the normal up-down windows), do they have working **counterbalance chains?**

Are the windows thermally **insulated** and with full **storms and screens?** Does the **hardware work?** What about the **locks, handles and security stops?**

If it is possible to gain outside access to the windows from a porch, fire escape, neighboring roof or the windows in the building next door, are there **window bars** or other protective **security** devices?

Walls and Ceilings

What are the **walls** like? Holes, cracks, chips, scaling, peeling? How about **sound transmission?** Are the **walls** thick or **thin?** Tap them and **listen.** Use the **boom box.** Are there **stains** on the **ceiling** or **walls?**

Floors

Are the **wooden floors** smooth, in **good** shape, properly **varnished** and sealed or painted? Are there **holes, bad tiles** or other **problems** with the flooring? If there is **carpeting,** is it clean, new, stain-spotted, tattered or **worn?** Is there a **concrete** slab **under** the tile or carpeted **flooring?** Is there **rotten flooring under tile or carpet,** such as old planking, broken tiles or bad linoleum?

Do the **floors** and **walls meet** at the floor line? Are they **sealed** so there are no **holes** or **cracks** that could allow dirt, smells, drafts and **mice** to enter? Are the **floors level?** Do they ripple, sink, rise or slant?

Inside Doors

Are there **doors** for **all** doorways and **rooms** that require them? Do the doors **open and close** properly? Do doors that require locks have them? Do **locks** and **hardware work?**

Rooms in General

Are the rooms **big enough for** your **furniture?** Are the rooms the **proper shape** for certain long or curved pieces? Will the dining table fit? Will you need new shades or curtains? Should you take measurements and make an apartment map of the place? Is there enough **sunlight** for your plants?

Will your **furniture fit through** the **doors** of the building, the angles on the stairways, the elevator, the apartment hallway and room doors? (Carry measurements of your large pieces to be sure.) Are there nearby restaurants or bars that will exhaust their **odors** into your living room or bedroom?

Smoke Detectors

Smoke detectors are required inside the apartment no more than 15 feet from each sleeping area and at the top of each flight of stairs and someplace in the central area of each floor of each apartment without a sleeping area. Do you see the required smoke detectors? Test the batteries by pushing the test button. (Use a broomstick or a chair, but **test them.**) Also test the unit with match smoke. If the smoke detectors don't work, find out why. The landlord should provide working units with batteries.

Bedrooms

Are they **big enough** for your **beds?** (Bed sizes are as follows: twin, 39″ × 75″; full (double), 54″ × 75″; queen, 60″ × 80″; king, 76″ × 80″.) Can you have a **water bed?** Will there be problems with **street noise** or the bar next door? Is there **fresh air** coming in from the window? Is the **air conditioner** fit? Power or outlet? What about the **closets?**

Closets

How many **closets** are there? If the closets have **metal doors,** do they operate properly or **fall off the tracks** and onto your feet? Do the closets have **hanger rods** or bars? Do they have **shelves?** Do they have side hooks? Are they conveniently located?

Bathrooms

Is the **sink clean?** Are there chips or mars? Are the **faucets** in good shape? Does the **spigot** drip? Are there rust or wear marks in the bowl? Does the sink **drain?** Does the drain leak? Are there stains or **wet** spots **underneath** the sink?

Does the **toilet** flush easily and completely **empty** with the toothpick test? Is the **toilet bowl** clean, not chipped, **cracked** or stained? Does the **toilet wobble** when sat on or pushed? Does the **toilet** fill and **shut off** within three minutes **after flushing?** Are there **stains** or **wetness** on the floor around the **toilet base?** Does the **floor sag** around the toilet?

How about the **bathtub?** Is it **clean,** unstained and free of scratches and mars? Are the tub and **shower** walls properly grouted? Are the **tiles** well stuck and **tight** to the walls? Is the **grout** at the edges of the tub (both along the walls and the floor) **solid, continuous** and without **mold** or **fungus** stains? Does the **tub drain** work? Does it drain **fast** enough? Are the **faucet fixtures** in **good** shape? Do they work, **shut off, drip?** Is there a working **shower head?** Is there a **shower-curtain rod?** Is the **hot water hot** enough? What about the **water pressure?** Could you fill the bathtub or take a shower with **no problem?** Is the **water** rust-free and **clean?**

Is there a **medicine cabinet?** Is it clean and in good shape? Are there **mirrors?** Can they be used for shaving, putting on makeup and grooming?

Is the bathroom **vented** to the **outside** of the building via a vent fan or an openable window?

What about lighting and **electrical** outlets? Are they convenient, **safely** away from water and **usable?**

Are there **holes** or leaks where the water **pipes** come into the bathroom? Any stain marks? Any signs that roaches or rodents could climb through the holes?

Is there a **linen closet** or some other type of **storage** for towels and supplies? Are there **towel rods?**

Kitchen

What is the condition of the **kitchen sink?** Is it **clean** and cleanable? Is it marred, scratched, stained, rusted or dented? Are **faucets** and controls **working?** Is there any **dripping?** If there is a **rinser hose**, does it **work?** Does the **sink drain** well? Is there a **strainer basket** to catch the gunk? Does the drain **seal?** Are there signs of **leaks** or **pests** under the sink?

Is the **stove** clean? Do all the burners or elements **work?** If it is a gas stove, are the pilot lights on? Does it look **safe?** Is it **adequate** for your needs?

Is the **refrigerator** working? Is it **clean?** Does the **door seal** tightly? Is it big enough? Is it frost-free or manually defrosting? Does the **freezer** freeze **cold** enough?

Are there adequate **kitchen cabinets and counter tops?** Is the kitchen **floor** in good shape and clean? Is the floor **cleanable?**

Can the **kitchen** be **ventilated** either through a window opening directly to the outside or through a stove hood fan that vents **to the outside?**

If you **own your appliances**, where will they go? Will they **fit?** Can they be **connected** easily?

Electrical Service

How many **circuits** does the apartment have? How are the circuits **divided?** Are there **enough circuits** for your needs?

How **many outlets** can you find in the average room? **Do all** the outlets and circuits **work?** (Use the circuit tester.) Are all the outlets the **legal three-prong ground** type or the unacceptable, old two-prongers? Is there **240-volt service** in the apartment for a large air conditioner?

How does the viewable wiring appear? Are there **modern** silent light **switches?** Have the switch plates and **outlets** been **painted over** multiple times? Ask the agent when the **apartment** was **rewired.** Where is the **circuit breaker** or **fuse** box located? How many circuits are there? (Do not confuse the two at the top—mains—with the ones on the sides, the actual circuits.) Do you have unlimited **24-hour access to the box** in case you blow a circuit? If not, why not? Who has the key, and what is his or her address and phone number?

Heating (and Cooling) System

What type of **heating system** is present? **Steam, hot-water, forced air, space heater, catalytic,** hot water or electric baseboard, **univent** (high-rise-style combination blower/radiator enclosed in a metal case, usually under windows)?

If there are **space heaters,** do they **vent** directly to the **outside?** Are there enough space heaters to heat the entire apartment? Do they leak **carbon monoxide?** Can a person be **burned** if the unit is touched? Is it **safe** for children and pets? Do the units **light** quickly and properly without exploding? Are there working **thermostatic** controls?

Is the apartment equipped with **steam** or **hot-water radiators?** Are there radiators **in each room?**

A **steam radiator** will have one pipe coming into it (low-pressure) or one pipe at either end (high-pressure). It will have a cylinder-shaped **air valve** on one end. Do all the radiators have **air valves** and **shutoff handles?** Are adjustable thermostatic air vents provided for low-pressure steam systems so that the tenant can control the heat?

A **hot-water radiator** will have feed pipes at either end and a small air bleeder/fill bleeder **spigot** at one end. Does the agent have a **bleeder valve key** to give you for the apartment?

If **heat** is supplied via a **high-pressure steam or hot-water** system, are there **cutoff valves** on both sides of the radiator? Are the radiators clean, rusted, dirty or **painted with** anything but high heat **aluminum paint?** Can any evidence of **leaking water,** rust stains or corrosion deposits be detected at the fittings (connections) under the air valve, spigot, on the legs or on the floor? Do you see **ceiling stains** from a leaky radiator on the floor above?

If there are **univents,** are they **clean** and painted? Do they have **filters** that need to be cleaned or replaced? Are the univents **quiet?** Do they have **thermostatic controls?** Do you see evidence of **leaks** around the base of the unit or directly overhead from a unit on the next floor? Will mold or fungus be a problem? Who pays for the electricity used by the electric motors?

If heat or cooling is supplied by a **forced-air system,** are there registers (hot-air vents) in every room? Is the air centrally heated and cooled or from the apartment unit itself? Is the furnace a standard heating/cooling unit, or is it a substitute floor, wall or closet furnace? Is there sufficient air flow into the furnace room to allow for efficient burning? Is there good air movement through the registers? Is there a cold-air return in each room? How **noisy** is the central air system or furnace when the fan is running? Is there a lot of **smudging** apparent at the registers indicating **dirty** filters, **heat exchange** and **ductwork?**

Catalytic heaters are special gas-fired units. They mount on outside walls or hang down from a ceiling. They are flat and look something like a gyros broiler. They get extremely hot but use direct radiation to heat, which means they do not heat the air as do normal systems and will heat unevenly.

Baseboard heating uses radiators that usually run the whole length of each room along an outside wall. They sit very low to the floor. If **hot water** is used, check for **leaks.** Make sure **cutoffs** are accessible for each radiator.

Electric baseboard and electric forced-air heating can be expensive and tends to be a very dry heat source, increasing the need for winter humidification. **How much** does it cost to run the electric heating? The use of electric baseboard heating in **older buildings** should raise the question of **safety** regarding the wiring system. **When** was the building **rewired** for such heat?

Is there a **thermostat** in the apartment to **control** heat if the tenant does not pay for his or her own heat?

If the **tenant pays** for **heating and cooling, what are** the Btu/cubic foot gas draws of the heating equipment and the **Btu/kilowatt draws** for the heating or cooling equipment? The **landlord should inform** you **as to** your **yearly** heating and cooling **costs** in addition to the monthly rent.

When **tenant pays** the bill and controls his or her own heat, is the **thermostat** a **modern** type with **set-back** features that allow tenant to run heat low while at work and while sleeping but high when at home and active? (This can save 10 to 20 percent on the heating bill.)

If the apartment is heated by **steam or hot-water boiler from an individual boiler** in the apartment, is the boiler in good shape? Does it have a local government **inspection and approval seal** on it?

Hot Water

Who pays for the hot water? Where is the **hot-water heater,** and how does it heat—gas or electric? Does the **landlord** supply the apartment with **hot water? How big** is the tank? What are the **tank's Btu and recovery Btu ratings?**

Pests

Do you see signs of **roaches or mice?** Are there **holes** in the floors or wood trim? Are there **roach droppings** the size and color of ground pepper? Are there **wet spots** under sinks and behind toilets where pests get water? **Leaks** around the tub where roaches or mice can get water? **Enlarged openings** where the pipes enter into the apartment, including plumbing and heating pipes?

Smells

Does the apartment **smell clean?** Are there any **gas, sewer,** mold, garbage, smoke or bathroom **odors?**

Radon Gas

Has there been a **radon gas** test? What was the picocurie per liter level of radon gas? Is it 4 pCi/l or less? Have radon gas safety procedures been initiated? Is the basement clean, dust-free and well ventilated?

Asbestos

Do you see the signs of **deteriorated heating pipe insulation?** What about "cocooned" furnace, broken plaster or old ceiling tiles? Is there an **asbestos certificate?**

Utilities and Storage Access

Where is the **storage area?** Can you get to it at all times? Does the area appear to be dry, **safe** from rats and safe from break-in? Is the area **locked** to outsiders?

Is there a laundry room? Is it clean, dry and fresh smelling? Are the machines antiques? How much does it cost to wash and dry? Is the laundry room well lit? Is it secure in the building? Is it protected with a locked door? Is there a TV and/or TV security?

Where is the **circuit breaker** or **fuse box?** Do you have 24-hour **unlimited access** to it? Where are the **utility meters?**

If you are really interested in the place, did you **ask for,** and was the agent willing to give up, a **sample of the application form and the lease?**

Comments?   **Notes**

Pass? Fail? Affordable? Safe?
Convenient? Trust the Agent?
Of the Units You Have Seen, How Do You Rank
   This Unit?
(First choice to last)
   1   2   3   4   5   6   7   8   9   10

Appendix

Move-in/Move-out Checklist

Use this list to summarize the physical condition of your apartment when you sign your lease, and then make a new list just after you have settled in. Getting a written document of conditions could save you a lot of grief and/or money later. Both you and your landlord should do the inspection together, and both of you should sign the list.

Apartment Conditions
Move-in/Move-out Checklist

Check one: ☐ Pre-check-in (before signing lease)

☐ Check-in (first ten days after move-in)

☐ Check-out (before or after move-out and/or key return)

Condition of Apartment Checklist/Exceptions Report

For apartment # _____ at _____

_____ to be made a rider to lease and attached and made part of lease

dated _____ for the above-described premises. This document contains

five pages.

Entries

Intercom system	☐ Excellent	☐ Passable	☐ Unacceptable.	State problem:_____.
Mailbox	☐ Excellent	☐ Passable	☐ Unacceptable.	State problem:_____.
Front door	☐ Excellent	☐ Passable	☐ Unacceptable.	State problem:_____.
Front door lock(s)	☐ Excellent	☐ Passable	☐ Unacceptable.	State problem:_____.
Rear door	☐ Excellent	☐ Passable	☐ Unacceptable.	State problem:_____.
Rear door lock(s)	☐ Excellent	☐ Passable	☐ Unacceptable.	State problem:_____.
Keys work	☐ Excellent	☐ Passable	☐ Unacceptable.	State problem:_____.
Ceilings	☐ Excellent	☐ Passable	☐ Unacceptable.	State problem:_____.
Lighting fixtures	☐ Excellent	☐ Passable	☐ Unacceptable.	State problem:_____.
Other:_____	☐ Excellent	☐ Passable	☐ Unacceptable.	State problem:_____.
Other:_____	☐ Excellent	☐ Passable	☐ Unacceptable.	State problem:_____.

Systems/General

Cleanliness	☐ Excellent	☐ Passable	☐ Unacceptable.	State problem:_____.
Water pressure	☐ Excellent	☐ Passable	☐ Unacceptable.	State problem:_____.
Drains	☐ Excellent	☐ Passable	☐ Unacceptable.	State problem:_____.
Clean windows	☐ Excellent	☐ Passable	☐ Unacceptable.	State problem:_____.
Window locks	☐ Excellent	☐ Passable	☐ Unacceptable.	State problem:_____.
Screens/storms	☐ Excellent	☐ Passable	☐ Unacceptable.	State problem:_____.
Heating system	☐ Excellent	☐ Passable	☐ Unacceptable.	State problem:_____.
Air conditioning	☐ Excellent	☐ Passable	☐ Unacceptable.	State problem:_____.
Thermostat	☐ Excellent	☐ Passable	☐ Unacceptable.	State problem:_____.
Smoke detectors	☐ Excellent	☐ Passable	☐ Unacceptable.	State problem:_____.
Fire extinguisher(s)	☐ Excellent	☐ Passable	☐ Unacceptable.	State problem:_____.
Air/water leaks	☐ Excellent	☐ Passable	☐ Unacceptable.	State problem:_____.
Fuse/breaker box	☐ Excellent	☐ Passable	☐ Unacceptable.	State problem:_____.

Stairways/Hallways

Treads	☐ Excellent	☐ Passable	☐ Unacceptable.	State problem:_____.
Railing	☐ Excellent	☐ Passable	☐ Unacceptable.	State problem:_____.
Flooring	☐ Excellent	☐ Passable	☐ Unacceptable.	State problem:_____.
Carpeting	☐ Excellent	☐ Passable	☐ Unacceptable.	State problem:_____.
Walls	☐ Excellent	☐ Passable	☐ Unacceptable.	State problem:_____.
Ceilings	☐ Excellent	☐ Passable	☐ Unacceptable.	State problem:_____.
Lighting fixtures	☐ Excellent	☐ Passable	☐ Unacceptable.	State problem:_____.
Outlets	☐ Excellent	☐ Passable	☐ Unacceptable.	State problem:_____.
Closet_____	☐ Excellent	☐ Passable	☐ Unacceptable.	State problem:_____.
Closet_____	☐ Excellent	☐ Passable	☐ Unacceptable.	State problem:_____.

Closet_____	☐ Excellent	☐ Passable	☐ Unacceptable.	State problem:_____.
Other:_____	☐ Excellent	☐ Passable	☐ Unacceptable.	State problem:_____.
Other:_____	☐ Excellent	☐ Passable	☐ Unacceptable.	State problem:_____.

Kitchen

General cleanliness	☐ Excellent	☐ Passable	☐ Unacceptable.	State problem:_____.
Sink	☐ Excellent	☐ Passable	☐ Unacceptable.	State problem:_____.
Floor	☐ Excellent	☐ Passable	☐ Unacceptable.	State problem:_____.
Walls	☐ Excellent	☐ Passable	☐ Unacceptable.	State problem:_____.
Windows (Do they work?)	☐ Excellent	☐ Passable	☐ Unacceptable.	State problem:_____.
Shades, curtains	☐ Excellent	☐ Passable	☐ Unacceptable.	State problem:_____.
Counters	☐ Excellent	☐ Passable	☐ Unacceptable.	State problem:_____.
Cabinets	☐ Excellent	☐ Passable	☐ Unacceptable.	State problem:_____.
Built-ins	☐ Excellent	☐ Passable	☐ Unacceptable.	State problem:_____.
Outlets	☐ Excellent	☐ Passable	☐ Unacceptable.	State problem:_____.
Stove (Are there racks?)	☐ Excellent	☐ Passable	☐ Unacceptable.	State problem:_____.
Fan/hood	☐ Excellent	☐ Passable	☐ Unacceptable.	State problem:_____.
Refrigerator (Are there racks and trays?)	☐ Excellent	☐ Passable	☐ Unacceptable.	State problem:_____.
Disposer	☐ Excellent	☐ Passable	☐ Unacceptable.	State problem:_____.
Dishwasher	☐ Excellent	☐ Passable	☐ Unacceptable.	State problem:_____.
Compactor	☐ Excellent	☐ Passable	☐ Unacceptable.	State problem:_____.
Ceiling	☐ Excellent	☐ Passable	☐ Unacceptable.	State problem:_____.
Lighting fixtures	☐ Excellent	☐ Passable	☐ Unacceptable.	State problem:_____.
Other:_____	☐ Excellent	☐ Passable	☐ Unacceptable.	State problem:_____.
Other:_____	☐ Excellent	☐ Passable	☐ Unacceptable.	State problem:_____.

Bathroom #1 (Location: _____)

General cleanliness	☐ Excellent	☐ Passable	☐ Unacceptable.	State problem:_____.
Sink	☐ Excellent	☐ Passable	☐ Unacceptable.	State problem:_____.
Vanity	☐ Excellent	☐ Passable	☐ Unacceptable.	State problem:_____.
Medicine cabinet	☐ Excellent	☐ Passable	☐ Unacceptable.	State problem:_____.
Outlets	☐ Excellent	☐ Passable	☐ Unacceptable.	State problem:_____.
Mirrors	☐ Excellent	☐ Passable	☐ Unacceptable.	State problem:_____.
Racks	☐ Excellent	☐ Passable	☐ Unacceptable.	State problem:_____.
Closet, shelves	☐ Excellent	☐ Passable	☐ Unacceptable.	State problem:_____.
Floor	☐ Excellent	☐ Passable	☐ Unacceptable.	State problem:_____.
Walls	☐ Excellent	☐ Passable	☐ Unacceptable.	State problem:_____.
Windows (Do they work?)	☐ Excellent	☐ Passable	☐ Unacceptable.	State problem:_____.
Shades, curtains	☐ Excellent	☐ Passable	☐ Unacceptable.	State problem:_____.
Toilet (Does it have a seat? Does it work?)	☐ Excellent	☐ Passable	☐ Unacceptable.	State problem:_____.
Shower	☐ Excellent	☐ Passable	☐ Unacceptable.	State problem:_____.
Curtain rod	☐ Excellent	☐ Passable	☐ Unacceptable.	State problem:_____.
Tub	☐ Excellent	☐ Passable	☐ Unacceptable.	State problem:_____.
Vent fan	☐ Excellent	☐ Passable	☐ Unacceptable.	State problem:_____.
Heater	☐ Excellent	☐ Passable	☐ Unacceptable.	State problem:_____.
Door and lock	☐ Excellent	☐ Passable	☐ Unacceptable.	State problem:_____.
Ceiling	☐ Excellent	☐ Passable	☐ Unacceptable.	State problem:_____.
Lighting fixtures	☐ Excellent	☐ Passable	☐ Unacceptable.	State problem:_____.
Other:_____	☐ Excellent	☐ Passable	☐ Unacceptable.	State problem:_____.
Other:_____	☐ Excellent	☐ Passable	☐ Unacceptable.	State problem:_____.

Bathroom #2 (Location: _____)

General cleanliness	☐ Excellent	☐ Passable	☐ Unacceptable.	State problem:_____.
Sink	☐ Excellent	☐ Passable	☐ Unacceptable.	State problem:_____.
Vanity	☐ Excellent	☐ Passable	☐ Unacceptable.	State problem:_____.

Medicine cabinet	☐ Excellent	☐ Passable	☐ Unacceptable.	State problem:_____.
Outlets	☐ Excellent	☐ Passable	☐ Unacceptable.	State problem:_____.
Mirrors	☐ Excellent	☐ Passable	☐ Unacceptable.	State problem:_____.
Racks	☐ Excellent	☐ Passable	☐ Unacceptable.	State problem:_____.
Closet, shelves	☐ Excellent	☐ Passable	☐ Unacceptable.	State problem:_____.
Floor	☐ Excellent	☐ Passable	☐ Unacceptable.	State problem:_____.
Walls	☐ Excellent	☐ Passable	☐ Unacceptable.	State problem:_____.
Windows (Do they work?)	☐ Excellent	☐ Passable	☐ Unacceptable.	State problem:_____.
Shades, curtains	☐ Excellent	☐ Passable	☐ Unacceptable.	State problem:_____.
Toilet (Does it have a seat? Does it work?)	☐ Excellent	☐ Passable	☐ Unacceptable.	State problem:_____.
Shower	☐ Excellent	☐ Passable	☐ Unacceptable.	State problem:_____.
Curtain rod	☐ Excellent	☐ Passable	☐ Unacceptable.	State problem:_____.
Tub	☐ Excellent	☐ Passable	☐ Unacceptable.	State problem:_____.
Vent fan	☐ Excellent	☐ Passable	☐ Unacceptable.	State problem:_____.
Heater	☐ Excellent	☐ Passable	☐ Unacceptable.	State problem:_____.
Door and lock	☐ Excellent	☐ Passable	☐ Unacceptable.	State problem:_____.
Ceiling	☐ Excellent	☐ Passable	☐ Unacceptable.	State problem:_____.
Lighting fixtures	☐ Excellent	☐ Passable	☐ Unacceptable.	State problem:_____.
Other:_____	☐ Excellent	☐ Passable	☐ Unacceptable.	State problem:_____.
Other:_____	☐ Excellent	☐ Passable	☐ Unacceptable.	State problem:_____.

Bedroom # 1 (Location: _____)

General cleanliness	☐ Excellent	☐ Passable	☐ Unacceptable.	State problem:_____.
Windows	☐ Excellent	☐ Passable	☐ Unacceptable.	State problem:_____.
Shades, curtains	☐ Excellent	☐ Passable	☐ Unacceptable.	State problem:_____.
Walls	☐ Excellent	☐ Passable	☐ Unacceptable.	State problem:_____.
Ceiling	☐ Excellent	☐ Passable	☐ Unacceptable.	State problem:_____.
Lighting fixtures	☐ Excellent	☐ Passable	☐ Unacceptable.	State problem:_____.
Outlets	☐ Excellent	☐ Passable	☐ Unacceptable.	State problem:_____.
Flooring	☐ Excellent	☐ Passable	☐ Unacceptable.	State problem:_____.
Carpeting	☐ Excellent	☐ Passable	☐ Unacceptable.	State problem:_____.
Closet, rod, shelf	☐ Excellent	☐ Passable	☐ Unacceptable.	State problem:_____.
Door and lock	☐ Excellent	☐ Passable	☐ Unacceptable.	State problem:_____.
Other:_____	☐ Excellent	☐ Passable	☐ Unacceptable.	State problem:_____.
Other:_____	☐ Excellent	☐ Passable	☐ Unacceptable.	State problem:_____.

Bedroom # 2 (Location: _____)

General cleanliness	☐ Excellent	☐ Passable	☐ Unacceptable.	State problem:_____.
Windows	☐ Excellent	☐ Passable	☐ Unacceptable.	State problem:_____.
Shades, curtains	☐ Excellent	☐ Passable	☐ Unacceptable.	State problem:_____.
Walls	☐ Excellent	☐ Passable	☐ Unacceptable.	State problem:_____.
Ceiling	☐ Excellent	☐ Passable	☐ Unacceptable.	State problem:_____.
Lighting fixtures	☐ Excellent	☐ Passable	☐ Unacceptable.	State problem:_____.
Outlets	☐ Excellent	☐ Passable	☐ Unacceptable.	State problem:_____.
Flooring	☐ Excellent	☐ Passable	☐ Unacceptable.	State problem:_____.
Carpeting	☐ Excellent	☐ Passable	☐ Unacceptable.	State problem:_____.
Closet, rod, shelf	☐ Excellent	☐ Passable	☐ Unacceptable.	State problem:_____.
Door and lock	☐ Excellent	☐ Passable	☐ Unacceptable.	State problem:_____.
Other:_____	☐ Excellent	☐ Passable	☐ Unacceptable.	State problem:_____.
Other:_____	☐ Excellent	☐ Passable	☐ Unacceptable.	State problem:_____.

Bedroom # 3 (Location: _____)

General cleanliness	☐ Excellent	☐ Passable	☐ Unacceptable.	State problem:_____.
Windows	☐ Excellent	☐ Passable	☐ Unacceptable.	State problem:_____.
Shades, curtains	☐ Excellent	☐ Passable	☐ Unacceptable.	State problem:_____.
Walls	☐ Excellent	☐ Passable	☐ Unacceptable.	State problem:_____.
Ceiling	☐ Excellent	☐ Passable	☐ Unacceptable.	State problem:_____.
Lighting fixtures	☐ Excellent	☐ Passable	☐ Unacceptable.	State problem:_____.

Outlets	☐ Excellent	☐ Passable	☐ Unacceptable. State problem:_____.
Flooring	☐ Excellent	☐ Passable	☐ Unacceptable. State problem:_____.
Carpeting	☐ Excellent	☐ Passable	☐ Unacceptable. State problem:_____.
Closet, rod, shelf	☐ Excellent	☐ Passable	☐ Unacceptable. State problem:_____.
Door and lock	☐ Excellent	☐ Passable	☐ Unacceptable. State problem:_____.
Other:_____	☐ Excellent	☐ Passable	☐ Unacceptable. State problem:_____.
Other:_____	☐ Excellent	☐ Passable	☐ Unacceptable. State problem:_____.

Living Room

General cleanliness	☐ Excellent	☐ Passable	☐ Unacceptable. State problem:_____.
Windows	☐ Excellent	☐ Passable	☐ Unacceptable. State problem:_____.
Shades, curtains	☐ Excellent	☐ Passable	☐ Unacceptable. State problem:_____.
Walls	☐ Excellent	☐ Passable	☐ Unacceptable. State problem:_____.
Ceiling	☐ Excellent	☐ Passable	☐ Unacceptable. State problem:_____.
Lighting fixtures	☐ Excellent	☐ Passable	☐ Unacceptable. State problem:_____.
Outlets	☐ Excellent	☐ Passable	☐ Unacceptable. State problem:_____.
Flooring	☐ Excellent	☐ Passable	☐ Unacceptable. State problem:_____.
Carpeting	☐ Excellent	☐ Passable	☐ Unacceptable. State problem:_____.
Fireplace	☐ Excellent	☐ Passable	☐ Unacceptable. State problem:_____.
Built-ins	☐ Excellent	☐ Passable	☐ Unacceptable. State problem:_____.
Door and lock	☐ Excellent	☐ Passable	☐ Unacceptable. State problem:_____.
Other:_____	☐ Excellent	☐ Passable	☐ Unacceptable. State problem:_____.
Other:_____	☐ Excellent	☐ Passable	☐ Unacceptable. State problem:_____.

Dining Room

General cleanliness	☐ Excellent	☐ Passable	☐ Unacceptable. State problem:_____.
Windows	☐ Excellent	☐ Passable	☐ Unacceptable. State problem:_____.
Shades, curtains	☐ Excellent	☐ Passable	☐ Unacceptable. State problem:_____.
Walls	☐ Excellent	☐ Passable	☐ Unacceptable. State problem:_____.
Ceiling	☐ Excellent	☐ Passable	☐ Unacceptable. State problem:_____.
Lighting fixtures	☐ Excellent	☐ Passable	☐ Unacceptable. State problem:_____.
Outlets	☐ Excellent	☐ Passable	☐ Unacceptable. State problem:_____.
Flooring	☐ Excellent	☐ Passable	☐ Unacceptable. State problem:_____.
Carpeting	☐ Excellent	☐ Passable	☐ Unacceptable. State problem:_____.
Built-ins	☐ Excellent	☐ Passable	☐ Unacceptable. State problem:_____.
Door and lock	☐ Excellent	☐ Passable	☐ Unacceptable. State problem:_____.
Other:_____	☐ Excellent	☐ Passable	☐ Unacceptable. State problem:_____.
Other:_____	☐ Excellent	☐ Passable	☐ Unacceptable. State problem:_____.

Den

General cleanliness	☐ Excellent	☐ Passable	☐ Unacceptable. State problem:_____.
Windows	☐ Excellent	☐ Passable	☐ Unacceptable. State problem:_____.
Shades, curtains	☐ Excellent	☐ Passable	☐ Unacceptable. State problem:_____.
Walls	☐ Excellent	☐ Passable	☐ Unacceptable. State problem:_____.
Ceiling	☐ Excellent	☐ Passable	☐ Unacceptable. State problem:_____.
Lighting fixtures	☐ Excellent	☐ Passable	☐ Unacceptable. State problem:_____.
Outlets	☐ Excellent	☐ Passable	☐ Unacceptable. State problem:_____.
Flooring	☐ Excellent	☐ Passable	☐ Unacceptable. State problem:_____.
Carpeting	☐ Excellent	☐ Passable	☐ Unacceptable. State problem:_____.
Fireplace	☐ Excellent	☐ Passable	☐ Unacceptable. State problem:_____.
Built-ins	☐ Excellent	☐ Passable	☐ Unacceptable. State problem:_____.
Door and lock	☐ Excellent	☐ Passable	☐ Unacceptable. State problem:_____.
Other:_____	☐ Excellent	☐ Passable	☐ Unacceptable. State problem:_____.
Other:_____	☐ Excellent	☐ Passable	☐ Unacceptable. State problem:_____.

Deck and Grounds

Decking	☐ Excellent	☐ Passable	☐ Unacceptable. State problem:_____.
Railings	☐ Excellent	☐ Passable	☐ Unacceptable. State problem:_____.
Grass	☐ Excellent	☐ Passable	☐ Unacceptable. State problem:_____.
Shrubs	☐ Excellent	☐ Passable	☐ Unacceptable. State problem:_____.

Miscellaneous

_____	☐ Excellent	☐ Passable	☐ Unacceptable. State problem:_____.
_____	☐ Excellent	☐ Passable	☐ Unacceptable. State problem:_____.
_____	☐ Excellent	☐ Passable	☐ Unacceptable. State problem:_____.
_____	☐ Excellent	☐ Passable	☐ Unacceptable. State problem:_____.

Exceptions and Differences: _____

_____

_____

_____

_____

_____

_____

_____

_____

_____

Lessor: _____ **Date:** _____

Lessee: _____ **Date:** _____

If move-out inspection—address to send security deposit return and interest due:

Address: _____

_____

C

Appendix

Sample Letters

Illegal Entry Warning Letters
Security Deposit Interest Letter
Security Deposit Refund Letter
Repair and Deduct Sample Letter: Notice of Intention To Repair and Deduct
Repair and Deduct Follow-Through Letter: Notice of Rent Setoff for Statutory
  Repairs
Notice of Intention To Reduce Rents
Rent Reduction Setoff Letter: Notice of Rent Setoff
Notice of Intention To Withhold Rents
Notice of Rent Withholding
Notice of Intention To Terminate Lease (for Cause)
Notice of Intention To Terminate Lease (Constructive Eviction)
Notice of Wrongful Enforcement of a Prohibited Clause
Notice to Cancel Month-to-Month (or Oral) Lease
Certificate of Delivery

Letters of complaints and requests to the landlord must contain specific information relating to a violation of a law or lease provision and specific references to what you will do and when. If these letters come from a tenants' union, each specific apartment and tenant must also be listed in the logical places.

Read chapters 7 and 8 thoroughly before you send one of these letters. There usually are fines and penalties, repayment requirements and even lawyers' fees and court costs assessed when the landlord fails to properly respond to your letters. Moreover, many times you can break your lease, reduce your rents or make repairs yourself and deduct the costs from your rent. Obviously, the laws can change. If you have any doubts, consult your tenants' union, community organization or attorney.

Make and keep several copies of your correspondence. Always send such letters and notices by certified mail, return receipt requested, and also by regular mail. Fill out the certificate of delivery, particularly when you deliver something by hand, but all the time as a precaution when getting ready for court.

Illegal Entry Warning Letters

Your tenants' rights law might consider frequent visits to your apartment by your landlord an act of harassment or abuse. As a matter of fact, many ordinances require two days prior notice before the landlord can enter your apartment (except in an emergency or other on-the-spot special occasions). If the landlord enters your apartment for an emergency, he or she may be obligated to give you a postinvasion notice within two days of the act. If the landlord violates these provisions, you may be able to break your lease and sue for penalties and damages.

The same is true for those repeated visits, with or without notice, that bug you and deprive you of your privacy or peace. Most laws require you to give a written warning telling the landlord to stop immediately. If you want to break the lease, tell him or her when you are leaving. Send your landlord the appropriate letter, such as one of the following:

Date

Dear Landlord:

On (date), you or your workmen entered my apartment (unit and address) without the required [two-day] notice (and/or outside of the legal limits of [8:00 A.M. to 8:00 P.M.]). You failed to inform me of this entry with written notice within [two] days of the occurrence. You are requested to deliver to me all notices, as provided by law. Please do not enter my apartment again without proper notice. If you do not start abiding by the provisions of the applicable laws within 24 hours, I will terminate this lease on (date, at least 15 days in the future).

Signed,

_____

Rattled Renter

or

Date

Dear Landlord:

Repeated entries into my apartment by you or your agents (unit and apartment address) (with or without proper notice) have the effect of harassing me. This is an abuse of my rights under applicable laws. You are hereby requested to cease and desist from these acts immediately, (today's date). If you do not abide by the provisions of the applicable laws, I will terminate this lease on (date, at least 15 days in the future but not more than 30 days after your deadline, and it ought to be at the end of a month).

Signed,

_____

Your loving lessee

Security Deposit Interest Letter

A special word is needed about security deposit interest. Almost everywhere, interest is due once a year, within 30 days after the renewal of your lease. It can be given to you in the form of a cash payment or a credit toward the rent for the month; it's the landlord's choice. In order to be sure you get this credit, you need to make a demand for the interest. On the renewal date of your lease, send the following letter. If you are making this request after you move out, send it within 30 days by certified mail.

Date

Dear Landlord:

I occupied apartment (unit number), (address), on (date). The annual calendar payment or credit of my security deposit interest is now due. Please forward or credit to me immediately, as provided by law, my security deposit interest. Send my money to me (in care of) at (address).

Sincerely,

_____

Harry D. Habitator

If you don't get the money or credit, a penalty may be due you as damages. The penalty can be double or treble your security deposit in some localities, plus interest and lawyers' fees.

Security Deposit Refund Letter

Date

Dear Landlord:

I vacated the apartment I occupied, (unit number), (address), on (date). Please forward to me immediately, as provided by law, my security deposit, (security deposit interest) (and any prepaid rent). Send my money to me (in care of) at (address).

Sincerely,

_____

Ayneeta Break, former tenant

Repair and Deduct Sample Letter:
Notice of Intention To Repair and Deduct

Date

Simon LeGree, Landlord
1234 Easy Street
Chicago, Illinois 60661

Sir:

I am a tenant of Sheridan's Folly, a courtyard building you manage at 3232 East 57th Place, Chicago, Illinois 60637, Apt. 1313. The lobby door unit does not close or lock properly, and the electric door buzzer won't release the door. Would you please fix this immediately? If the work is not completed before (15 days from the date of the letter), I will make arrangements to have the work done and deduct these repairs from my next month's rent.

Respectfully,

_____

Terry Tenant

Repair and Deduct Follow-Through Letter:
Notice of Rent Setoff for Statutory Repairs

To: (Name of person or company appearing as lessor on lease)
Regarding: 3232 East 57th Place, Chicago, Illinois 60637, Apt. 1313

On (date), a letter was sent to you regarding certain maintenance and repair items that required correction before ("when or else" date). Since these corrections were not satisfactorily completed by you on that date, the repairs were completed by ([others at my request] or [me]). Here is the rent for (current month), in the amount of $(total rent), which is the total monthly rent. This consists of $(total of the paid work/parts receipts), which is the cost of repairs for which copies of the paid receipts are submitted, and a (check or money order) for $(balance due). This rent is submitted in compliance with [Municipal Tenants' Rights Ordinance]. A copy of the original letter is attached. Please send me a rent receipt indicating the total credits given to me for this payment.

Respectfully,

_____

Terry Tenant

It is best to pay your rent in person so you can get an immediate receipt, but certified mail (return receipt) is also good. Just keep copies of everything, including a photocopy of the check or money order. Put a certificate of delivery on the back (or attached to it), fill it out and sign it.

Notice of Intention To Reduce Rents

One of your options in dealing with apartment problems is to give your landlord a certain number of days (commonly 14) to make the repair or else accept a reduced amount of rent. You can take this route instead of opting for repair and deduct or breaking the lease. In most cases, you'll be complaining about a leaking ceiling, bad radiator or exploding stove. But you can also deal with a bad neighbor this way—thus, the flavor of my sample letter. Substitute your own needs. As long as you take a reduction, a *setoff* as it is called, you preclude your other options. You can, of course, start to pay the landlord full fare and simultaneously give notice to break the lease. See chapter 7 for the details, and further on in this appendix for lease-breaking letters.

NOTICE OF INTENTION TO REDUCE RENT

Date:
To: (Name of person or company appearing as lessor on lease)
Re: Needed action for Unit 4B, 3712 North Wrigley Park, Chicago, Illinois 60613.

This is to inform you that certain action needs to be taken in my building. (The tenant in Unit 3B, immediately under my apartment, creates disturbances related to loud parties, fights and music playing. I am unable to sleep because of the noise. I have spoken to the tenant and called the police on several occasions. Would you please stop these disturbances?) (The front door lock is broken.) If you do not correct this situation within [7] days of the date of this letter, under the [Municipal Code of _____, Chapter _____], I will reduce my monthly rent payments by ($_____) per day for each and every day from the date of this letter until (the disturbances permanently stop)(repairs are satisfactorily completed). Should the situation not be corrected, I will seek other legal recourse as well.

Respectfully,

_____

Nick Schloffin

Rent Reduction Setoff Letter: Notice of Rent Setoff

Date:

To: (Name of person or company appearing as lessor on lease)

On (date), a letter was sent to you regarding certain maintenance and repair items that required correction. Since these corrections were not completed by you within [7] days from that date, the rental value of the premises is reduced by ($ amount stated in first letter) per day, starting with the date of that letter. (The work was not completed until [date] for [X days] of reduced value during the month(s) of [immediate past month(s)].) or (The work remains incomplete with [X days] of reduced value during the month(s) of [immediate past month(s)].) Here is the rent for (current month) in the amount of $ (total monthly rent), which is the total monthly rent, consisting of $ (total reduction) in credits, which is the reduced value of rent, and a (check or money order) for $(balance due), the cash balance. This rent is submitted in compliance with (city)(state) laws. A copy of the original letter is attached. Please send me a rent receipt indicating the total credits given to me for this payment.

Respectfully,

_____

Nick Schloffin

Deliver this letter in person or by certified mail. Photocopy everything, including the check. Attach a copy of the certificate of delivery. Keep a copy of the letter.

Notice of Intention To Withhold Rents

Date:

To: (Name of person or company appearing as lessor on lease)

Re: (12193 Rancho Frio Road, Brisk, Montana, Apt. 3)

This is to inform you that repairs to the heater and roof have not been made as requested by phone yesterday. The snow continues to blow in, and the toilet froze over last night. Please be advised that unless all necessary repairs are completed [48 hours from now] by 5:00 P.M., September 31, all rents will be withheld commencing with today's date and deducted from any future rent payments after repairs are satisfactorily completed.

Stiffly,

_____

Will Chills

Notice of Rent Withholding

Date:
To: (Name of person or company appearing as lessor on lease)
Re: (12193 Rancho Frio Road, Brisk, Montana, Apt. 3)

This is to inform you that all rents are being withheld because of the repair, living and habitability issues described in my letter to you of (date of intention to withhold) and your failure to make satisfactory corrections. This action is taken in accordance tenants' rights law (chapter and verse).

I will continue to withhold rents until conditions are satisfactorily achieved. Payment of back rents will be determined on the reduced value of the rental unit.

Stiffly,

_____

Will Chills

Breaking a Written Lease

A written lease can be broken with many tenants' rights ordinances under the following situations: when there is a material noncompliance with the lease or landlord's responsibility to maintain the premises after a notice to cure; when the apartment cannot be moved into; when the apartment sustains fire or other casualty damage and is therefore uninhabitable.

For each problem, a letter with the proper notice must be sent.

Notice of Intention To Terminate Lease (for Cause): Violation of [Municipal Code] or Lease Provision

Date:
To: (Landlord)

This is to inform you that I will terminate my lease for the premises I rent (apartment number and address) if you do not immediately comply as follows:

Within (ten) days of the date of this letter, correct the following problems with my (apartment) (building): (State the problem here. It could be a heat problem, a leak or a bad neighbor.)

If you fail to comply satisfactorily and completely by the expiration of the ten-day period, under law, I will terminate my lease and vacate the premises on or before (date, at least 15 days after the landlord receives the notice and no more than 30 days after your ten-day deadline).

With highest regards, I remain, but not for long,

_____

Teuta Lou

Notice of Intention To Terminate Lease: Uninhabitable Conditions (Constructive Eviction)

Date:
To: (Landlord)

This is to inform you that I hereby immediately terminate my lease for the premises I rent (apartment number and address) because the unit is not habitable due to (fire, broken furnace, collapsed roof, no running water or essential services). These conditions occurred within the past 14 days and constitute a material noncompliance with my lease or the [Municipal Code] and do not allow for continued legal occupancy. I will vacate the premises on or before (date). You are required to return to me my security deposit and all prepaid rent from the date of the occurrence of the problem.

Respectfully,

_____

Notice of Wrongful Enforcement of a Prohibited Lease Clause

Date:
To: (Landlord)

This is to inform you that I will (seek) (demand) compensation for (attempted) wrongful enforcement of a prohibited lease clause for the premises I rent (apartment number and address) if you do not immediately comply as follows:

Cease immediately to enforce a lease provision prohibited under the law as of the date of this letter, namely: (repeatedly entering my apartment at any time without prior notice for a nonemergency reason, claiming it as your right under clause 7 of my lease) or (charging me more than the legal late fee).

Furthermore, if you do not cease immediately, this lease will terminate (at least 14 days after landlord receives notice and not more than 30 days after your deadline).

Urgently,

_____

Hattie Nuff

Notice To Cancel Month-to-Month (or Oral) Lease

Date:
To: (Landlord)

This is to inform you that I will terminate my lease for the premises I rent (apartment number and address) on (date).

_____

Ima Gonne

No reason is needed. This notice must be sent at least [31] days before the termination is effective. It must be effective after the last day of your regular rental period. Oral leases typically run on a calendar month. You must send the termination notice before the beginning of the last month of occupancy. Thus, to move out September 30, you must send your notice before the end of August. If you send it September 1, then you are legally stuck until October 31. Get it?

Where you are allowed a shorter notice period, it must be sent prior to the last 10 or 20 days of the rental period—that is, before the 10th or the 20th, so the days don't go over into a new rental period.

Certificate of Delivery

Attach this to *your* copy of whatever official notices or letters you send to your landlord. Use the appropriate delivery method and delete the other method. If you don't know who you gave it to, delete that part too. If you send the notices or letters by certified mail, also send them by regular mail at the same time. Do not send the certificate to the landlord; keep it to use later, in case you go to court.

Certificate of Delivery

I, (name of person delivering notice) did deliver the attached notice by: personally giving a true copy of same to an owner, partner, employee or agent of the Lessor—namely, (name of person or company)—at (address) on (date),

or

by mailing a true copy of same by depositing it with the U.S. Postal Service at (address of post office), certified mail, return receipt requested, and regular mail, on (date).

Under penalty provided by law, the undersigned certifies that the delivery of this notice was made as stated above.

_____   _____

(Signature of deliverer/mailer)   (Date)

Appendix

Sample Rider to the Lease

You will have to make up your own list based on specific conditions. This is just an example in a proper form. Make your rider short so as not to totally overwhelm your landlord. If you have a tenant's rights law, all the code violations problems can be handled after you move in by means of repair and deduct and abatements.

Rider to Lease to be attached to Lease and made part of Lease proper for premises located at _____

_____

between Lessee, _____,

and Lessor (owner, manager and/or agent; address and phone number), _____

_____

_____.

1. Apartment will be repainted by Lessor prior to start of Lease period. The bathroom walls will be painted hard-enamel white; the kitchen walls will be chrome yellow; the kitchen ceiling will be white. The east wall of the living room will be sky-blue pink, and the rest of the apartment will be mauve.

2. The Lessor will repair the kitchen stove and will install a new 14-cubic-foot refrigerator prior to start of Lease period.

3. A doorbell/buzzer/intercom system will be operating prior to start of Lease period.

4. Front- and back-door deadbolt locks will be installed by Lessor, and all keys will be changed from those of the previous tenants.

5. Lessee will be allowed to install shelving on walls. Lessee will restore walls to original condition, filing and sanding screw holes, or Lessor will accept shelving supports to remain after termination of Lease.

6. Indoor hanging plants and outdoor window boxes are permitted. Lessee will fill plant hanger holes or allow hooks to remain at termination of Lease. Lessee will stabilize outdoor plant boxes so they are not in danger of falling.

7. Lessor permits picture hooks, curtain rods, door chains and pot hangers to be installed by Lessee.

8. Lessor will supply disposable air filters for furnace five times a year in January, March, May, September and November.

9. Lessor will supply and install storm windows, weather stripping, caulking and screens for all windows.

10. Installation of a burglar alarm is permitted, including installation of small-gauge wires and detector mechanisms.

11. Storage in the basement is included as part of Lease.

12. Permission is granted for Lessee to install a portable dishwasher in the kitchen.

13. Permission is granted for Lessee to install air conditioners in windows where Lessee so desires to install them.

14. Lessee is granted permission to wallpaper ceiling in bedroom. Lessor will be given approval power as to wallpaper. Paper will be a permanent addition to the apartment, and Lessor will not require its removal at termination of Lease.

15. Three new electrical circuits will be installed in Lessee's apartment. Lessor will provide electricians and materials. The new circuits will be located as follows: one 20-amp circuit in kitchen over counter; one 15-amp circuit in large bedroom near window (for 110-volt air conditioner); one 220-volt, single-phase circuit in living room near north window (for air conditioner). Cost of such work will be split 50/50 between Lessor and Lessee. Lessor will pay for all costs, and Lessee will reimburse Lessor. Cost of work will be approved prior to start of work. Work will be performed within the first 30 days of Lease period.

16. Lessor will pay for repairs of stove, refrigerator, garbage disposal and furnace.

17. Permission is granted for Lessee to park Moped next to back door.

18. All work to be performed (except wiring) will be completed prior to commencement of Lease. Failure to comply with this agreement may result in cancellation of Lease by Lessee, and the return to Lessee of all monies advanced plus other damages to Lessee.

19. As the terms herein change and modify the Lease, this agreement shall hold force and be in effect, and the other clauses so affected are considered null and of no force.

_____   _____
Tenant (Lessee)   Date

_____   _____
Lessor (or agent)   Date

E

Appendix

Universal Tenants' Rights Rider to the Lease

This is also a sample of a suggested rider. It is expressly for tenants who are not covered by a tenants' rights law and wish to ensure their rights contractually. This rider can be tied to almost any lease to protect against sleepers and hard-to-live-with rules.

Rider to Lease to be attached to Lease and made part of Lease proper.

For premises located at _____ ,

between _____ ,

Lessee, and _____ , Lessor (owner, manager and/or agent),

whose business address and phone number are _____

_____ .

1. Lessor warrants, covenants and guarantees the following: that the premises described above are habitable, safe and secure; that there are no latent or potential defects that may affect habitability; that the premises are in compliance with the building code ordinances of the city of _____ and all other applicable regulations of all jurisdictions of city, county, state and federal agencies; that Lessor will maintain building in a like condition for term of Lease.

2. Lessor warrants that Lessor, his agents and assigns will maintain and repair all appliances and equipment that Lessor conveys as part of Lease. The Lessor will maintain the premises in a healthful, clean, safe and sanitary manner and cause others to do likewise. Lessor will maintain and operate and cause to operate properly all essential services, including all plumbing, heating, electrical and water-heating equipment in building, and will repair same immediately. Lessor will supply extermination services on a regular basis and control all vermin.

3. Lessor will issue a written rent receipt for each and every payment of monies tendered as payment for Lessee's rents. Receipt shall be issued at time money is tendered. No monies shall be owing if issuance of a receipt shall be refused.

4. Lessor holds harmless Lessee for damages occurring to the above-described premises when damages are caused by Lessor's poor materials, improper workmanship or incorrect applications or installations. Lessee is further held harmless in the event of damages caused by unknown third parties or circumstances beyond Lessee's control.

5. Lessor will grant a rent setoff if Lessor fails to maintain building in compliance with the building codes; fails to maintain adequate and sufficient essential services; fails to maintain the habitability of the premises at least at the level established at the time the Lease commenced; or fails to make improvements in accordance with other attachments and agreements to the Lease. The setoff will be determined by the decreased fair market value of the premises.

6. Lessor will grant Lessee a rent credit in the form of a rent setoff as reimbursement for any and all payments Lessee makes on behalf of the Lessor in order to maintain essential services including water, gas, oil, coal and electricity; and to make repairs necessary to maintain premises' habitability conditions including, but not limited to, repairs for furnace, water heater, stove, refrigerator, toilets and all other plumbing, windows, storm windows, screens, doors, door locks, floors, walls and ceilings. Lessee will inform Lessor in advance of repairs as to problems and cost of repairs. If Lessor does not respond, Lessee will take all necessary actions.

7. The attached Lease may be canceled prior to the termination date on the face for the following reasons: (a)Lessee is transferred to a new work location further than 60 miles from above-described premises; (b)Lessee dies; (c)Lessor fails to maintain essential services or repair major appliances as promptly as necessary; (d)fire and/or any other conditions make premises unsafe, untenable or uninhabitable. Notice of cancellation will be as follows: transfers—a two-month (60 days) written notice is required (the termination date will coincide with the end of a calendar month); death of lessee—45 days after notice or knowledge of death; fire—to take effect immediately upon receipt of notice; inhabitability—five days from date of notice to make repairs or cancel Lease. (e)Lease may also be canceled by either party when the other party substantially violates any agreement of the Lease or of the attached riders. Costs and damages may also be recovered by either party through action at law if the Lease or attachments are breached.

8. Lessee (tenant) absolutely does not grant any power of attorney to Lessor or his assigns. Lessee does not waive any rights of notice nor does Lessee confess judgment. Lessee does not agree to pay any court or other legal costs on behalf of Lessor unless these are assessed in open court. Lessee will not limit its remedies for damages as they are set forth within the body of the Lease but will retain full rights to action at law in cases of breach or damage against Lessee.

9. Lessor will not unreasonably refuse or reject proposed tenants if Lessee wishes to reassign Lease before termination. It is understood that Lessee will advertise, screen and show the above-described apartment, and these shall be Lessee's sole costs and duties regarding reassignment. All other fees will be borne by assignee and/or Lessor.

10. Lessor warrants that the above-described premises will be delivered in a completed and habitable condition and conveyed to Lessee on the first day of the term of the Lease. Lessor will pay cash damages for all lodging, food, moving and storage expenses and lost income caused by failure to deliver premises on time. If premises is not delivered within 10 days of start of Lease, Lessor will pay all the above expenses plus the difference in rent for another apartment if another apartment of similar type is not available at the rent on the face of the Lease here attached and Lessee cancels this Lease under clauses 7 (c), (d) or (e) of this attachment.

11. The attached Lease shall remain in force until the termination date on the front, regardless of change of ownership. The security deposit shall be transferred and conveyed to any new owner or agent, and the new owner or agent will have the control of same.

12. The attached Lease is renewable at the end of the present term. The amount of rent for renewal shall be reasonable and in keeping with the fair market value of the services and housing offered. Failure to renew Lease because of lawful complaints, tenant activities or action filed by Lessee against Lessor for breaches of the Lease or applicable codes, ordinances, statutes and regulations is prohibited. Lessee shall have recourse to recover damages, including reasonable lawyer's fees and moving expenses. If building is sold, converted to condominiums or no longer habitable, this clause does not apply.

13. The tendering of rents to Lessor is absolutely conditional upon proper performance, by Lessor, of all covenants of Lease agreement, this Universal Rider and all other agreements herein attached. The Lessor's duties shall not be mitigated by any alleged breach by Lessee, which shall be considered independently.

14. In the event of a dispute, the parties agree to a good-faith effort to resolve the issue(s) through the use of mediation with a qualified community mediation service or certified mediation practitioner prior to Lease termination or any action at law. The cost, if any, will be shared mutually by all parties.

_____   _____

Tenant (Lessee)   Date

_____   _____

Lessor (or Agent)   Date

Tenants' Union Building Conditions Survey

This is a short-form housing survey. We originally developed a five-page questionnaire but found it was too cumbersome. This sample should be reworked to reflect the specific problems you have. It should state the name of the owner, management company or building. In addition to surveying conditions, it reveals what rents are, how they have changed and what type of support you have in your organizing attempts.

(Name and address of organization)
(Name of person sending letter)
(Address of organization)
(Phone number)

Dear Tenant,

    For too long _____ Management Company has been making promises to the people who live in the buildings that it owns or manages. And for too long these promises have gone unfulfilled. Each of us has spoken to the company and asked it to fix, finish, install or replace something. Most of the time these things have just not been done. Because we ask alone, individually, we can't bring enough pressure on _____ to get action. Therefore, we, the residents of a _____ Company building at _____, are forming a tenants' union to bring pressure on _____. When we do this, things will start getting fixed and the landlord will listen to our problems. We have found that only through organizing together *all* the tenants in the building can we get things done.

    We insist that the building and apartments where we live be safe, clean and well repaired. We insist that we as tenants be respected as people and not treated like a commercial commodity, pushed around and robbed once a month for the rent.

    For starters, here is a survey that will enable you and us to see what problems exist. Will you please take five minutes and fill it out? Will you join us, so that all of us can live in decent, clean apartments with the dignity we deserve?

Tenants' Union Organizing Committee

Building Survey

Your Name: _____

Address: _____

Phone: _____ Best time to call: _____

1. Does your electrical service work properly (outlets, switches, lights, fuses)?
   ☐ Yes ☐ No

2. Do your appliances work properly (stove, refrigerator)?   ☐ Yes ☐ No

3. Does your plumbing work properly (leaks, pressure, hot water)?
   ☐ Yes ☐ No

4. Do you have all the doors, windows, storm windows, screens that you need?
   ☐ Yes ☐ No

5. Of the ones you have, do all of them work properly (close, lock, unbroken)?
   ☐ Yes ☐ No

6. Are all of your walls and ceilings free of loose paint, plaster, holes and leaks?
   ☐ Yes ☐ No

7. During the winter is your apartment warm enough without being too hot?
   ☐ Yes ☐ No

8. Is your apartment free of roaches and mice?   ☐ Yes ☐ No

9. Are the public areas of your building kept clean and in good repair?
   ☐ Yes ☐ No

10. Do your building's outside doors and mailboxes lock properly?   ☐ Yes ☐ No

11. Is there enough lighting in public areas at night?   ☐ Yes ☐ No

12. Has the landlord responded to your complaints about building problems promptly and courteously?   ☐ Yes ☐ No

13. Has the landlord kept promises to you about repairing and maintaining your building?   ☐ Yes ☐ No

14. If you have any problems other than those listed or want to detail any of these questions, please do. (Use the back if you need more room.) _____

_____

_____

_____

15. Have you had an unjustified rent raise recently?   ☐ Yes ☐ No

16. How much has your rent been raised in the last two years? From $_____ to $_____ .

17. Would you be willing to join a tenants' union to pressure the landlord into maintaining the building properly and keeping the rents fair?   ☐ Yes ☐ No

18. Would you be willing to help organize a meeting of other interested tenants in your building who want to act and bring the landlord into line?
   ☐ Yes ☐ No

Appendix

Sample Tenants' Association Organizational Bylaws and Charter

This is the set of bylaws established by our tenants' association. It states our purposes and establishes a written set of procedures. Use this as a sample and starting point for your own group, and modify the charter to fit your particular situation.

The length of the term of office should be practical—long enough so that someone can learn the ropes and short enough that he or she isn't worn to a frazzle. In our group we wanted to be egalitarian. We didn't want a leader per se, so we called our chief officer the "chair." I think it is bad policy to have a few elites in charge of the association. You must spread the work around in order to get continuing support. If your group is going to incorporate, you must have bylaws and officers, so a charter is a necessary step. If you do not incorporate, a charter is still a good idea. Our charter was developed by the entire association and put in working, practical form by Jerry Smeltzer and David deVries.

Tenants' Association Charter and Bylaws

I. Name

This organization shall be known as the _____ Tenants' Association, hereafter also known as the Association or the ____TA.

II. Purpose

To organize tenants, occupants and residents and to collectively and mutually defend tenants' rights, both legally and morally, in all dealings with the landlord, manager and owner of the building.

To educate ourselves to enable us to survive as tenants with dignity.

To mutually aid and assist all residents for purposes relating to, but not limited to, the health, safety, welfare, security and comfort of each resident.

To mutually and collectively protect ourselves so we may pursue our daily lives as tenants without interference or threat from the landlord, manager or owner.

To assist tenants in other buildings with their own attempts to form their own tenants' groups by providing information and advice, and to join in citywide and statewide tenants' activities.

III. Membership

A. None but actual residents in the building may become members.

B. All residents over 14 years of age are eligible for voting membership in the Association.

C. Residents may become members by notifying the treasurer of the Association and paying dues.

D. Members may leave the Association by notifying the secretary in writing.

E. Members will be considered resigned from the Association if they fail to pay dues for three months and/or fail to attend meetings or respond to notices of meetings. Members who contact the treasurer for the purpose of informing the secretary of their continued interest will be considered reactivated if they pay their dues.

F. Membership is prohibited to any representative, agent or direct employee of the landlord, manager and owner. When rent concessions are granted to residents by the landlord for work performed, the entire membership shall evaluate the relationship between the landlord and those particular residents. If a conflict of interest is determined to exist, then those particular residents will be barred from membership or asked to resign. When no conflict exists, the residents will be admitted and/or their membership continued.

G. All members shall agree to abide by the bylaws of the Association and by the ordinances and rules it shall pass. Payment of dues will constitute acceptance of the bylaws.

IV. Meetings

A. Regular business meetings shall be held on the fourth Monday of every month at 8:30 P.M.

B. Special meetings may be called by any member of the Association through application to the secretary, who must notify all members of the purpose, time and place of the meeting.

C. The secretary shall call all meetings to order.

D. A quorum for any meeting shall be more than half of all members in good standing.

E. Meetings shall be held within the building.

F. Order of Business
   1. Call to order
   2. Reading of previous meeting's minutes
   3. Reports of committees and officers
   4. Treasurer's report
   5. Unfinished business
   6. New business
   7. Nominations and elections
   8. Good and welfare
   9. Adjournment

G. The chair shall at all times keep the meeting in order. He or she shall have the authority to rule any member out of order if the member becomes unruly, speaks out of turn or interrupts another member.

H. To pass any motion, action or ordinance, a majority of all those present and voting is needed. Under no circumstances shall any motion, ordinance or action pass if it receives less than 25 percent of the total number of members of the Association.

I. Proxy votes will be acceptable if the absent member previously submits a written notice to the secretary and states what that member's vote will be. No other proxy or absentee votes will be allowed.

J. Motions defeated may be reintroduced once in the same meeting.

K. Robert's rules of order may be employed if required.

V. Officers

A. *Secretary/Treasurer.* The secretary's duties shall include retaining copies of all records, correspondence and minutes; carrying out all correspondence and making minutes of all meetings; sending out notices of all meetings; notifying members of all pertinent events and activities; calling meetings to order; counting written ballots with the chair; admitting residents to membership; keeping membership rolls; formally writing up all approved legislation; acting in the stead of the chair when the chair is absent. As treasurer, he or she shall retain all financial records; keep books; issue receipts; collect dues; collect other funds; make deposits and issue checks; pay all bills and approved demands.

B. *Chair.* The chair of the Association shall preside over all meetings of the Association; appoint committees and receive committee reports; approve all correspondence; act as spokesperson for the Association; negotiate, represent and defend Association policies, actions and members to the landlord, manager and owner; oversee the daily operations or problems of the Association.

C. All officers shall be elected for a period of six months.

D. No more than one member from the same dwelling unit shall hold office simultaneously.

E. An officer shall not succeed himself or herself more than once (two consecutive terms only), nor shall any person hold a position as an officer for more than three consecutive terms combined.

F. An officer may be recalled from office at a special meeting called for that purpose. It shall require a two-thirds quorum to impeach the officer and a majority vote of that quorum to remove the officer.

G. New elections will be held immediately to replace the officer recalled.

VI. Dues and Finances

A. The sources of revenue for the Association shall be regular monthly dues from the membership; proceeds from special benefits; special assessments; the interim collection of rents; and other sources.

B. All funds will be placed in the regular operations account of the Association, with the exception of rent monies.

C. All rent monies shall be placed in a separate account. These monies will be used to pay the landlord rents due and owing; or pay qualified workmen and suppliers to make necessary and required repairs and to supply necessary and required materials; or pay the courts, as so ordered; or refund members' rents as required.

D. Three signatures will be required to release funds from the banking accounts. The treasurer will sign and obtain two cosignatures from among the membership.

E. Expenditures of funds will be made with the general knowledge and approval of the membership.

F. Dues shall be paid to the Association treasurer.

G. The treasurer shall also collect the rents from all members as required and when necessary.

H. An amended dues structure will be allowed for students and other members not fully employed. The structure will be determined by the membership at large.

VII. Amendments to the Bylaws

These bylaws may be amended by a majority vote conforming to Chapter IV, Section I after notification to all members of intent to change the bylaws.

VIII. Ratification

These bylaws will be ratified when 51 percent of all residents eligible for membership vote for ratification at a special meeting called for that purpose and affix their signatures herein.

Signatures of the founding members:

_____

_____

_____

_____

_____

Appendix

Collective Bargaining Agreement

This is a contract between the tenants' association and the owner or manager of a building. It grants recognition and rights. This is what every building ought to have to protect tenants. The struggle to get such an agreement signed is long and difficult, but it is well worth it.

You must attach to the back of a general agreement a specific list of demands, repair schedules, concessions, arrangements and so on. Consult your community group or a lawyer to make sure you have everything you need in the agreement before offering the contract to the building management.

Good luck, friends, and congratulations!

The credit for this contract goes to David deVries, an association member who researched and prepared the first draft.

Collective Bargaining Agreement and Contract

between

_____ and _____
                Agent   Tenants' Association

Definitions:

Landlord: _____ Management Company, located at _____,
and authorized representatives and agents and their assignees.

Tenants' Association: The sole agent for the tenants, residents and occupants of the (above) building and their designated and authorized representatives, agents and assignees.

Building: The multiple-unit building described as located at _____,
_____, County of _____, ss.

I. Recognition of Association

A. The Landlord hereby recognizes the Tenants' Association as the sole representative of the tenants, residents and occupants in regard to all matters pertaining to the maintenance, upkeep, security, safety and general condition of the building and property on which the building is situated.

B. The Landlord shall have the right to negotiate with individual tenants on such matters as length and condition of lease and amount of rent.

C. The Tenants' Association reserves the right to enter into negotiations with the Landlord on behalf of an individual tenant if said tenant so requests the Association's representations.

D. (1) The Landlord hereby recognizes the right of the Tenants' Association to recruit tenants and potential tenants into the Association, and the Landlord shall not deny the Association access to tenants and potential tenants.

  (2) The Landlord shall advise all potential tenants of the existence of the Association prior to the signing of any lease and shall indicate how the Association may be contacted.

  (3) The Landlord shall advise the Association of all new tenants within 15 days of move-in.

II. Continuity

A. This Agreement and Contract shall remain in force regardless of the person, persons, company, corporation or trust that/who shall own and/or manage this Building.

B. This Agreement shall remain in force indefinitely subject to renegotiation.

III. Renegotiation

A. Either party shall have the right to request renegotiation of this Agreement.

IV. Good Faith

A. It is agreed by both parties that they will bargain in good faith regarding, but not limited to, section I of this Agreement.

B. Agreements reached by the parties to this Contract shall be written, and authorized representatives of both parties will affix their signatures to such documents.

C. It shall constitute a breach of good faith, and a breach of this Agreement, for the Landlord to offer special concessions or other inducements or threats to an individual tenant in an attempt to disrupt or destroy the Tenants' Association or discourage the tenant from participating in the activities of the Association.

D. It shall constitute a breach of good faith, and a breach of this Agreement, for the Landlord to discriminate against a tenant by reason of that tenant's membership in the Tenants' Association or his or her participation therein as regards renewal of lease, amount of rent and all other matters.

E. It shall be a breach of good faith, and a breach of this Contract, to render an unfavorable reference for a tenant because of his or her participation in the Tenants' Association or his or her membership therein.

F. It shall constitute a breach of good faith, and a breach of this Contract, to evict a tenant, occupant or resident of the building for Association membership, activity or participation, including taking part in such actions as lawful picketing of the Landlord, other lawful actions against the Landlord or rent strikes.

G. It shall constitute a breach of good faith, and a breach of this Contract, for the Landlord to include in any lease with any individual tenant or possible tenant in the above Building any part or portion of a lease that is contradictory or in conflict with this Agreement.

H. It shall constitute a breach of good faith, and a breach of this Contract, for the Landlord to (1) prohibit the Association from distributing written materials to all residents concerning Association activities; (2) prohibit Association representatives from contacting residents within the physical confines of the Building or property; (3) prohibit the Association from erecting bulletin or notice boards in public areas of the premises or placing notices in public places.

V. Payment of Rents

A. Payment of rents to management are absolutely dependent upon the Landlord's performance of each and every covenant of this Agreement and all other agreements and attachments hereto. The Landlord covenants and warrants that the above Building is habitable and in substantial compliance with the building, electrical, water, fire and plumbing codes of the city of _____ and all other codes, regulations, ordinances, laws and court decisions that in any way apply. The Landlord further covenants and warrants that he or she will maintain the Building in a habitable condition for the length of each and every lease.

B. Failure to maintain each and every dwelling unit, all public and common areas and all other parts of the Building in a safe, well-repaired, secure, sanitary and lawful manner strikes at the very essence of this Agreement.

C. Failure by the Landlord to properly perform his or her duties under this clause is good and sufficient reason for all rents to be withheld until such time as compliance is demonstrated.

D. The Tenants' Association may take any other action it deems necessary to protect the health, safety and welfare of its membership, including hiring outside contractors to perform urgent or necessary tasks, and paying for the same from withheld rents, provided that no such act shall be done until after the Landlord is duly notified and fails to take satisfactory action promptly.

VI. Grievance Procedure

A. Authorized representatives of both parties shall meet jointly not less than once every two weeks on a regular basis to present, negotiate and resolve grievances arising out of this Agreement, its attachments and other agreements and arrangements reached under this Agreement.

B. Emergency meetings of the above joint grievance committee may be called on a 24-hour notice by any member of the grievance committee. Such meetings shall be called in writing, and the notice shall state the specific reason for the emergency meeting. Notice must be delivered to the chief representative of each party.

C. All grievances shall be presented in writing.

D. All settlements and resolutions shall be in writing and signed by representatives of both parties.

E. The grievance committee will establish a priority of grievances; (1) Class I grievances shall be considered the most urgent with immediate resolution required; (2) Class II grievances will be considered serious grievances with prompt attention required; (3) Class III grievances will be considered minor situations that require correction within a reasonable time; (4) Class IV grievances relate to long-term problems and need considerable time to correct.

F. The joint grievance committee shall be authorized to negotiate final settlements.

G. Mediation shall be employed if the joint committee cannot adequately resolve a grievance. A mutually acceptable and neutral mediator shall be approved by the joint committee.

H. Upon failure to resolve a complaint by performance, negotiation or mediation, the Tenants' Association may take any action it deems necessary to protect the health, safety, security and welfare of its membership including (1) withholding rents; (2) hiring outside contractors to perform urgent or necessary tasks and paying for the same from withheld rents and/or deducting the amount of the payments from future rents; and (3) taking action at law.

The Landlord shall be notified in writing prior to any such actions.

VII. Contract

Upon the signing by both parties to this Agreement, this Collective Bargaining Agreement shall become a binding and legal Contract between the two parties and shall be made a part of each and every lease signed between management and Tenants' Association members, now and in the future. Further, that where conflict exists between this Agreement (and its attachments) and the lease, only this Agreement shall survive, and the other shall be considered null and void.

_____   _____
For the Association   Date

_____   _____
For the Landlord   Date

I

Appendix

Lease Cancellation Agreement

When you cancel your lease before expiration, or if there is some confusion as to when a written lease is supposed to expire (because of notice or renewal provisions), use this agreement to make sure you are off the hook.

Lease Cancellation Agreement

The lease for the premises located at _____, Unit _____, is hereby terminated and cancelled effective on _____. Lessee will vacate the premises on or before _____. Lessor will return all prepaid rents, security deposit and security deposit interest to Lessee on or before _____ by delivering same to _____.

_____   _____
Lessee (Tenant)   (Date)

_____   _____
Lessor (Landlord/Agent)   (Date)

Lease Assignment Agreement

If you are moving early and have found a replacement tenant but your landlord won't cancel your lease, use this form to get out from under. Remember, with a *sublet* you are still 100 percent responsible for the lease. With an assignment, you typically are not.

Assignment of Lease

The lease for the premises located at _____, Unit _____, is hereby assigned to _____, whose current address is _____. Lessee conveys the lease and possession of the above premises effective on _____. Assignee pays over to Lessee the sum of $_____, in compensation for security deposit, interest and prepaid rents held by Lessor, and Lessee acknowledges receipt. Upon the effective date, Assignee agrees to and assumes all responsibility for the rents, the premises, the terms, conditions and rules of the lease and any damages claimed by Lessor, until the lease expires or is terminated according to law or agreement. Lessee is released from the lease as of the effective date of the assignment and is held harmless from further action in regards to the lease or this assignment.

This Assignment is to be made part of the lease and attached to the lease, a copy of which has been given to Assignee, receipt of which is acknowledged.

_____   _____
Assignee (New tenant)   (Date)

_____   _____
Lessee (Current tenant)   (Date)

_____   _____
Lessor (if required)   (Date)

K

Appendix

Uniform Residential Landlord and Tenant Act

ARTICLE I
GENERAL PROVISIONS AND DEFINITIONS

PART I
SHORT TITLE, CONSTRUCTION, APPLICATION
AND SUBJECT MATTER OF THE ACT

SECTION 1.101. [*Short Title.*] This Act shall be known and may be cited as the "Uniform Residential Landlord and Tenant Act."

SECTION 1.102. [*Purposes; Rules of Construction.*]
(a) This Act shall be liberally construed and applied to promote its underlying purposes and policies.
(b) Underlying purposes and policies of this Act are
   (1) to simplify, clarify, modernize, and revise the law governing the rental of dwelling units and the rights and obligations of landlords and tenants;
   (2) to encourage landlords and tenants to maintain and improve the quality of housing; and
   (3) to make uniform the law with respect to the subject of this Act among those states which enact it.

SECTION 1.103. [*Supplementary Principles of Law Applicable.*] Unless displaced by the provisions of this Act, the principles of law and equity, including the law relating to capacity to contract, mutuality of obligations, principal and agent, real property, public health, safety and fire prevention, estoppel, fraud, misrepresentation, duress, coercion, mistake, bankruptcy, or other validating or invalidating cause supplement its provisions.

SECTION 1.104. [*Construction Against Implicit Repeal.*] This Act being a general act intended as a unified coverage of its subject matter, no part of it is to be construed as impliedly repealed by subsequent legislation if that construction can reasonably be avoided.

Note: This is reproduced with the kind permission of the National Conference of Commissioners on Uniform State Laws. For the full version with additional legal language and legal commentary, send $7.00 to the National Conference at 676 North St. Clair Street, Chicago, IL 60611 (312-915-0195).

Section 1.105. [*Administration of Remedies; Enforcement.*]

(a) The remedies provided by this Act shall be so administered that an aggrieved party may recover appropriate damages. The aggrieved party has a duty to mitigate damages.

(b) Any right or obligation declared by this Act is enforceable by action unless the provision declaring it specifies a different and limited effect.

Section 1.106. [*Settlement of Disputed Claim or Right.*]   A claim or right arising under this Act or on a rental agreement, if disputed in good faith, may be settled by agreement.

Part II
Scope and Jurisdiction

Section 1.201. [*Territorial Application.*]   This Act applies to, regulates, and determines rights, obligations, and remedies under a rental agreement, wherever made, for a dwelling unit located within this state.

Section 1.202. [*Exclusions from Application of Act.*]   Unless created to avoid the application of this Act, the following arrangements are not governed by this Act:

(1) residence at an institution, public or private, if incidental to detention or the provision of medical, geriatric, educational, counseling, religious, or similar service;

(2) occupancy under a contract of sale of a dwelling unit or the property of which it is a part, if the occupant is the purchaser or a person who succeeds to his interest;

(3) occupancy by a member of a fraternal or social organization in the portion of a structure operated for the benefit of the organization;

(4) transient occupancy in a hotel, or motel [or lodgings [subject to special taxes]];

(5) occupancy by an employee of a landlord whose right to occupancy is conditional upon employment in and about the premises;

(6) occupancy by an owner of a condominium unit or a holder of a proprietary lease in a cooperative;

(7) occupancy under a rental agreement covering premises used by the occupant primarily for agricultural purposes.

Part III
General Definitions and
Principles of Interpretation: Notice

Section 1.301. [*General Definitions.*]   Subject to additional definitions contained in subsequent Articles of this Act which apply to specific Articles or Parts thereof, and unless the context otherwise requires, in this Act

(1) "action" includes recoupment, counterclaim, set-off, suit in equity, and any other proceeding in which rights are determined, including an action for possession;

(2) "building and housing codes" include any law, ordinance, or governmental regulation concerning fitness for habitation, or the construction, maintenance, operation, occupancy, use or appearance of any premises or dwelling unit;

(3) "dwelling unit" means a structure or the part of a structure that is used as a home, residence, or sleeping place by one person who maintains a household or by 2 or more persons who maintain a common household;

(4) "good faith" means honesty in fact in the conduct of the transaction concerned;

(5) "landlord" means the owner, lessor, or sublessor of the dwelling unit or the building of which it is a part, and it also means a manager of the premises who fails to disclose as required by Section 2.102;

(6) "organization" includes a corporation, government, governmental subdivision or agency, business trust, estate, trust, partnership or association, 2 or more persons having a joint or common interest, and any other legal or commercial entity;

(7) "owner" means one or more persons, jointly or severally, in whom is vested (i) all or part of the legal title to property or (ii), all or part of the beneficial ownership and a right to present use and enjoyment of the premises. The term includes a mortgagee in possession;

(8) "person" includes an individual or organization;

(9) "premises" means a dwelling unit and the structure of which it is a part and facilities and appurtenances therein and grounds, areas, and facilities held out for the use of tenants generally or whose use is promised to the tenant;

(10) "rent" means all payments to be made to or for the benefit of the landlord under the rental agreement;

(11) "rental agreement" means all agreements, written or oral, and valid rules and regulations adopted under Section 3.102 embodying the terms and conditions concerning the use and occupancy of a dwelling unit and premises;

(12) "roomer" means a person occupying a dwelling unit that does not include a toilet and either a bath tub or a shower and a refrigerator, stove, and kitchen sink, all provided by the landlord, and where one or more of these facilities are used in common by occupants in the structure;

(13) "single family residence" means a structure maintained and used as a single dwelling unit. Notwithstanding that a dwelling unit shares one or more walls with another dwelling unit, it is a single family residence if it has direct access to a street or thoroughfare and shares neither heating facilities, hot water equipment, nor any other essential facility or service with any other dwelling unit;

(14) "tenant" means a person entitled under a rental agreement to occupy a dwelling unit to the exclusion of others.

SECTION 1.302. [*Obligation of Good Faith.*] Every duty under this Act and every act which must be performed as a condition precedent to the exercise of a right or remedy under this Act imposes an obligation of good faith in its performance or enforcement.

SECTION 1.303. [*Unconscionability.*]

(a) If the court, as a matter of law, finds

(1) a rental agreement or any provision thereof was unconscionable when made, the court may refuse to enforce the agreement, enforce the remainder of the agreement without the unconscionable provision, or limit the application of any unconscionable provision to avoid an unconscionable result; or

(2) a settlement in which a party waives or agrees to forego a claim or right under this Act or under a rental agreement was unconscionable when made, the court may refuse to enforce the settlement, enforce the remainder of the settlement without the unconscionable provision, or limit the application of any unconscionable provision to avoid an unconscionable result.

(b) If unconscionability is put into issue by a party or by the court upon its own motion the parties shall be afforded a reasonable opportunity to present evidence as to the setting, purpose, and effect of the rental agreement or settlement to aid the court in making the determination.

SECTION 1.304. [*Notice.*]
(a) A person has notice of a fact if
  (1) he has actual knowledge of it,
  (2) he has received a notice or notification of it, or
  (3) from all the facts and circumstances known to him at the time in question he has reason to know that it exists.
  A person "knows" or "has knowledge" of a fact if he has actual knowledge of it.
(b) A person "notifies" or "gives" a notice or notification to another person by taking steps reasonably calculated to inform the other in ordinary course whether or not the other actually comes to know of it. A person "receives" a notice or notification when
  (1) it comes to his attention; or
  (2) in the case of the landlord, it is delivered at the place of business of the landlord through which the rental agreement was made or at any place held out by him as the place for receipt of the communication; or
  (3) in the case of the tenant, it is delivered in hand to the tenant or mailed by registered or certified mail to him at the place held out by him as the place for receipt of the communication, or in the absence of such designation, to his last known place of residence.
(c) "Notice," knowledge or a notice or notification received by an organization is effective for a particular transaction from the time it is brought to the attention of the individual conducting that transaction, and in any event from the time it would have been brought to his attention if the organization had exercised reasonable diligence.

PART IV
GENERAL PROVISIONS

SECTION 1.401. [*Terms and Conditions of Rental Agreement.*]
(a) A landlord and a tenant may include in a rental agreement terms and conditions not prohibited by this Act or other rule of law, including rent, term of the agreement, and other provisions governing the rights and obligations of the parties.
(b) In absence of agreement, the tenant shall pay as rent the fair rental value for the use and occupancy of the dwelling unit.
(c) Rent is payable without demand or notice at the time and place agreed upon by the parties. Unless otherwise agreed, rent is payable at the dwelling unit and periodic rent is payable at the beginning of any term of one month or less and otherwise in equal monthly installments at the beginning of each month. Unless otherwise agreed, rent is uniformly apportionable from day-to-day.
(d) Unless the rental agreement fixes a definite term, the tenancy is week-to-week in case of a roomer who pays weekly rent, and in all other cases month-to-month.

SECTION 1.402. [*Effect of Unsigned or Undelivered Rental Agreement.*]
(a) If the landlord does not sign and deliver a written rental agreement signed and delivered to him by the tenant, acceptance of rent without reservation by the landlord gives the rental agreement the same effect as if it had been signed and delivered by the landlord.
(b) If the tenant does not sign and deliver a written agreement signed and delivered to him by the landlord, acceptance of possession and payment of rent without reservation gives the rental agreement the same effect as if it had been signed and delivered by the tenant.

(c) If a rental agreement given effect by the operation of this section provides for a term longer than one year, it is effective for only one year.

SECTION 1.403. [*Prohibited Provisions in Rental Agreements.*]
(a) A rental agreement may not provide that the tenant:
    (1) agrees to waive or forego rights or remedies under this Act;
    (2) authorizes any person to confess judgment on a claim arising out of the rental agreement;
    (3) agrees to pay the landlord's attorney's fees; or
    (4) agrees to the exculpation or limitation of any liability of the landlord arising under law or to indemnify the landlord for that liability or the costs connected therewith.
(b) A provision prohibited by subsection (a) included in a rental agreement is unenforceable. If a landlord deliberately uses a rental agreement containing provisions known to him to be prohibited, the tenant may recover in addition to his actual damages an amount up to [3] months' periodic rent and reasonable attorney's fees.

SECTION 1.404. [*Separation of Rents and Obligations to Maintain Property Forbidden.*] A rental agreement, assignment, conveyance, trust deed, or security instrument may not permit the receipt of rent free of the obligation to comply with Section 2.104(a).

ARTICLE II

LANDLORD OBLIGATIONS

SECTION 2.101. [*Security Deposits; Prepaid Rent.*]
(a) A landlord may not demand or receive security, however denominated, in an amount or value in excess of [1] month[s] periodic rent.
(b) Upon termination of the tenancy property or money held by the landlord as security may be applied to the payment of accrued rent and the amount of damages which the landlord has suffered by reason of the tenant's noncompliance with Section 3.101 all as itemized by the landlord in a written notice delivered to the tenant together with the amount due [14] days after termination of the tenancy and delivery of possession and demand by the tenant.
(c) If the landlord fails to comply with subsection (b) or if he fails to return any prepaid rent required to be paid to the tenants under this Act the tenant may recover the property and money due him together with damages in an amount equal to [twice] the amount wrongfully withheld and reasonable attorney's fees.
(d) This section does not preclude the landlord or tenant from recovering other damages to which he may be entitled under this Act.
(e) The holder of the landlord's interest in the premises at the time of the termination of the tenancy is bound by this section.

SECTION 2.102. [*Disclosure.*]
(a) A landlord or any person authorized to enter into a rental agreement on his behalf shall disclose to the tenant in writing at or before the commencement of the tenancy the name and address of
    (1) the person authorized to manage the premises; and
    (2) an owner of the premises or a person authorized to act for and on behalf of the owner for the purpose of service of process and receiving and receipting for notices and demands.

(b) The information required to be furnished by this section shall be kept current and this section extends to and is enforceable against any successor landlord, owner, or manager.

(c) A person who fails to comply with subsection (a) becomes an agent of each person who is a landlord for:

(1) service of process and receiving and receipting for notices and demands; and

(2) performing the obligations of the landlord under this Act and under the rental agreement and expending or making available for the purpose all rent collected from the premises.

SECTION 2.103. [*Landlord to Deliver Possession of Dwelling Unit.*] At the commencement of the term a landlord shall deliver possession of the premises to the tenant in compliance with the rental agreement and Section 2.104. The landlord may bring an action for possession against any person wrongfully in possession and may recover the damages provided in Section 4.301(c).

SECTION 2.104. [*Landlord to Maintain Premises.*]

(a) A landlord shall

(1) comply with the requirements of applicable building and housing codes materially affecting health and safety;

(2) make all repairs and do whatever is necessary to put and keep the premises in a fit and habitable condition;

(3) keep all common areas of the premises in a clean and safe condition;

(4) maintain in good and safe working order and condition all electrical, plumbing, sanitary, heating, ventilating, air-conditioning, and other facilities and appliances, including elevators, supplied or required to be supplied by him;

(5) provide and maintain appropriate receptacles and conveniences for the removal of ashes, garbage, rubbish and other waste incidental to the occupancy of the dwelling unit and arrange for their removal; and

(6) supply running water and reasonable amounts of hot water at all times and reasonable heat [between [October 1] and [May 1]] except where the building that includes the dwelling unit is not required by law to be equipped for that purpose, or the dwelling unit is so constructed that heat or hot water is generated by an installation within the exclusive control of the tenant and supplied by a direct public utility connection.

(b) If the duty imposed by paragraph (1) of subsection (a) is greater than any duty imposed by any other paragraph of that subsection, the landlord's duty shall be determined by reference to paragraph (1) of subsection (a).

(c) The landlord and tenant of a single family residence may agree in writing that the tenant perform the landlord's duties specified in paragraphs (5) and (6) of subsection (a) and also specified repairs, maintenance tasks, alterations, and remodeling, but only if the transaction is entered into in good faith.

(d) The landlord and tenant of any dwelling unit other that a single family residence may agree that the tenant is to perform specified repairs, maintenance tasks, alterations, or remodeling only if

(1) the agreement of the parties is entered into in good faith and is set forth in a separate writing signed by the parties and supported by adequate consideration;

(2) the work is not necessary to cure noncompliance with subsection (a)(1) of this section; and

(3) the agreement does not diminish or affect the obligation of the landlord to other tenants in the premises.

(e) The landlord may not treat performance of the separate agreement described in subsection (d) as a condition to any obligation or performance of any rental agreement.

SECTION 2.105. [*Limitation of Liability.*]
(a) Unless otherwise agreed, a landlord who conveys premises that include a dwelling unit subject to a rental agreement in a good faith sale to a bona fide purchaser is relieved of liability under the rental agreement and this Act as to events occurring after written notice to the tenant of the conveyance. However, he remains liable to the tenant for all security recoverable by the tenant under Section 2.101 and all prepaid rent.
(b) Unless otherwise agreed, a manager of the premises that include a dwelling unit is relieved of liability under the rental agreement and this Act as to events occurring after written notice to the tenant of the termination of his management.

ARTICLE III
TENANT OBLIGATIONS

SECTION 3.101. [*Tenant to Maintain Dwelling Unit.*] A tenant shall
(1) comply with all obligations primarily imposed upon tenants by applicable provisions of building and housing codes materially affecting health and safety;
(2) keep that part of the premises that he occupied and uses as clean and safe as the condition of premises permit;
(3) dispose from his dwelling unit all ashes, garbage, rubbish, and other waste in a clean and safe manner;
(4) keep all plumbing fixtures in the dwelling unit or used by the tenant as clean as their condition permits;
(5) use in a reasonable manner all electrical, plumbing, sanitary, heating, ventilating, air-conditioning, and other facilities and appliances including elevators in the premises;
(6) not deliberately or negligently destroy, deface, damage, impair, or remove any part of the premises or knowingly permit any person to do so; and
(7) conduct himself and require other persons on the premises with his consent to conduct themselves in a manner that will not disturb his neighbors' peaceful enjoyment of the premises.

SECTION 3.102. [*Rules and Regulations.*]
(a) A landlord, from time to time, may adopt a rule or regulation, however described, concerning the tenant's use and occupancy of the premises. It is enforceable against the tenant only if
(1) its purpose is to promote the convenience, safety, or welfare of the tenants in the premises, preserve the landlord's property from abusive use, or make a fair distribution of services and facilities held out for the tenants generally;
(2) it is reasonably related to the purpose of which it is adopted;
(3) it applies to all tenants in the premises in a fair manner;
(4) it is sufficiently explicit in its prohibition, direction, or limitation of the tenant's conduct to fairly inform him of what he must or must not do to comply;
(5) it is not for the purpose of evading the obligations of the landlord; and
(6) the tenant has notice of it at the time he enters into the rental agreement, or when it is adopted.

(b) If a rule or regulation is adopted after the tenant enters into the rental agreement that works a substantial modification of his bargain it is not valid unless the tenant consents to it in writing.

SECTION 3.103. [*Access.*]

(a) A tenant shall not unreasonably withhold consent to the landlord to enter into the dwelling unit in order to inspect the premises, make necessary or agreed repairs, decorations, alterations, or improvements, supply necessary or agreed services, or exhibit the dwelling unit to prospective or actual purchasers, mortgagees, tenants, workmen, or contractors.

(b) A landlord may enter the dwelling unit without consent of the tenant in case of emergency.

(c) A landlord shall not abuse the right of access or use it to harass the tenant. Except in case of emergency or unless it is impracticable to do so, the landlord shall give the tenant at least [2] days' notice of his intent to enter and may enter only at reasonable times.

(d) A landlord has no other right of access except
  (1) pursuant to court order;
  (2) as permitted by Sections 4.202 and 4.203(b); or
  (3) unless the tenant has abandoned or surrendered the premises.

SECTION 3.104. [*Tenant to Use and Occupy.*] Unless otherwise agreed, a tenant shall occupy his dwelling unit only as a dwelling unit. The rental agreement may require that the tenant notify the landlord of any anticipated extended absence from the premises [in excess of [7] days] no later than the first day of the extended absence.

ARTICLE IV
REMEDIES

PART I
TENANT REMEDIES

SECTION 4.101. [*Noncompliance by the Landlord—In General.*]

(a) Except as provided in this Act, if there is a material noncompliance by the landlord with the rental agreement or a noncompliance with Section 2.104 materially affecting health and safety, the tenant may deliver a written notice to the landlord specifying the acts and omission constituting the breach and that the rental agreement will terminate upon a date not less than [30] days after receipt of the notice if the breach is not remedied in [14] days, and the rental agreement shall terminate as provided in the notice subject to the following:

  (1) If the breach is remediable by repairs, the payment of damages or otherwise and the landlord adequately remedies the breach before the date specified in the notice, the rental agreement shall not terminate by reason of the breach.

  (2) If substantially the same act or omission which constituted a prior noncompliance of which notice was given recurs within [6] months, the tenant may terminate the rental agreement upon at least [14 days'] written notice specifying the breach and the date of termination of the rental agreement.

  (3) The tenant may not terminate for a condition caused by the deliberate or negligent act or omission of the tenant, a member of his family, or other person on the premises with his consent.

(b) Except as provided in this Act, the tenant may recover actual damages and obtain injunctive relief for noncompliance by the landlord with the rental agreement or Section 2.104. If the landlord's noncompliance is willful the tenant may recover reasonable attorney's fees.

(c) The remedy provided in subsection (b) is in addition to any right of the tenant arising under Section 4.101(a).

(d) If the rental agreement is terminated, the landlord shall return all security recoverable by the tenant under Section 2.101 and all prepaid rent.

SECTION 4.102. [*Failure to Deliver Possession.*]

(a) If the landlord fails to deliver possession of the dwelling unit to the tenant as provided in Section 2.103, rent abates until possession is delivered and the tenant may

  (1) terminate the rental agreement upon at least [5] days' written notice to the landlord and upon termination the landlord shall return all prepaid rent and security; or

  (2) demand performance of the rental agreement by the landlord and, if the tenant elects, obtain possession of the dwelling unit from the landlord or any person wrongfully in possession and recover the actual damages sustained by him.

(b) If a person's failure to deliver possession is willful and not in good faith, an aggrieved person may recover from that person an amount not more than [3] months' periodic rent or [threefold] the actual damages sustained, whichever is greater, and reasonable attorney's fees.

SECTION 4.103. [*Self-Help for Minor Defects.*]

(a) If the landlord fails to comply with the rental agreement or Section 2.104, and the reasonable cost of compliance is less than [$100], or an amount equal to [one-half] the periodic rent, whichever amount is greater, the tenant may recover damages for the breach under Section 4.101(b) or may notify the landlord of his intention to correct the condition at the landlord's expense. If the landlord fails to comply with [14] days after being notified by the tenant in writing or as promptly as conditions require in case of emergency, the tenant may cause the work to be done in a workmanlike manner and, after submitting to the landlord an itemized statement, deduct from his rent the actual and reasonable cost or the fair and reasonable value of the work, not exceeding the amount specified in this subsection.

(b) A tenant may not repair at the landlord's expense if the condition was caused by the deliberate or negligent act or omission of the tenant, a member of his family, or other person on the premises with his consent.

SECTION 4.104. [*Wrongful Failure to Supply Heat, Water, Hot Water or Essential Services.*]

(a) If contrary to the rental agreement or Section 2.104 the landlord willfully or negligently fails to supply heat, running water, hot water, electric, gas or other essential service, the tenant may give written notice to the landlord specifying the breach and may

  (1) take reasonable and appropriate measures to secure reasonable amounts of heat, hot water, running water, electric, gas, and other essential service during the period of the landlord's noncompliance and deduct their actual and reasonable costs from the periodic rent; or

  (2) recover damages based upon the diminution in the fair rental value of the dwelling unit; or

(3) procure reasonable substitute housing during the period of the landlord's noncompliance, in which case the tenant is excused from paying rent for the period of the landlord's noncompliance.

(b) In addition to the remedy provided in paragraph (3) of subsection (a) the tenant may recover the actual and reasonable cost or fair and reasonable value of the substitute housing not in excess of an amount equal to the periodic rent, and in any case under subsection (a) reasonable attorney's fees.

(c) If the tenant proceeds under this section, he may not proceed under Section 4.101 or Section 4.103 as to that breach.

(d) Rights of the tenant under this section do not arise until he has given notice to the landlord or if the condition was caused by the deliberate or negligent act or omission of the tenant, a member of his family, or other person on the premises with his consent.

SECTION 4.105. [*Landlord's Noncompliance as Defense to Action for Possession or Rent.*]

(a) In an action for possession based upon nonpayment of the rent or in an action for rent when the tenant is in possession, the tenant may [counterclaim] for any amount he may recover under the rental agreement or this Act. In that event the court from time to time may order the tenant to pay into court all or part of the rent accrued and thereafter accruing, and shall determine the amount due to each party. The party to whom a net amount is owed shall be paid first from the money paid into court, and the balance by the other party. If no rent remains due after application of this section, judgment shall be entered for the tenant in the action for possession. If the defense or counterclaim by the tenant is without merit and is not raised in good faith, the landlord may recover reasonable attorney's fees.

(b) In an action for rent when the tenant is not in possession, he may [counterclaim] as provided in subsection (a) but is not required to pay any rent into court.

SECTION 4.106. [*Fire or Casualty Damage.*]

(a) If the dwelling unit or premises are damaged or destroyed by fire or casualty to an extent that enjoyment of the dwelling unit is substantially impaired, the tenant may

(1) immediately vacate the premises and notify the landlord in writing within [14] days thereafter of his intention to terminate the rental agreement, in which case the rental agreement terminates as of the date of vacating; or

(2) if continued occupancy is lawful, vacate any part of the dwelling unit rendered unusable by the fire or casualty, in which case the tenant's liability for rent is reduced in proportion to the diminution in the fair rental value of the dwelling unit.

(b) If the rental agreement is terminated the landlord shall return all security recoverable under Section 2.101 and all prepaid rent. Accounting for rent in the event of termination or apportionment shall be made as of the date of the fire or casualty.

SECTION 4.107. [*Tenant's Remedies for Landlord's Unlawful Ouster, Exclusion, or Diminution or Service.*] If a landlord unlawfully removes or excludes the tenant from the premises or willfully diminishes services to the tenant by interrupting or causing the interruption of heat, running water, hot water, electric, gas, or other essential service, the tenant may recover possession or terminate the rental agreement and, in either case, recover an amount not more than [3] months' periodic rent or [threefold] the actual damages sustained by him, whichever is greater, and reasonable attorney's fees. If the rental agreement is terminated the landlord shall return all security recoverable under Section 2.101 and all prepaid rent.

PART II

LANDLORD REMEDIES

SECTION 4.201. [*Noncompliance with Rental Agreement; Failure to Pay Rent.*]

(a) Except as provided in this Act, if there is a material noncompliance by the tenant with the rental agreement or a noncompliance with Section 3.101 materially affecting health and safety, the landlord may deliver a written notice to the tenant specifying the acts and omissions constituting the breach and that the rental agreement will terminate upon a date not less than [30] days after receipt of the notice. If the breach is not remedied in [14] days, the rental agreement shall terminate as provided in the notice subject to the following. If the breach is remediable by repairs or the payment of damages or otherwise and the tenant adequately remedies the breach before the date specified in the notice, the rental agreement shall not terminate. If substantially the same act or omission which constituted a prior noncompliance of which notice was given recurs within [6] months, the landlord may terminate the rental agreement upon at least [14] days' written notice specifying the breach and the date of termination of the rental agreement.

(b) If rent is unpaid when due and the tenant fails to pay rent within [14] days after written notice by the landlord of nonpayment and his intention to terminate the rental agreement if the rent is not paid within that period, the landlord may terminate the rental agreement.

(c) Except as provided in this Act, the landlord may recover actual damages and obtain injunctive relief for noncompliance by the tenant with the rental agreement or Section 3.101. If the tenant's noncompliance is willful the landlord may recover reasonable attorney's fees.

SECTION 4.202. [*Failure to Maintain.*] If there is noncompliance by the tenant with Section 3.101 materially affecting health and safety that can be remedied by repair, replacement of a damaged item, or cleaning, and the tenant fails to comply as promptly as conditions require in case of emergency or within [14] days after written notice by the landlord specifying the breach and requesting that the tenant remedy it within that period of time, the landlord may enter the dwelling unit and cause the work to be done in a workmanlike manner and submit the itemized bill for the actual and reasonable cost or the fair and reasonable value thereof as rent on the next date periodic rent is due, or if the rental agreement has terminated, for immediate payment.

SECTION 4.203. [*Remedies for Absence, Nonuse and Abandonment.*]

(a) If the rental agreement requires the tenant to give notice to the landlord of an anticipated extended absence [in excess of [7] days] pursuant to Section 3.104 and the tenant willfully fails to do so, the landlord may recover actual damages from the tenant.

(b) During any absence of the tenant in excess of [7] days, the landlord may enter the dwelling unit at times reasonably necessary.

(c) If the tenant abandons the dwelling unit, the landlord shall make reasonable efforts to rent it at a fair rental. If the landlord rents the dwelling unit for a term beginning before the expiration of the rental agreement, it terminates as of the date of the new tenancy. If the landlord fails to use reasonable efforts to rent the dwelling unit at a fair rental or if the landlord accepts the abandonment as a surrender, the rental agreement is deemed to be terminated by the landlord as of the date the landlord has notice of the abandonment. If the tenancy is from month-to-month or week-to-week, the term of the rental agreement for this purpose is deemed to be a month or a week, as the case may be.

SECTION 4.204. [*Waiver of Landlord's Right to Terminate.*] Acceptance of rent with knowledge of a default by the tenant or acceptance of performance by him that varies from the terms of the rental agreement constitutes a waiver of the landlord's right to terminate the rental agreement for that breach, unless otherwise agreed after the breach has occurred.

SECTION 4.205. [*Landlord Liens; Distress for Rent.*]
(a) A lien or security interest on behalf of the landlord in the tenant's household goods is not enforceable unless perfected before the effective date of this Act.
(b) Distraint for rent is abolished.

SECTION 4.206. [*Remedy after Termination.*]   If the rental agreement is terminated, the landlord has a claim for possession and for rent and a separate claim for actual damages for breach of the rental agreement and reasonable attorney's fees as provided in Section 4.201(c).

SECTION 4.207. [*Recovery of Possession Limited.*]   A landlord may not recover or take possession of the dwelling unit by action or otherwise, including willful diminution of services to the tenant by interrupting or causing the interruption of heat, running water, hot water, electric, gas, or other essential service to the tenant, except in case of abandonment, surrender, or as permitted in this Act.

PART III
PERIODIC TENANCY; HOLDOVER; ABUSE OF ACCESS

SECTION 4.301. [*Periodic Tenancy; Holdover Remedies.*]
(a) The landlord or the tenant may terminate a week-to-week tenancy by a written notice given to the other at least [10] days before the termination date specified in the notice.
(b) The landlord or the tenant may terminate a month-to-month tenancy by a written notice given to the other at least [60] days before the periodic rental date specified in the notice.
(c) If the tenant remains in possession without the landlord's consent after expiration of the term of the rental agreement or its termination, the landlord may bring an action for possession and if the tenant's holdover is willful and not in good faith the landlord may also recover an amount not more than [3] month's periodic rent or [threefold] the actual damages sustained by him, whichever is greater, and reasonable attorney's fees. If the landlord consents to the tenant's continued occupancy, Section 1.401(d) applies.

SECTION 4.302. [*Landlord and Tenant Remedies for Abuse or Access.*]
(a) If the tenant refuses to allow lawful access, the landlord may obtain injunctive relief to compel access, or terminate the rental agreement. In either case the landlord may recover actual damages and reasonable attorney's fees.
(b) If the landlord makes an unlawful entry or a lawful entry in an unreasonable manner or makes repeated demands for entry otherwise lawful but which have the

effect of unreasonably harassing the tenant, the tenant may obtain injunctive relief to prevent the recurrence of the conduct or terminate the rental agreement. In either case the tenant may recover actual damages [not less than an amount equal to [1] month's rent] and reasonable attorney's fees.

ARTICLE V

RETALIATORY CONDUCT

SECTION 5.101. [RETALIATORY CONDUCT PROHIBITED.]

(a) Except as provided in this section, a landlord may not retaliate by increasing rent or decreasing services or by bringing or threatening to bring an action for possession after:

    (1) the tenant has complained to a governmental agency charged with responsibility for enforcement of a building or housing code of a violation applicable to the premises materially affecting health and safety; or

    (2) the tenant has complained to the landlord of a violation under Section 2.104; or

    (3) the tenant has organized or become a member of a tenant's union or similar organization.

(b) If the landlord acts in violation of subsection (a), the tenant is entitled to the remedies provided in Section 4.107 and has a defense in any retaliatory action against him for possession. In an action by or against the tenant, evidence of a complaint within [1] year before the alleged act of retaliation creates a presumption that the landlord's conduct was in retaliation. The presumption does not arise if the tenant made the complaint after notice of a proposed rent increase or diminution of services. "Presumption" means that the trier of fact must find the existence of the fact presumed unless and until evidence is introduced which would support a finding of its nonexistence.

(c) Notwithstanding subsections (a) and (b), a landlord may bring an action for possession if:

    (1) the violation of the applicable building or housing code was caused primarily by lack of reasonable care by the tenant, a member of his family, or other person on the premises with his consent; or

    (2) the tenant is in default in rent; or

    (3) compliance with the applicable building or housing code requires alteration, remodeling, or demolition which would effectively deprive the tenant use of the dwelling unit.

(d) The maintenance of an action under subsection (c) does not release the landlord from liability under Section 4.101(b).

Index